Until Our Minds Rest in Thee

Until Our Minds Rest in Thee

Open-Mindedness, Intellectual Diversity,
and the Christian Life

JOHN ROSE

CASCADE *Books* • Eugene, Oregon

UNTIL OUR MINDS REST IN THEE
Open-Mindedness, Intellectual Diversity, and the Christian Life

Copyright © 2019 John Rose. All rights reserved. Except for brief quotations in critical publications or reviews, no part of this book may be reproduced in any manner without prior written permission from the publisher. Write: Permissions, Wipf and Stock Publishers, 199 W. 8th Ave., Suite 3, Eugene, OR 97401.

Cascade Books
An Imprint of Wipf and Stock Publishers
199 W. 8th Ave., Suite 3
Eugene, OR 97401

www.wipfandstock.com

PAPERBACK ISBN: 978-1-5326-6254-6
HARDCOVER ISBN: 978-1-5326-6255-3
EBOOK ISBN: 978-1-5326-6256-0

Cataloguing-in-Publication data:

Names: Rose, John, author.
Title: Until our minds rest in thee : open-mindedness, intellectual diversity, and the Christian life / by John Rose.
Description: Eugene, OR : Cascade Books, 2019 | Includes bibliographical references.
Identifiers: ISBN 978-1-5326-6254-6 (paperback) | ISBN 978-1-5326-6255-3 (hardcover) | ISBN 978-1-5326-6256-0 (ebook)
Subjects: LCSH: Virtues. | Virtue epistemology.
Classification: BD176 .R67 2019 (print) | BD176 .R67 (ebook)

Manufactured in the U.S.A.　　　　　　　　　　　　　　　NOVEMBER 11, 2019

Table of Contents

PART I:

Open-Mindedness and Intellectual Diversity before Grace

Introduction 3

Chapter 1: The Start of the Inquiry 21

Chapter 2: Corresponding Vices and Accompanying Intellectual Virtues 33

Chapter 3: Semblances 60

Chapter 4: The Semblance of Strong Fallibilism 80

Chapter 5: The Virtue of Open-Mindedness 106

Chapter 6: The Value of Intellectual Diversity 117

PART II:

Open-Mindedness and Intellectual Diversity after Grace

Chapter 7: Intellectual Diversity after Grace 139

Chapter 8: Infused Open-Mindedness 166

Chapter 9: Open-Mindedness and Intellectual Diversity after Death 186

Bibliography 199

Part I

Open-Mindedness and Intellectual Diversity before Grace

Meno: How will you look for it, Socrates, when you do not know at all what it is? How will you aim to search for something you do not know at all? If you should meet with it, how will you know that this is the thing you did not know?

PLATO, *FIVE DIALOGUES*

Introduction

Terminology

"Intellectual virtues" in this project are synonymous with good habits of mind that entail both a willful moral dimension and a mental dimension that concerns the reception, formation, and exchange of beliefs and ideas. "Open-mindedness," one of these intellectual virtues, is a noncontradictory active receptivity or open disposition towards new ideas and beliefs, a studious appetite to learn from the broadest possible range of teachers and sources. "Intellectual diversity" means a variety of disagreeing—meaning conflicting and thus noncomplimentary—beliefs and opinions as encountered in a local, lived manner.

Summary of the Argument

In its distilled form, the thesis of this book is that open-mindedness, as defined above, *is* an intellectual virtue, in keeping with the standards of the neo-Aristotelian tradition, while intellectual diversity, lacking in any (philosophically demonstrable) utilitarian value, is nevertheless something virtuous people should naturally find themselves surrounded by out of a desire for friendship (defined in an Aristotelian fashion) with others, and something Christians should naturally find themselves surrounded by for *missional* reasons, born out of an inability to rest content with intellectual fragmentation. The current chapter is largely an argument for the relevance of and the need for a book on these subjects. Much of the evidence it marshals is sociological, and many of its moral pleas assume certain virtue ethics premises. The next two chapters are philosophical in style. Chapter 2 first discusses open-mindedness' corresponding vices, which, much like a photographic negative, can help bring open-mindedness into focus. It then looks at those virtues that tend to accompany open-mindedness. Much like people, you can tell a lot about a habit by the friends it keeps. Chapter 3 covers open-mindedness' "semblances," or traits that could easily be mistaken for open-mindedness but are not the real thing, some of which are actual vices, and others of which are morally neutral. A fallibilism-based form of intellectual humility receives the most attention of any of these semblances in chapter 4. Finally, chapter 5 returns to the proposed definition of virtuous open-mindedness, describing it in detail and offering examples of it in action. Chapter 6 turns to the subject of intellectual diversity, critiquing the philosophical arguments for its utilitarian value as somehow conducive to arriving at truth. Chapter 7 begins the second half of the book, with its explicitly theological turn. It discusses how the addition of the theological virtues changes the way Christians should view intellectual diversity. Chapter 8 considers the difference that the theological virtues of faith, hope, and love make to the virtue of open-mindedness (how they "elevate" and "perfect" the virtue by changing its end, in the language of virtue ethics). As the final and most speculative part of the project, chapter 9 explores the fate of open-mindedness and intellectual diversity in the Christian afterlife, arguing (as my title hints) that open-mindedness, in both its acquired and infused forms, becomes superfluous and thus passes away—blessed minds being finally *closed* minds—and that intellectual diversity (having already been characterized as a lamentable result of the fall of man) similarly ceases to be.

Thinking With and Outside the Tradition

The definition of "intellectual virtues" given above is somewhat out of step with the Thomistic tradition, to which this project otherwise tries to adhere as much as possible. Augustine and Aquinas did not believe that intellectual virtues met the high standard of a habit that "cannot be misused." As I argue later, their analysis is indeed true of many possible definitions of open-mindedness, but not all.[1] It is understandable that Augustine and Aquinas thought this way about intellectual virtues. To them, such virtues—like science, art, and understanding—were not virtues in the *highest* sense (as the moral virtues were) because grasping or failing to grasp knowledge does not render a person morally praiseworthy

---

1. Aquinas, *Summa Theologica*, I-II.56.3; hereafter *ST* in footnotes.

or blameworthy. According to the traditional view, it is only when the conversation turns to *why* a person wants to acquire knowledge or *what they'll do* with that knowledge once they acquire it, that the intellectual sphere has been left and the moral sphere entered. Intellectual virtues, on this account, always reside in the intellect, make of the intellect its subject, and perfect the intellect's acts such as understanding, reasoning, judging, etc. By contrast, moral virtues reside in the appetite, the source of passions and desires, which, when perfected by the moral virtues, lead to upright feelings and actions. Intellectual virtues seek truth, whereas moral virtues seek goodness. Again, this is the inherited Thomistic framework for virtue specification, labels, and relationships. It is a sensible system. After all, there is no obvious reason to think that an ethical mathematician is any more likely to arrive at a correct proof than a conniving colleague of comparable mental powers. Indeed, there is something intuitive about this type of thinking towards the division between moral and intellectual virtues. And yet, largely (though not entirely[2]) overlooked by Aquinas and Aristotle are, I believe, other intellectual virtues (open-mindedness among them) that span this hard divide by contributing to human moral excellence regardless of whether or not they lead to truth, while also revealing the ways in which how we arrive at beliefs—right down to our basic epistemologies—is colored by our moral character. These habits wobble between the intellectual and moral. Philosopher Linda Zagzebski speaks of such intellectual virtues as having "terms that have the same name as a moral virtue," as in the cases of intellectual charity and intellectual courage—all of which "probably borrow most of their stereotype from the stereotype of the parallel moral virtue, with the proviso that it is in the domain of intellectual inquiry or belief."[3] Just as Aristotle regarded prudence as formally moral but materially intellectual in its actual

---

2. To be fair, Aquinas does treat prudence or *iudicium* in a manner similar to that in which open-mindedness are treated in this project. And in response to the question of whether belief (including but not limited to faith) can be meritorious, Aquinas draws a distinction between "the scientist's assent to a scientific fact and his consideration of that fact." Because "the assent of science is not subject to free-will, . . . the scientist [being] obliged to assent by force of the demonstration," scientific assent is not meritorious; however, "the actual consideration of what a man knows scientifically is subject to his free-will, for it is in his power to consider or not to consider." For this reason, "scientific consideration may be meritorious if it be referred to the end of charity, i.e. to the honor of God or the good of our neighbor." *ST* II-II.2.9.

3. Zagzebski, CCT conference paper, 149.

content, many of these intellectual virtues pull the reverse trick: they are materially moral while in pursuit of formally intellectual ends.

Ways in Which This Project is Untraditional

Because this book aims to open up a new topic, describing the contours of an under-theorized virtue, I expect some will resist what I have to say. Others will no doubt discover details that I have left out. My project is also highly interdisciplinary by the standards of most projects in theological ethics. I have felt free to grab from texts in a wide array of fields and to integrate their claims. My writing style is informal at times and intentionally so, motivated by a desire to make the work more democratic, more accessible, and of greater interest to a more general audience. At times, I take on a rather personal tone, in full awareness that this may appear at odds with the academic ideal of a neutral, objective observer; indeed, one of the recurring themes of this work is the unmasking of assumptions about moral neutrality in the ways in which we arrive at and exchange our beliefs.

This project is also unusual because its method and arguments are bound up with each other and, to a certain degree, stand and fall with one another. I hope that it practices what it preaches, since the variety of virtue ethics I employ teaches (and thus argues) by *example*, not syllogisms. For this reason, what follows may seem overly anecdotal or impressionistic at times. Readers may also find themselves wondering, "Why *these* examples?—surely there are others that could have been used." I've chosen them simply because they are nicely representative of a set of views or because they are interesting, and I do not regard this latter criterion as superficial; given the practical nature of this project, choice of style will presumably influence readers' attentiveness and thus the work's effectiveness on their minds.

There is, no doubt, a confrontational aspect to this project. It attempts to bring to people's attention the lack of open-mindedness and intellectual diversity (at the local, lived level) in our country today and to propose a partial answer to this problem. In particular, my project has an eye toward higher education. It is only natural that a project examining the life of the mind should concern itself with the dealings of the institution in society most dedicated to cultivating that life. And yet this is not the only reason I use numerous examples from higher education.

It is also because the intellectual virtues—and open-mindedness in particular—are being neglected and under-cultivated among the minds in higher education, which is unfortunate, because virtues are constitutive of human flourishing. I've been motivated by what I've seen around me, yes, but also by what I've seen in myself. It's a moral rebuke, but also a moral exhortation ("friend, come up higher" in the spirit of Luke 14:10). We can do better. We were *made* for better, something virtue ethicists who believe in a universal human nature and teleology are committed to believing. The good news is that every vice has a corresponding virtue.

Large portions of this text, however, neither exhort nor recommend but merely try to clarify, using philosophy, what we mean by certain concepts, showing in some cases that what we think of as a normative habit is actually amoral, or perhaps that what we consider to be a strong philosophical case for the value of intellectual diversity isn't so.

Within the guild of higher education, institutions with Christian identities receive special attention in the second half of this book, which considers how the theological gifts or graces alter how Christians should think about open-mindedness and intellectual diversity. It is my hunch that what many perceive as confusion on the part of these institutions regarding their self-understandings—some say "identity crises"—can in part be traced back to simultaneous commitments to remain true to their confessional mission statements or denominational identities and to be open-minded (in the best sense of the word) and respectful of intellectual diversity in our modern pluralist world,[4] without (and here is where the confusion comes in) being sure of how to do this. As is discussed in the latter half of this book, these institutions are different from their secular counterparts in an important way: members of their communities are to

---

4. The work of religion scholar Leonard Swidler, for example, represents a way of thinking that sees the lesson to be learned from modern pluralism as the realization that people (out of intellectual humility and in order to avoid violence) should assume a non-absolutist position with regard to the truth claims of their particular traditions. He writes, "[w]hereas the understanding of truth in the West was largely absolute, static, monologic, or exclusive up to the last century, it has subsequently become deabsolutized, dynamic, and dialogic—in a word: relational. All statements about reality are now seen to be related to the historical context, intentionality, perspective, language, and interpretation of the speaker. . . . [M]y perception and description of the world are true only in a limited sense, that is, only as seen from my place in the world." This is what it means to be a modern religious believer. Importantly, this project criticizes such a version of intellectual humility and its accompanying form of modern religious belief (Swidler, "Understanding Dialogue," 12). Special thanks to Ellen Charry for bringing this text to my attention.

assume that their intellectual relationships are graced by the theological virtues, which should change their character.

As mentioned, I make no pretense about trying to remain removed from my claims, but rather am at times speaking to myself, reflecting and regretting my personal intellectual vices, and asking my readers, "You, too?" Virtue ethicists believe that attention needs to be paid to agents' actions, since it is in these actions where things finally come to pass. Importantly, I include here what might be called mental actions, not always perceivable to an outside viewer, but no less real for it, whose reality is ascribed on appeal to external evidence they help explain. These are inclinations of the mind that are worthy of praise or criticism. I pay attention to how we actually form our views. Most people don't believe what they do about important matters because of the arguments in dry books or dissertations; instead, a mix of anecdotes, intentional personal habits, impressions, and personal experiences—all chastened by rational arguments, to be sure—play a large role in influencing beliefs. According to the version of virtue ethics I'll be using, there's nothing wrong with this, and so I'll be following suit at many points.

I confess that, in choosing my topic and style, I consciously wanted to challenge typical publications in the humanities today, which are often narrow in their focus and sometimes suffer from a lack of intellectual creativity, a logical result of institutionally agreed-upon lines of inquiry, scholarly standards, styles of composition, and disciplinary boundaries. My own discipline of theology, for instance, suffers from a lack of integration between its pastoral, practical, biblical, and systematic approaches. As William Deresiewicz, a professor of English at Yale, notes in a recent work,[5] our present system of higher education discourages and vexes students with noncompliant, risk-taking intellectual temperaments. Deresiewicz's observation accords with French philosopher Frédéric Gros's biting criticism of the majority of humanities scholarship today:

> Our first question about the value of a book . . . or a musical composition [is]: can they walk? Books by authors imprisoned in their studies, grafted to chairs, are heavy and indigestible. They are born of a compilation of the other books on the table. They are fattened geese: crammed with citations, stuffed with references, weighed down by annotations. They are weighty, obese, *boring*, and are read slowly, with difficulty. Books made from other books, by comparing lines with other lines, by

---

5. Deresiewicz, *Excellent Sheep*.

repeating what others have said of what still others have thoroughly explained. They verify, specify, rectify; a phrase becomes a paragraph, a whole chapter. A book becomes the commentary of a hundred books on a single sentence from another book.[6]

Whatever else this project is, it is not the kind of scholarship Gros criticizes here. If, in trying to avoid this fate, I also fail to make a scholarly contribution to my field, then no doubt that avoidance was not worthwhile. My hope is to do both.

Anticipated Objections

The transition from a philosophical mode to an overtly theological mode in the latter half of the book may strike some—particularly those less interested in theology than in secular, philosophical investigations of the ethical life—as a wrong turn or, worse, a sleight of hand. If secular readers were to stop reading at this point and consider the rest to be of interest only to Christian readers, or to be epistemically less credible than the first part, then I would consider this project a failure. My hope is that the philosophical portion of the text will lead such readers to want to know more about how good habits will be transformed by additional "theological virtues," on the promise that these virtues are actually "perfected" by the gifts of grace. The same goes for Christians skeptical of the philosophical approach to Christian ethics, who, having a lower estimation of the capacity of pure philosophy to make insights into the ethical life, prefer instead to begin any analysis in Christian ethics with a basis in a specifically Christian faith in the person of Jesus Christ; should those readers skip ahead to the second section, I would again consider this a failure on my part. It is my hope that the first chapter, on the relevance of my topic within a greater contemporary societal context, will motivate both audiences to read the "other" section, if only out of a desire to meet the challenges our society faces today. Here I am appealing to what I hope is a shared democratic spirit among my readers, regardless of specific religious beliefs or lack thereof.

The style of virtue ethics I employ assumes a universal, objective human nature, with universally appealing and beneficial traits of the mind that deserve the title of virtue. In the modern humanities, this line of thought has been criticized for giving insufficient attention to the role

---

6. Gros, *Philosophy of Walking*, 19–20.

that power dynamics, race, class, and gender play in the formation and practice of these supposed virtues. Furthermore, such talk of universal virtues has been criticized as overlooking the contextual nature of all such claims, as local to certain times and places, and therefore not necessarily true to people from other cultures. According to this view, virtues and vices are contextual and can only be "true" within a set of shared experiences, practices, etc.

To the first of these criticisms, the best response is that any such ideological critique must presume a notion of justice in its own right, one that can be practiced by individuals acting in just (i.e., virtuous) ways. Far from being at odds with virtue ethics, the approach of ideological critique requires (or tacitly assumes) a form of virtue ethics of its own. As legal scholar Martha Nussbaum remarks about the work of philosopher and gender theorist Judith Butler, deconstructive modes of scholarship (sometimes called ideological critique) must finally presume and marshal normative beliefs to achieve their goals. We are all invested in final causes, whether we realize it or not. Those like Butler who are leery of any normative notions of universal human nature and flourishing on the grounds that such theories are inherently colonizing or oppressive (or inevitably become oppressive) overlook the ways in which their reluctance to endorse any such notions are palatable to them only when they can assume (as they can as college professors) an

> audience of like-minded readers who agree (sort of) about what the bad things are—discrimination against gays and lesbians, the unequal and hierarchical treatment of women—and who even agree (sort of) about why they are bad (they subordinate some people to others, they deny people freedoms that they ought to have).[7]

But not everyone in the world holds the same assumptions about such things being "bad," and this is where the refusal to take a step in the direction of Aristotle becomes so costly.

This is not to say that there isn't value in the kind of ideological critique provided by scholars like Butler, who bring to our attention forms of structural oppression, for instance, that can result from making normative arguments about what is good for human beings. But my project makes the assumption, shared by Nussbaum, that critiques like Butler's presume and need these norms as well. As Nussbaum writes, "It

---

7. Nussbaum, "Professor of Parody," 43.

is one thing to say that we should be humble about our universal norms, and willing to learn from the experience of oppressed people. It is quite another thing to say that we don't need any norms at all."[8] We need these norms to give reasons for why, as Butler wishes to say, the subversion of unjust gender norms is a good thing (i.e., *just*). Or as philosopher José Medina puts it, we can't *just* perform ideological critiques of power structures of knowledge and epistemologies.

> After the epistemic regimes are shattered, we have to undertake a process of reconstruction with the pieces we are left with, not in order to a produce a new overarching regime, but in order to make our heterogeneous (and sometimes conflicting) epistemic practices livable, to make them properly communicated and, whenever possible, coordinated, so that . . . these practices don't dissolve into chaos. . . . *Guerilla* pluralism has a lot to offer in terms of epistemic disruptions and processes of unlearning, but very little in terms of epistemic regrouping and resuming processes of collective learning. If we *only* had the epistemic subversions and insurrections of this *guerilla* pluralism, we would be doomed to relativism.[9]

Fortunately, we are not doomed to relativism, because we know what epistemic justice looks like.

To the second objection—that of virtue ethics being too circumscribed in particular cultural contexts to be persuasive to anyone (let alone everyone) outside its cultural matrix of origin—I offer the admission that virtue ethics of this kind *is* self-referential, as well as the proposal that such a challenge be settled on empirical grounds: i.e., are virtues and vices intelligible and persuasive across cultures, or are they incommensurable? My project wagers that the first is true. Philosopher Jonathan Lear expressed this criticism in its inverse form by worrying about how a self-referential, self-confirming virtue ethic could ever *correct* itself in the face of divergent opinion on an ethical matter. "How," he asks, "can we avoid dismissing any challenge to our virtue as a brave person dismisses a coward's demurrals? From within the perspective of the alleged virtue, it is not at all clear how we might come to recognize that our perspective was distorted by illusion."[10] The answer to Lear's

---

8. Nussbaum, "Professor of Parody," 45.

9. Medina, *Epistemology of Resistance*, 297. Special thanks to Mark L. Taylor for suggesting this work to me.

10. Lear, *Open Minded*, 189.

worry is that such recognition happens all the time. What we thought was courage—perhaps a daredevil doing stunts—we come to understand as false courage or lesser courage after grappling with arguments about what constitutes a true virtue or witnessing examples of higher forms of courage in other people. While Lear might reply that the distinction between virtue and semblance just made is also the product of our particular perspective, the proper response to this objection resembles the first rejoinder: it happens all the time that, upon reflection, people coming from different perspectives are indeed able to recognize this virtue/semblance distinction as well.

It is also possible that readers of this book might, ironically, regard its arguments to be closed-minded in kind themselves insofar as they make a number of assumptions that it has neither the time nor the space to fully defend. Such an accusation, however, would presume a definition of open-mindedness that this project does not seek to defend and, in fact, criticizes in later chapters.

A Basic Assumption

My approach and its arguments implicitly reject what has been called the "postmodern turn" in theology. Representative of this flavor of scholarship is the theologian David Hart, whose understanding of the reality of the postmodern position in which Christian theology now finds itself leaves no space for the kind of virtue ethics practiced here. Hart writes,

> In a world of ungovernable plurality, composed of an endless multiplicity of narratives, there can be no grand metanarrative that extracts itself from, and then comes to comprise, all the finite and culturally determined narratives that throng the horizons of meaning; no discourse can triumph over the particularities of all the stories that pass one another by in the general congress of cultures; there is no overarching dialectic by which a single and rationally ascertainable truth might be set above all merely contingent truths.[11]

Amid the plurality of narratives for the world and competing notions of what words can mean—especially norm-laden words—virtue ethics maintains that there are still empirical observations to be made about what it means to be human (recall that Aristotle was a biologist first).

---

11. Hart, *Beauty of the Infinite*, 5.

Importantly, Christian virtue ethics maintains that these observations and arguments can be made in a nonviolent way, in contrast to the postmodern Nietzschean assumption—very much endorsed by Hart—that human claims to universal truth are always ambitions for conquest, power, and empire, never free of deceit or aggression. My project assumes, with Aristotle, that there exists a form of rhetoric (to use Hart's word) that is nonviolent prior to and apart from the peaceful form of Jesus Christ which Hart holds up as our only hope. Without this, a virtue ethics that begins with a purely philosophical treatment of habits as virtues or vices would be guilty of a kind of intellectual violence, a kind of power grab that it fails to see in itself but that motivates its will and determines its choices.

A final potential objection to my project concerns its epistemological and metaphysical assumptions. Philosophers are fond of making a distinction between what is termed "the order of being" and "the order of knowing." As a property of propositions or claims, "truth" pertains to the order of being. What we say or believe either does or does not match up to what is, in reality, the case. Matters like confidence and certainty, by contrast, are things in the "order of knowing," where the subject matter is the properties of the knowers themselves. The two orders, according to the way the distinction is typically run by philosophers, are entangled but are not, importantly, identical—thus, the necessity of the distinction. For instance, assent (which belongs in the category of the order of knowing) does not always imply views about the truth of something (which, again, pertains to the order of being). One can, after all, assent without reservation to something without having any idea as to its truth, just as someone can, in theory, take something to be true while not assenting to it. Or so this way of thinking goes about the distinction between the two orders.

The distinction between the order of being (what is the case) and order of knowing (how we get to know what is the case) has implications for our epistemic judgement about matters—in other words, what our degree of confidence is and should be in what we take ourselves to know. John Henry Newman, for instance, draws a distinction between certainty and certitude, the first being a case in which doubt is absent, the second being a case in which doubt is believed to be impossible—that it can never, even in theory, affect one's confidence about the claim in question. Some philosophers think the latter degree of epistemic confidence is itself impossible to achieve, others that it is simply rare (exceptions might be made for the principle of noncontradiction, of the truth of one's own existence, etc.).

A related line can be drawn between the act of assenting to a doctrine or claim, on the one hand, and grasping what a doctrine or claim means, on the other hand. For Christians, this difference is apparent when a person offers religious submission or assent to a church teaching (taking it to be true) without full (or even partial) understanding of what is meant by the teaching.

On the face of it, it is hard to argue with the descriptions of the two orders—being and knowing—given above, and their implications for epistemic confidence. The descriptions are commonsensical, and people (especially philosophers) are likely to agree with them when presented with the arguments, even if they disagree about the specific contents of the order of being (that is, what is true), just as they disagree about which claims deserve our epistemic confidence. They are free to do so without disputing the distinction. It is important to acknowledge that this project, for the most part, ignores this distinction, based on the belief that it is of little help in adjudicating between the morality of various intellectual habits. Part I's opening epigraph—Meno's putting forth the so-called "Learner's Paradox"—is intended to function as a reminder (or stated belief) that this paradox has never been solved. It is the assumption of this book that intellectual claims of all kinds—whether in the realm of virtue ethics or any other branch of learning—begin with fundamental confidence in certain claims about reality. It is no less the case when we change our minds about what is true, for to do so, as Meno points out, requires us to know what the truth looks like when we find it, or, to put it the way Wittgenstein does,[12] changing our minds requires us to know what it is like to (i.e., to know what would make one) change one's mind.

This project assumes a kind of (epistemic) anthropology of humans as believing, convicted creatures, who cannot be otherwise. Doubt, on this view, is always derivative of more fundamental generative beliefs (we doubt things for *reasons*), just as degrees of self-understood confidence are merely downstream ways of expressing views about which we are confident. To deny one argument is always to first affirm another. Indeed, this notion even applies to the very idea of making a distinction between the order of being and the order of knowing, since such a distinction is a conclusion about the world, one about the relation of our

---

12. Wittgenstein, *On Certainty*, §32.

minds to the inventory of the universe of which they are part. Ironically, the distinction cannot be made without (unknowingly) assuming its own falsity. Not unlike denying the free will of human beings, the distinction may be true (in the order of being as viewed from, say, the perspective of God), but the very act of placing confidence in it requires us to suspend or surrender it, to admit that one is not behaving as though it were true. We must begin from and always return to—as knowers and agents—an epistemic ground we regard as the common terrain of the orders of being and knowing, where they touch.

This human nature is one that humans cannot escape any more than we can escape the fact that we are normative creatures. Thus, this project, when discussing what knowers regard as true, does not remind readers that such claims are not necessarily true, because it assumes that, functionally (and thus as regards virtue), such a distinction is of no practical consequence and is thus unhelpful. This project tries to focus its attention on where the real (epistemic) action is, so to speak (or what is doing the heavy lifting), where the casual map of our beliefs is at its most basic and revealing level. For this is also the world in which we live: the misleading picture of our knowledge as having frontiers (on the one side, the things we know, and on the other side, those things we know we don't know) is of a piece with a picture of knowledge as having a fuzzy boundary that represents degrees of certainty about given propositions. Both pictures need correction. Our universe of knowledge is, yes, ever expanding, from the inside out, but it lacks a boundary, for to posit one is to know what would lie on the other side, and to do so is to include and relate such statements to what is on the near side of the line.[13] Learned ignorance and hedged confidence, alike, are born of learnedness and confidence. Much like our physical universe, our world of our knowledge is expanding into . . . nothing.

Why Open-Mindedness as a Topic?

The very phrase "intellectual virtues" may sound like a confusion of categories. After all, we don't call people "good" because they're smart. Moral actions are supposed to entail a movement of the will. On the other hand,

---

13. As Ludwig Wittgenstein puts it, "[I]n order to draw a limit to Thinking, we should have to be able to think both sides of this limit (we should therefore have to be able to think what cannot be thought." Wittgenstein, *Tractatus*, 27.

we do speak of "charitable" interpretations and know what they look like when we see them, just as we know what "willful" ignorance feels like when we engage in it. Habits like these have both moral and intellectual dimensions; they are "go-between" or "border-crossing" habits, because they are willful actions of the mind.

Intellectual virtues in general are a hot topic today. In the wake of the 2016 presidential election, there have been renewed calls for greater civic empathy across political lines, citing the fact that Americans of different political convictions are increasingly unable to understand each other, let alone persuade each other of their views. In her concession speech, Hilary Clinton told her supporters that they "owed" President-elect Trump "an open mind," though without going on to specify what, precisely, this should entail.

In recent years, multiple centers for the study of the academic virtues have sprung up, numerous initiatives to examine them have been undertaken by universities and think tanks, and a recent spate of literature has been published on the subject. Why, now, have intellectual virtues finally come into their own? A few reasons stand out. First, analytic philosophers in the field of epistemology are gradually realizing that claims about evidence and reasons for beliefs have an inherent moral component (or at least make value judgments) and that the application of virtue theory holds out the possibility of helping solve old epistemological puzzles that historically have been approached by bracketing moral considerations for the sake of objectivity. Second, virtue ethicists in the neo-Aristotelian tradition are themselves becoming interested in how moral character affects the life of the mind. And third, Christian philosophers today are having to think harder about how to make rational arguments for continued confidence in their faith claims in the face of increasing intellectual diversity in the society and world which they inhabit. Among the intellectual virtues, the habit of open-mindedness deserves special interest because it holds out the promise of helping inspire theologians to identify and work to alleviate some of the mental hang-ups preventing real dialogue between separate schools of thought, not only because of what the habit promotes, but also because the topic doesn't lend itself to rehearsed points and counterpoints. It gets us out of our mental ruts. Given how many non-Christians are personally invested and interested in it, open-mindedness might render the same service to dialogue between Christians and nonbelievers.

Among the intellectual virtues, several—intellectual humility, tolerance, and open-mindedness, for instance—suffer from a degree of vagueness. If asked, many people will affirm these traits as admirable but become tongue-tied or frustrated when asked to define them. It should not be surprising, then, that some suspect these "virtues" as stalking horses or proxy concepts standing in for deeper, hidden, and more partisan commitments. But this dismissal is too broad and too fast, especially in the case of a philosophically chastened open-mindedness. When properly defined, open-mindedness can be defended as a *bona fide* virtue with both intellectual and moral dimensions, in accordance with the standards of the admittedly diverse Christian virtue-ethics tradition. The meaning and usage of the concept of open-mindedness is ambiguous, often confusing. If open-mindedness were as well understood as it is frequently invoked in our society, the first part of this book would be unnecessary. Thus, one goal of this work is to bring greater clarity to its meaning.

By the close of this project, some readers may wonder if the habit of mind I've described is better labeled "studiousness," the medieval Christian term for a well-ordered intellectual appetite that seeks to engage new ideas and learn from others. While there is much overlap, I have not used the term "studiousness" for two reasons: (1) "open-mindedness" in this book connotes a *wide*ness of mind that can be underemphasized in descriptions of studiousness as *keen*ness of mind (though the two are complementary), and (2) the concept of "open-mindedness" has a certain kind of capital among modern people that "studiousness" does not; indeed, a great many people who are suspicious of normative arguments based in human nature (as overly universalizing) and religious traditions (as overly dogmatic) are so on the grounds of wanting to remain "open-minded," and are thus personally invested in the concept.

"Open-mindedness" is frequently referred to in connection with such topics as pluralism or multiculturalism—things that are very much in the background of this work but are not its real concern. Nor is this work concerned with political conceptions of tolerance. Rather, this is an examination of the moral life of open-mindedness: what lies behind it, alongside it, and awaiting it.

Why the Virtue Ethics Approach?

The virtue ethics approach, as best expressed by Aristotle and Thomas Aquinas, is attractive for the ways in which it bypasses so many of the anxieties and antinomies afflicting modern moral philosophy. Instead of, say, debating the foundations of morality up front, virtue ethics begins by pointing us to instances of virtue in practice, whose truth and goodness speak for themselves. Consider an example: a boy goes to visit his sick grandmother in the hospital, not out of a sense of guilt, or to impress a girlfriend, or because his parents expect him to. He does it simply because it is the right thing to do. Is his action *intelligible*? Assume for the sake of argument that no hermeneutic of suspicion can explain away his action, reducing it to mere behavior. Do such actions occur? Most people say they do. Skeptics who persist in asking, "But what were the *consequences* of his action?" or "How can we be *positive* that his action is good?" should not be argued with. Instead, they should be shown the action again . . . and again, and told, "Get it? Now you try." At this point, virtue ethics has its foot in the door. Questions about action, end, and circumstance—the standard Thomistic verbiage and tools—will, in time, need to be asked and answered before we can conclude that this particular visit to this particular grandmother by this particular boy on this particular day was right and good, but they will be "answered" with further, future actions on the part of the boy. In short, keep watching.

So, to Meno's famous question "Can virtue be taught?" the virtue ethicist's answer is yes and no. No, not in the way geometry can be taught, but yes, in that it can be displayed through examples, over and over again, or, better, through action of the same kind but in different circumstances and (perhaps) ordered to different ends; thus, the anecdotal style of this book, a kind of "this is what open-mindedness does *not* look like" and "this is what open-mindedness *does* look like" strategy. As the political scientist John Agresto says of great literature, "Some of it holds up mirrors labeled 'courage' or 'friendship' or 'smallness of soul,' to see if we can see ourselves in there. . . . [I]t has us walk with Virgil through the dismal rings of hell and ask at which circle Virgil might turn 'round on us, then walk away and leave us."[14] What, then, of novel, disorienting, self-transforming applications of familiar virtue terms? What about cases in which you do not see yourself in a virtue's mirror (to use Agresto's language) but rather as something alien and strange? In such cases, virtues

---

14. Agresto, "Suicide of the Liberal Arts," para. 5.

like open-mindedness help us determine whether we need to revise our current understanding of a particular virtue or whether the novel application is in fact a misapplication.

By beginning with normative content in hand—by refusing to separate the "is" from the "ought" when it comes to human nature and flourishing—virtue ethicists avoid having to face epistemological questions empty-handed. Praxis informs theory. This project begins with judgments we already make about virtue and vice without assuming that all of us make all of the same judgments. This approach enables us to identify the object of our inquiry and the agreement in concept and judgment that we need in order to consider our disagreements about particular cases. Of course, further and more philosophical questions can be (and often are) asked at this point, such as: How is it that people, regardless of factors like race, wealth, etc., *can* see the reasonableness of actions like the grandson's and admire their goodness? Why, for that matter, is it that people want to be *better* persons? Why does even a self-understood nihilist want to be a better version of himself? Why does it feel good to do the right thing? These questions all lead to bigger discussions about natural law, metaphysics, etc., but none of these discussions have to be asked or answered for this project to be effective. That's part of the beauty of a low-flying virtue ethics approach. I wish to be clear that if this method of advocating for virtue ethics is valid, it does not commit the error of presuming a "view from nowhere," a criticism I levy against several semblances of open-mindedness in later chapters. Instead, I wish it to be "a view from everywhere"—by which I do not mean a view that is everywhere on display or always quickly convincing. Rather, I mean that it presumes that, at least at a very rudimentary level, we can identify certain actions or habits in others worthy of admiration, creating the desire in ourselves to imitate them, to make them our own, and that, in so doing, we become better versions of ourselves.

The Standards of Virtue Ethics

The standard litmus test administered by virtue ethicists for whether or not a habit is a virtue first looks at the constancy of the habit. For a habit to be a virtue, it must always be virtuous. Consider the virtue of temperance. There is never a bad time to be temperate. There is nothing situational about the rightness of temperance. The same can be said of open-mindedness. As earlier defined, it is not something we engage in only occasionally or momentarily, and there is never an inappropriate time to be open-minded. It is, moreover, an ongoing, stable disposition of the will. Aristotle's definition of virtue as experiencing "an emotion at the right time, toward the right objects or people, for the right reason, and in the right manner" fits open-mindedness.[15] So does Aquinas's definition (which follows Augustine's general definition): "Virtue is a good quality . . . by which we live righteously, of which no one can make bad use, which God brings about in us, without us."[16] In this mold, open-mindedness perfects our passions. It has cognitive and affective aspects that work together in such a way that will and intellect are simultaneous and harmonious. Likewise, as is key in Christian virtue ethics, open-mindedness can be shown to have a strong unity with other already-accepted virtues rather than existing in a kind of moral isolation.

To better understand how virtue ethics works, I offer the following metaphor: Habits in general (rather than, say, completely involuntary movements) can be identified easily, much like members of the plant family. But it is trickier to identify which habits are virtues and which are vices, just as it can become difficult to tell one flower from another. We must know essential characteristics to avoid doppelgängers—the false morals of the false morels, so to speak. We can be helped in this task by learning which other plants/virtues tend to be found alongside the plant/virtue in question, and which help them grow (what biologists call the phenomenon of "mutualism"). Knowing all these things also helps us cultivate these virtues in ourselves (pun intended).

---

15. Aristotle, *Nicomachean Ethics* II.6; hereafter *NE* in footnotes.
16. *ST* I-II.55.4.

1

The Start of the Inquiry

The Need for This Project

AN ESSAY ON A proposed virtue (if the arguments and examples are sound) should not require a section on "relevance," provided its readers are human beings. That's because any essay on virtues is relevant to us as human beings who want to be better people. Nevertheless, in the case of open-mindedness and our attitudes toward intellectual diversity, much more can and should be said about their *extra* relevance in our current cultural context.

First, there is a trend toward social segregation in the modern United States, which, I wish to argue, has at least partially been driven by (and helped further drive) a decline in the habit of open-mindedness and an increasingly incorrect attitude toward intellectual diversity—an attitude motivated neither by charity nor by a desire for intellectual union. The story of this social segregation is well told by the sociologist Bill Bishop in his book, *The Big Sort: Why the Clustering of Like-Minded America is Tearing Us Apart*. Bishop argues that the disintegration of America's cultural fabric did not begin with the cultural revolution of the late 1960s, though its ideology would later contribute to the divide, but rather in the mid-1970s, when an influx of wealth changed how and to what extent Americans migrated around the country.

Many got richer, says Bishop, at the same time that we started to lose faith in the organizing principles and institutions that had theretofore defined us and created our social arrangements: family, government, newspapers, class, land, and, above all, *church*. Such things "were replaced over the next thirty years with a new order based on individual choice"—a freedom made possible by greater economic means.[1] "Today we seek our own kind in like-minded churches, like-minded neighborhoods, and like-minded sources of news and entertainment." This is not a good thing. "As a result," Bishop argues, "we now live in a giant feedback loop, hearing our own thoughts about what's right and wrong bounced back to us by the television shows we watch, the newspapers and books we read, the blogs we visit online, the sermons we hear, and the neighborhoods we live in."[2] Open-mindedness is hard to find, and intellectual diversity—a variety of opinions within a functional community—is something people are choosing to avoid if they have the means to do so.[3]

As America's long-reigning social establishment, mainline Protestantism is more a victim of Bishop's "big sort" than, as is commonly thought, a cultural force whose initial decline served as a catalyst for the trend. From the founding of our country until 1965, membership in mainline churches grew every year. Then the mainline churches began to decline, both in numbers and cultural influence. A new model of Protestantism emerged from the resulting vacuum, but did not cause the

---

1. Bishop, *Big Sort*, 39.
2. Bishop, *Big Sort*, 39.
3. While individuals who practice the habit of open-mindedness are naturally going to find themselves in environments of intellectual diversity, being surrounded by intellectual diversity does not necessarily make one more inclined toward open-mindedness. Like "courage" or "fortitude," open-mindedness as a virtue is not something that can be easily quantified. Nevertheless, social scientists have tried to measure the effect of diversity (including intellectual diversity) upon the levels of tolerance in populations. Sociologists Oliver Christ and Katharina Schmid, for instance, have found that "[a]lthough mixed social environments can provoke conflict, where this diversity promotes positive intergroup contact, prejudice is reduced." Prejudice, they say, is partially "a function of where you live"—and yet prejudice is not synonymous with closed-mindedness, but with the extent to which individuals fail "to value and endorse diversity." Christ et al., "Contextual Effect of Positive Intergroup Contact," 3996–4000. Political scientist Robert Putnam, on the other hand, has found that levels of trust, altruism, and voluntary community participation actually *fall* (at least in the short term) among inhabitants of an ethnically diverse neighborhood (with presumably diverse worldviews among them). Putnam writes, "Inhabitants of diverse communities tend to withdraw from collective life, to distrust their neighbors, regardless of the color of their skin, to withdraw even from close friends, to expect the worst from their community and its leaders, to volunteer less, give less to charity and work on community projects less often, to register to vote less, to agitate for social reform more, but have less faith that they can actually make a difference, and to huddle unhappily in front of the television. . . . Diversity, at least in the short run, seems to bring out the turtle in all of us." Putnam, "*E Pluribus Unum*."

decline.⁴ Bishop reminds us that there was no "religious right" in 1965. Mainliners left of their own accord. The upstart evangelical model offered church to people on their own terms, a principal the mainline initially was slow to adopt but has since embraced, as witnessed, for example, by divisions in Anglicanism and Presbyterianism over gay marriage. Religion scholar Martin Marty, on whom Bishop relies for analysis, laments this trend. According to Marty, the purpose of the older church was to build community within a specific geographic area, rather than carry out evangelicalism's "great commission" of church-building around particular cultural preferences. America's social fabric has weakened from the loss of this older mission.⁵ "What society needs," says Marty, "are town meeting places where people with very different commitments can meet and interact," and such places need not function like debating clubs.⁶ Churches once performed this role but no more. Today, people are free to go (intellectually) undisturbed. *E pluribus, pluribus.*

Higher education, as a sphere of our social order, is a case in point. William Deresiewicz's *Excellent Sheep* is among a spate of new books claiming that America's meritocracy, whose members are granted acceptance through institutions of higher education, has lost touch with regular people.⁷ There is a growing perception that our new establishment

---

4. For a possible explanation of why it occurred, see Bottum, "Death of Protestant America."

5. See also Murray, *Coming Apart*. Murray deals only with white America, where he sees widening class divisions caused more by cultural habits (out-of-wedlock births, etc.) than economic forces. Contrary to the rhetoric of the religious right, says Murray, our meritocracy is practicing healthier, more traditional, civic habits than lower middle-class whites, whose traditional religious affiliation is quickly eroding.

6. As quoted in Bishop, *Big Sort*, 173. Political scientist Patrick Deneen sees a similar phenomenon among students at college today: "Students [at college] today are taught . . . that the only remaining political matter at hand is to equalize respect and dignity according to all people, even as those institutions are mills for sifting the economically viable from those who will be mocked for their backward views on trade, immigration, nationhood, and religious beliefs. The near unanimity of political views represented on college campuses is echoed by the omnipresent belief that an education must be economically practical, culminating in a high-paying job in a city populated by like-minded college graduates who will continue to reinforce their keen outrage over inequality while enjoying its bounteous fruits." Deneen, *Why Liberalism Failed*, 12.

7. Deresiewicz, *Excellent Sheep*. Deresiewicz visited my undergraduate seminar in the fall of 2018 and was unsurprised by the relative homogeneity of the class in terms of the students' socioeconomic backgrounds, as well as their attitudes towards politics and religion, a general trend among those who inhabit elite institutions of

is failing to represent and hold together society in the way their WASP predecessors did, however imperfectly. In short, we have a ruling class but no real establishment, whether political or religious—the decline of the former helping explain the decline of the latter. The meritocracy's insularity, according to this theory, has left it unable to relate to the values and life experiences of a majority of citizens: privileges, zip codes, alma maters, buying habits, income brackets, etc.[8] According to Deresiewicz, our governing class exists in a cultural bubble that breeds intellectual conformity, groupthink, and institutional feedback loops—and *vice versa*, all working in mutual reinforcement. The system of educational advancement within elite institutions now virtually requires a blinkered focus on résumé-building and hoop-jumping. This, in turn, fosters unconscious groupthink.[9] Intellectual bubbles are not only dangerous epistemically but also harmful socially.[10]

---

higher education, faculty included. All of which helps make possible, Deresiewicz remarked, the fact that, "We live in a time when progressive opinion has hardened into something approaching religious dogma. There's a right way to think and a right way to talk. Secularism is taken for granted, environmentalism is a sacred cause. Issues of identity, particularly the holy trinity of race, gender, and sexuality occupy the center of the discourse. The assumption on the Left is that we are already in full possession of moral truth. . . . There is really nothing to discuss."

8. See also Packer, *Unwinding*, and Hayes, *Twilight of the Elites*. Hayes speaks of a growing distrust on the part of average Americans towards the meritocracy, which, to judge by the behavior of congress, corporate CEOs, professional sports owners and athletes, etc., over the last decade, is failing practically and morally without being held accountable. Americans, says Hayes, are losing faith in institutions because they are losing faith in the meritocratic processes that have been, for the last forty or so years, used to select those institutions' leaders. Legal scholar Amy Chau offers a complimentary explanation, writing that "The Great Enlightenment principles of modernity—liberalism, secularism, rationality, equality, free markets—do not provide the kind of tribal group identity that human beings crave and have always craved." Chua, *Political Tribes*.

9. Attempting to explain how the 2008 financial crisis could have come as such a surprise to people "in the know," David Brooks notes that these experts were "part of the same overlapping social networks, and inevitably [began] to perceive the world in similar . . . ways. They thrive[d] in institutions where people are not rewarded for being cantankerous intellectual bomb-throwers." Brooks, "Why Partyism is Wrong," para. 2.

10. At a 2017 lecture at Duke University, theologian Alan Jacobs remarked that exposure to intellectual diversity, when done properly, is *good* for society. Regarding the distinction between *pain* and *harm*, Jacobs explained that "It does not follow that all pain is harmful. In the game we call undergraduate education, . . . some level of mental and emotional pain is part and parcel of the game. And that is not always and inevitably bad. . . . [T]he task of the undergraduate student is to embrace this kind

Higher education is a case in point. To take an example close to home, in the run-up to the 2012 presidential election, 157 (or 99 percent) of Princeton University faculty and staff who reported making political donations gave to Barack Obama's campaign; a single visiting lecturer in the School of Engineering reported a contribution to Mitt Romney, along with a dormitory custodian.[11]

Social psychologists José Duarte et al. have made a more scientific case study of the lack of political diversity within their own guild.[12] As they write, "Psychologists have demonstrated the value of diversity— particularly diversity of viewpoints—for enhancing creativity, discovery, and problem solving. But one key type of viewpoint diversity is lacking in academic psychology in general and social psychology in particular: political diversity."[13] Duarte et al. note recent surveys that have found that 58–66 percent of social science professors in the United States identify as liberals, while only 5–8 percent identify as conservatives. Self-identified Democrats outnumber Republicans by at least an 8:1 ratio. Duarte et al. document a similar situation in the humanities where surveys find that 52–77 percent of humanities professors self-identify as "liberal," while only 4–8 percent self-identify as "conservative," and that Democrats outnumber Republicans by at least a 5:1 ratio. In psychology, Duarte et al.'s own field, the imbalance is even stronger: 84 percent identify as "liberal" while only 8 percent identify as "conservative"—a 10.5:1 ratio. A 2018

---

of bruising, such pain, and the task of teachers and administrators is, if they can, to structure the game in such a way that that *pain* doesn't escalate into *harm*. And if we can manage that, then it's good for students, good for the university, and good for the society at large." Jacobs, "Embrace the Pain."

11. Liu, "99% of Donors."

12. "There has never been an extensive or representative survey of the political attitudes of social psychologists, but we do have two imperfect sources of evidence. One of the largest gatherings of social psychologists is the presidential symposium at [The Society for Personality and Social Psychology's] annual meeting. At the 2011 meeting in San Antonio, Texas, Jonathan Haidt asked the roughly one thousand attendees to identify themselves politically with a show of hands. He counted the exact number of hands raised for the options 'conservative or on the right' (3 hands), 'moderate or centrist' (20 hands), and 'libertarian' (12 hands). For the option 'liberal or on the left,' it was not possible to count, but he estimated that approximately 80% of the audience raised a hand (i.e., roughly 800 liberals). The corresponding liberal-conservative ratio of 267:1 is surely an overestimate; in this non-anonymous survey, many conservatives may have been reluctant to raise their hands. But if conservatives were disproportionately reluctant to self-identify, it illustrates the problem we are raising." Duarte et al., "Political Diversity," 7.

13. Duarte et al., "Political Diversity," 7.

study by Samuel Abrams of Sarah Lawrence College found that the ratio of liberals to conservatives among college administrators is even more skewed, as much as 25:1 in the New England region.[14] For the purposes of this project with its focus on open-mindedness and intellectual diversity, these statistics are not problematic *in themselves*, provided they at least partially reflect society as whole. Far from it, though. As Duarte et al. note, in the United States as a whole, the ratio of liberals to conservatives is about 1:2, remarkably different from the makeup of the faculties of institutions of higher education they survey.[15]

Duarte et al.'s main complaint is that this lack of political diversity is having a negative effect on the quality of research in their own field, because the prejudices to which it leads prevent a wider range of projects that might be helpful to the field:

> Field studies demonstrating discrimination against research projects that are unflattering to liberals and their views, and survey results of self-reported willingness to engage in political discrimination all point to the same conclusion: political discrimination is a reality in social psychology. Conservative graduate students and assistant professors are behaving rationally when they keep their political identities hidden, and when they avoid voicing the dissenting opinions that could be of such great benefit to the field. Moderate and libertarian students may be suffering the same fate.[16]

I hesitate to use political examples in this chapter because they can stir such strong emotions in people, especially when plenty of apolitical examples, *no less intense* for those involved, are available. Consider a merely glancing survey of departmental infighting within the academy today: Keynesians versus classical economists, sociologists for and against using normative categories when studying human behavior, English Literature scholars for/against the use of literary theory, continental versus analytic philosophers, political scientists for/against the quantification of their field's methods, biologists who insist natural selection occurs only at the level of the gene versus those who maintain it is a multilevel process, etc. Political wedge issues have the advantage of broader relatability than the issues in the previous list and, precisely *because* they evoke such

---

14. Abrams, "Think Professors are Liberal?"
15. Duarte et al., "Political Diversity," 6.
16. Duarte et al., "Political Diversity," 33–34.

strong passions in people, serve as a good "stress test" for the value and workability of intellectual diversity.

Cultural bubbles such as those that exist in the current academy work against local intellectual diversity and are liable to political partisanship, a prejudice on the rise in America. Legal scholar Cass Sunstein discovered strong "partyism" when surveying parents about how pleased they would be if their son or daughter married someone with different political sympathies. Perhaps more surprising, sociologist Shanto Iyengar has shown, using blind experiments, that clues of political affiliations colored would-be employers' evaluations of applicants' résumés *even more* than clues about the applicants' race.[17] In another study, Iyengar shows the great extent to which Americans are now, by default, assuming bad motives for the beliefs of those with different fundamental beliefs, particularly political ones.[18]

Sunstein, using Iyengar's sociological data, laments the fact that such partyism is leading to legislative gridlock and making it harder to govern society. The cost of partyism more relevant to this project is that it tears our social fabric and leads to the loss of *friendship*.[19] As Aristotle argued, friendship,[20] not legislation, is the basis of society. And since friendship is "realized in [people] living together and sharing in discussion and

17. Iyengar and Westwood, "Fear and Loathing."

18. "We show that Democrats and Republicans not only increasingly dislike the opposing party, but also impute negative traits to the rank-and-file of the out-party." Iyengar et al., "Affect, Not Ideology," 405, 407.

19. Though the kind of friendship referred to here is union-seeking, it does not achieve this goal by ignoring real differences. Philosopher Alexander Nehamas, for instance, describes friendship as "a mechanism of individuality," as it sparks "the need to come to know people and things as intimately as possible, in their particularity, and understand just what makes them different from every other thing." Friendship, then, "highlights distinction." But, importantly, it doesn't stop there. Where there is sufficient charity and intellectual virtue (words Nehamas does not use, to be fair), friendship can lead people to greater agreement. As Nehamas reminds us, "Many significant moral and social developments have occurred not so much because their proponents convinced the world with their arguments but because (to cite two parochial examples), as more women entered the workplace and more homosexuals began to live openly, the others got used to their presence and some of them gradually became able to treat them with trust and respect [in the context of newly formed friendships]. The net result of such changes is the creation of common psychological, institutional and cultural ground between us—they make us more similar to one another than we used to be, and that is where *their* value lies." Nehamas, "Good of Friendship," 290–91.

20. In the Aristotelian way of thinking, "friendship" means the true kind of friendship in which two virtuous people will each other's good.

thought,"[21] the possibility for friendship is damaged when partyism creates social self-segregation. Quite apart from congressional infighting, there is a non-instrumentalist cost to what this entails for friendships from an Aristotelian perspective, in which friends are "the greatest of external goods."[22] Friendship is bound up with human flourishing, according to Aristotle, who claims that friendship "is a virtue or implies virtue, and is besides most necessary with a view to living. For without friends, no one would choose to live, though he had all the other goods."[23] Friendship makes us better people, as "it stimulates [us] to noble actions—'two going together'—for with friends men are more able to both think and act."[24] The Bible affirms as much: from the beginning, God decided it was not good for man to be alone, and did not rest until Eve was created.

Because Sunstein, as a legal scholar, gives insufficient attention to the cultivation of virtues in his scholarship, he is unable either to see or speak to the loss of individual virtue entailed in these trends. Insofar as partyism is strong in us, we are not open-minded (as I will define open-mindedness) but instead suffer from intellectual vices.[25] That is a loss in itself, regardless of partyism's effect on governance.[26]

Neither Bishop, Marty, or Sunstein entertain the possibility that churches, among leading cultural institutions, historically stood in a unique position to facilitate peaceful, charitable, intellectually diverse exchanges—that, in short, they were a check on partyism because their members assumed that basic, shared religious beliefs ran deeper and were more fundamental than any political beliefs that might divide them. Political disagreements were, as the church's setting reminded people, framed and superseded by some creedal and cultural beliefs (the latter formed by religious beliefs), until, as Bishop says, mainline Protestantism ceased to be America's social glue and moral currency for national conversations about important matters. This development helps explain

21. Aristotle, *NE* 9.9.
22. Aristotle, *NE* 9.9
23. Aristotle, *NE* 8.1.
24. Aristotle, *NE* 8.1.
25. See Jacobs, *How to Think*.
26. "Partyism is real, and it is increasing, and it has serious adverse effects both in daily life and in the political domain. It makes governance more difficult and, in some cases, even impossible." Sunstein, "Partyism," 26. Sunstein, later and elsewhere, has remarked, however, that "partyism" is an issue of character and that greater virtue could mitigate against it.

the unproductive, frustrated, and shrill tone that characterizes so much of the political dialogue in America today. David Brooks, seconding this theory, writes that politics has become hyper-moralized because "straight moral discussion has atrophied. There used to be public theologians and philosophers who discussed moral issues directly"—e.g., Reinhold and H. Richard Niebuhr's 1932 exchange about just war (and the Christian morality of US military intervention abroad) in the pages of *The Christian Century* occasioned by Japan's attack of China—but, says Brooks, "that kind of public intellectual is no longer prominent, so moral discussion is now done under the guise of policy disagreement."[27]

The Myth of Moral Neutrality

The problems generated by partyism and the under-cultivation of virtues like open-mindedness cannot be solved or politically managed through laws that are morally neutral. In *The Next Religious Establishment*, political scientist Eldon Eisenach describes the long process that culminated in our current culture wars.[28] Like Bishop, Eisenach recognizes the death of the Protestant establishment but adds that something must replace it; we cannot remain without a shared national identity if our laws are to be coherent. Simply agreeing to disagree on fundamental questions that shape our politics is unsustainable. As Eisenach writes, "Multiculturalism as a principle and not as a set of concrete facts and historical struggles requires that we view America as an aggregate of separate tribes or autonomous cultures. This portrait must then include governance by imperial rules if the tribes are not to be at each other's throats."[29] While any such governors may claim to practice a kind of high-minded neutrality, Eisenach sees false consciousness at work. His stock example is the supposed neutrality of today's judicial interpretations of the wall of separation between church and state and the protection of religious liberties. These interpretations, he writes, "do not rest on their own foundations of truth but ride on the cultural and religious understandings that prevail."[30] A new, truly secular establishment has not yet been built because it *cannot* be built, insofar as all national establishments must be founded on

---

27. Brooks, "Why Partyism is Wrong," para. 13.
28. Eisenach, *Next Religious Establishment*.
29. Eisenach, *Next Religious Establishment*, x.
30. Eisenach, *Next Religious Establishment*, 3.

shared normative and universal beliefs; in short, all establishments are at heart forms of "religion." We can become post-Christian but never post-religious (in Eisenach's description).[31]

According to Eisenach, the false neutrality of the secular state described in the "secularization thesis" of the West is on display in church-state jurisprudence. Its incoherence is unmasked by historicist and pragmatist accounts of the principals of religious freedom as existing within the frameworks of shared history, as opposed to ahistorical accounts of these principals as standing above and outside time.

---

31. Columnist Ross Douthat observes that Americans today are quite divided on the questions of our shared national identity and founding myth (i.e., there is no ruling establishment at the present). The older national myth, which Douthat calls the "settlers" narrative, demanded that immigrants assimilate to the norms of certain European traditions. Gradually, however, a liberal narrative began to challenge this older way of thinking, largely because of the way in which the old narrative failed to properly include and address the experiences of mistreated groups such as blacks and Native Americans. Still, as Douthat observes, "for a great many Americans the older narrative still feels like the real history. They still see themselves more as settlers than as immigrants, identifying with the Pilgrims and the Founders, with Lewis and Clark and Davy Crockett and Laura Ingalls Wilder. They still embrace the Iliadic mythos that grew up around the Civil War, prefer the melting pot to multiculturalism, assume a Judeo-Christian civil religion rather than the 'spiritual but not religious' version." The problem, in trying to bring such people into agreement with those proposing a more liberal narrative, is that, "so far we haven't found a way to correct the story while honoring its full sweep—including all the white-male-Protestant-European protagonists to whom, for all their sins, we owe so much of our inheritance." We are, in other words, between establishments and without a clear vision of who or what the next one could (or should) be. Indeed, Douthat worries that "Maybe no unifying story is really possible. Maybe the gap between a heroic founders-and-settlers narrative and the truth about what befell blacks and Indians and others cannot be adequately bridged." Douthat, "Who Are We?," para. 9. Political scientist Mark Lilla makes a similar point in a recent article that begins by recognizing the current lack of a shared American identity, and proceeds to argue that whatever this identity is to be, it cannot be defined in terms of what "we are not" as a people. On the question of diversity, Lilla points out that there exists a liberal belief that, in politics, "we should become aware of and 'celebrate' our differences. Which is a splendid principle of moral pedagogy—but disastrous as a foundation for democratic politics in our ideological age." An obsession with seeing the world and approaching ethical questions through the lens of race, gender, sexuality, etc., had left American liberalism—despite all its popularity in higher education, the courts, and the media—unable to "become a unifying force capable of governing." Indeed, it has done the opposite. As Lilla concludes, "It is at the level of electoral politics that identity liberalism has failed most spectacularly, as we have just seen. National politics in healthy periods is not about 'difference,' it is about commonality. And it will be dominated by whoever best captures Americans' imaginations about our shared destiny." Lilla, "End of Identity Liberalism," paras. 2, 9.

"[W]henever a state of religious freedom is declared achieved by the courts by applying a universal principle, what has actually resulted is only a temporary settlement concerning the prevailing limits of toleration. Toleration is not a principled and equal freedom for all religions under an endless horizon of neutrality, but a particular and historical legitimating of a particular practice and patterns of toleration."[32]

Religion scholar Winnifred Sullivan, in her book *The Impossibility of Religious Freedom*, similarly notes that modern church-state jurisprudence relies on clearly defined notions of what constitutes legitimate religion, something it cannot do with impartiality. She writes, "There is a sense in which religion moved from 'norm' to 'fact' in modernity. Laws guaranteeing religious freedom meant that religion no longer would provide norms for society, but that religion must prove itself as a social fact in court."[33] This is impossible to do without taking cultural sides—thus the title of Sullivan's book. She profiles a federal court case about what kinds of grave memorials are acceptable as "religious" in nature at a Florida cemetery. This "experiment in living with pluralism," as Sullivan calls it, occurred when there were complaints about aboveground decorations on graves—mostly Roman Catholic and Orthodox Jewish—in a cemetery of mostly Protestant graves without such decorations. Using the Bible and a bit of theology, the judge ruled that such displays were "non-religious" on the basis that "true religion" in the court of law should be construed as private, individual, textual, and voluntary beliefs—which, as it happens, correctly characterizes what modern liberal Protestantism thinks religion is. Its opposite—public, coercive, and communal religion—is thus "false religion" despite the fact that it is practiced by such global faiths as Roman Catholicism and Islam.[34] Moral neutrality cannot help

---

32. Eisenach, *Next Religious Establishment*, 137.

33. Sullivan, *Impossibility of Religious Freedom*.

34. For a history of the role of anti-Catholicism in this story, see Hamburger, *Separation of Church and State*. The book's self-summary: "[S]eparation became a constitutional freedom largely through fear and prejudice. Jefferson supported separation out of hostility to the Federalist clergy of New England. Nativist Protestants (ranging from nineteenth-century Know Nothings to twentieth-century members of the K. K. K.) adopted the principle of separation to restrict the role of Catholics in public life. Gradually, these Protestants were joined by theologically liberal, anti-Christian secularists, who hoped that separation would limit Christianity and all other distinct religions. Eventually, a wide range of men and women called for separation. Almost all of these Americans feared ecclesiastical authority, particularly that of the Catholic Church, and, in response to their fears, they increasingly perceived religious liberty to require a separation of church from state. American religious liberty was thus

solve these problems. But a better understanding and greater practice of open-mindedness, and a correct appraisal of the value and place of intellectual diversity in our modern pluralist society—all approached through philosophical virtue ethics and, yes, theology—*can* help. The next chapter begins to take up this project.

---

redefined and even transformed. In the process, the First Amendment was often used as an instrument of intolerance and discrimination."

2

Corresponding Vices and Accompanying Intellectual Virtues

Historical Precedent

AT VARIOUS POINTS IN his *Summa Theologica*, Aquinas suggests that moral character can negatively or positively affect the operations of the intellect, even to the point that we can speak of a mind being sinful. If true, the established Thomist axiom that that which is in the will is always first in the intellect is not necessarily reversed, but merely nuanced in these special occasions. For it is possible to imagine such occurrences as moments when will and intellect are simultaneously harmonized without any kind of sequential relationship[1]—in which we should not speak of a

---

1. If reserved for instances of intellectual virtues or vices, theologian Daniel Westberg's description of will and intellect in Aquinas is helpful: "[For Aquinas] reason and will do not work in sequence but in harmony, *at the same time*. The intellectualist account pictures the will having to follow what the intellect concludes; the voluntarist account says that the will is free to decide on an action no matter what the intellect comes up with. Thomas's teaching is neither of these, but that the two operate together: that when a decision is made it expresses the agent's understanding as well as his desires." Westberg, "Did Aquinas Change His Mind?," 51. Westberg later adds: "[For Aquinas], intellect and will are not two similar but distinct faculties of the mind, one doing one job and one another (in which case they would operate sequentially), but are actually two different *kinds* of potencies according to Thomas. Using his metaphysical basis, the intellect is the term for a person's ability to recognize reality and truth, while the will is the person's ability to be attracted toward good specified in this way.... Apprehension and inclination are simultaneously necessary for action just as pitch and rhythm are both essential for music (which must involve sound frequencies as well as motion forward in time)." Westberg, "Did Aquinas Change His Mind?," 53.

will to believe, to use William James's phrase, but rather something more like the possibility of virtuous or vicious reasoning.

Aquinas, for instance, talks of "blindness of mind," and notes how a mind can fail to attend to the things it should for two reasons: (1) a man's will is intentionally turned away from considering something, as described in Psalm 35:4, "He would not understand, that he might do well"; or (2) a man's mind is too preoccupied with other things he loves more, as in Psalm 57:9, "Fire [of concupiscence] hath fallen on them and they shall not see the sun." Aquinas says that "[o]n either of these ways blindness of mind is a sin."[2] The carnal vices of gluttony and lust, according to Aquinas, can prevent people from directing their attention away from corporeal matters towards more important intelligible things, such as spiritual matters. Aquinas does, though, grant that those who are slaves to these vices "can know some truths," while quickly adding that "their uncleanness is a clog on their knowledge."[3] The corresponding virtues of abstinence and chastity, on the other hand, "dispose man very much to the perfection of intellectual operation. Hence it is written (Daniel 1:17) that 'to these children' on account of their abstinence and continency, 'God gave knowledge and understanding in every book, and wisdom.'"[4]

Analogies and Metaphors

Many of the terms and turns of phrases I use in this chapter emerge out of an effort to project language and ideas typically reserved for descriptions of moral virtues (or internal to specific disciplines) onto the life of the mind. To accomplish this, I use analogies that may at first appear strained or odd, like a mixing of categories. When necessary, I have even permitted myself to invent new terminology.

To continue a metaphor used in chapter 1, corresponding vices are those plants (those ecological conditions) that thwart the germination and choke the growth of the virtue in question. They are weeds. They poison the soil from which habits sprout. They steal sunlight and resources away from the desired virtuous plants. Accompanying virtues, in the metaphor, are plants that help the virtue in question grow and that, in turn, are helped to grow by the virtue in question; that is, they are in a

2. *ST* II-II.15.1.
3. *ST* II-II.15.1.
4. *ST* II-II.15.1.

symbiotic relationship with the virtue in question. They improve the soil for it. They might climb the virtue like a grapevine, or act as a trellis for the virtue's ascent.

As for the conceptual work of the virtue ethicist, consider the analogy of a person mining for a particular type of stone. Miners know what set of aggregates, when found, indicate that they are on the wrong track because the mineral they're after does not form, does not naturally occur, alongside of such aggregates. These are the corresponding vices. The accompanying virtues are the rocks that, when found, make us think we're on the right track. In some ways, the winnowing of the possible definitions for a virtuous form of open-mindedness is a bit like separating the ore or dross from the pure metal in a mining washplant through a series of screens and agitators (or litmus tests). What comes out the other end, after all the semblances have been disqualified and discarded on the tailings pile, is our best hope for finding the virtuous precious stone in question.

Corresponding Vices

Because it isn't very helpful to say that the opposite of open-mindedness is *closed*-mindedness, we need to go deeper and investigate the cluster of corresponding vices that might, together, constitute something like a "closed" mind.

Below I organize these corresponding vices into a few groups. The first are all forms of prejudice. The second group concerns intellectual vices that grow primarily from pride. And the third group contains vices of omission, particularly those that reveal a lack of desire for collective intellectual unity. As true open-mindedness requires an openness to learning from the widest possible group of potential teachers, prejudice is its enemy. As true open-mindedness requires a form of intellectual humility, any intellectual pride is its enemy. And as true open-mindedness desires intellectual unity with those who disagree, any vice that works against this desire is its enemy. Think of these three genuses of intellectual vices as cardinal vices and all the others as their subspecies. Just like many virtues, some vices could be placed in more than one category, a fact that only reinforces the purpose of this exercise: to show that true virtues (and vices) naturally maintain certain internal relationships with one another.

Prejudice

Partisanship. In its most general sense, partisanship is the intellectual vice that gives undue preference to beliefs confirming the rightness of one's own affiliations and discounts the beliefs of (and the potential of instruction from) others and their schools of thought. Partisanship can be thought of in economic terms. What might be called "intellectual protectionism" is a vice by which a person subsidizes (and therefore gives unfair advantage to) his ideas or those like his own, and those from people in his own institutions—just as an economic nativist might do for domestic products—while placing tariffs on (i.e., taxing) "foreign" ideas by receiving them with less than full charity and presenting them to others in a way that is less than fully reasonable. In its extreme form, protectionism might also entail all-out embargos on any ideas originating from certain ideological circles. As philosopher José Medina says of closed-mindedness driven by and blinded by prejudice generated by partisan loves,

> [It] can be narrowly used, targeting very specific experiences and perspectives that one's mind comes closed off to. But it usually involves a lack of openness to a whole range (no matter how broad or narrow) of experiences and viewpoints that can destabilize (or create trouble for) one's own perspective. Among the obvious examples of [prejudicial] closed-mindedness, we can mention the white supremacist who has deemed the voices and perspectives of members of other racial groups as unworthy of epistemic respect and, therefore, is not open to listen to them and to learn from them; or the sexist man who systematically undermines the epistemic authority of women, gives them no credibility and pathologizes their perception, reasoning, and testimony.[5]

The football fan who thinks that the referees are favoring the opposing team in every game he watches is a partisan. So is the employer who won't hire anyone without his same Ivy League pedigree, despite the presence of plenty of worthy applicants from other colleges. These are moral failings, at odds with open-mindedness. Undue love for a group can lead to a closed mind in which appetite corrupts apprehension.

The vice of partisanship occurs in varying degrees. The further one gets from the corresponding virtue of intellectual democratism—the expansion of those who one considers to be his epistemic peers to include

---

5. Medina, *Epistemology of Resistance*, 35.

everyone (the peerhood of all believers, to adapt a Reformation battle cry)—the more partisan one is. As a rule of thumb, degrees of anti-democratism all limit the number and variety of interlocutors (and thus potential teachers) and act as conversation stoppers or at least restrictors.

Partisanship comes in many flavors. What I'll call "intellectual speciesism" occurs when one takes seriously only a certain species of argument (perhaps *analytical* philosophy, for example) with regard to big questions. Individuals guilty of this vice actively discriminate against other types of arguments. What might be called "discriminatory perspectivalism" occurs when a person believes that anyone who has not experienced what he or she has in a given arena has no status as an epistemic peer (which is not to say that their opinions must be seen as *equally* credible by the open-minded person). Take, for example, a veteran who believes that only those who have experienced war firsthand should be entitled to an opinion about the morality of warfare. Or a man who believes that men alone have epistemic authority in discussions about what constitutes healthy masculinity, or the ethics of male initiation, or the wisdom of Robert Bly's *Iron John*. Virtue ethics, it must be admitted, has historically been guilty of discriminatory perspectivalism in its prejudice against youth. The attitude, found at times in Aristotle, that says, "no one under the age of 50 (because they lack sufficient life experience) has wisdom on questions of philosophical ethics" is an expression of intellectual prejudice. The most extreme form of this vice is, one might argue, Cartesianism, because it begins with the assumption that we should grant epistemic trust or authority to no one but ourselves. In other words, the solipsist is the most intellectually prejudiced and least open-minded of all.

Consider the following passage from C. S. Pierce:

> If the settlement of opinion is the sole object of inquiry, and if belief is of the nature of a habit, why should we not attain the desired end, by taking as answer to a question any we may fancy, and constantly reiterating it to ourselves, dwelling on all which may conduce to that belief, and learning to turn with contempt and hatred from anything that might disturb it? This simple and direct method is really pursued by many men. I remember once being entreated not to read a certain newspaper lest it might change my opinion upon free-trade. "Lest I might be entrapped by its fallacies and misstatements," was the form of expression. "You are not," my friend said, "a special student of political economy. You might, therefore, easily be deceived by fallacious

arguments upon the subject. You might, then, if you read this paper, be led to believe in protection. But you admit that free-trade is the true doctrine; and you do not wish to believe what is not true." I have often known this system to be deliberately adopted.[6]

Pierce is rightly critical of such a closed-minded approach to the development and preservation of one's beliefs. For the sake of this project, it is important to note that intellectual virtues, including open-mindedness, cannot coexist with the belief that the settlement of opinion is the sole object of inquiry, since intellectual virtues presume that part of the goal of inquiry is the right action, the mental flourishing, of the person whose opinions are under discussion.

Intellectual inoculation. By taking a small piece of another's argument, in a weakened form, removed and isolated from its greater intellectual context or biological support system (much like a vaccine or weakened virus), a person commits the vice of intellectual self-inoculation. It entails an effort (conscious or not) to make it easy to defeat the wider argument in question, allowing one to be free to ignore or simply dismiss the remainder of the other person's perspective. Note that this is not the same as making "straw men" of others' arguments, which suggests making a caricature of an opponent's argument. Consider the person who begins (and ends) their appraisal of Henry David Thoreau by pointing out that his way of thinking was individualistic and gives us no grounds to seek social justice for the poor and the oppressed. If the individual is satisfied with this easy dismissal, he or she is guilty of what I'm calling intellectual inoculation. They have freed themselves, protected themselves, from having to take seriously Thoreau's greater project (admittedly complex with respect to these matters), and its values of self-sufficiency, simplicity, and living in accord with nature.

A priori attribution of vicious ulterior motives to interlocutors. This habit is a form of prejudice, since it means denying a fair hearing to another point of view. Claiming that someone unknown to you who opposes (on ostensible constitutional grounds) the placement of the Ten Commandments on the lawn of city hall is actually "merely out to get religion" and motivated by ill feeling towards Christianity or Judaism is an instance of

---

6. Pierce, "Fixation of Belief," 1–15, as quoted in Kelly, "Disagreement," 4.

this vice. It is intellectual prejudice to assume, in an unreflective manner, that supporters of same-sex marriage "really just want to destroy the institution of marriage," even if they claim to value it and want to preserve it, while expanding it to a new group of people. Philosopher Michael Ruse was guilty of this vice when, instead of engaging and potentially learning from philosopher Michel Foucault's arguments about how power structures can affect societal norms, he declared, "Foucault's end-game was gay rights. That's what his whole project was about."[7] Ruse, in the same address, went on to describe professional historians of science like Foucault as academics with "axes to grind—homosexual rights, feminism, and so forth"—that went to work "digging up dirt" on Newton, Darwin, and Freud. In other words, these historians and philosophers, despite their stated motivations, were on a mission to justify, morally, their liberal causes; according to Ruse, they went about trying to find power structures in the history of scientific discovery so as to so relativize all truth claims that nothing could stand in the way of justifying their liberal normative projects. Ruse's prejudice was further apparent in his question, "Does anyone other than benighted feminists and demented and disappointed Marxists, and the lunatic fringe in cultural studies, really think that Copernicus was wrong or Darwin, or Watson and Crick?"[8]

Declaring this a vice—one opposed to open-mindedness—does not mean denying that some people do indeed have vicious ulterior motives. Sometimes we *should* attribute such motives to another. There will be times when a person's commitments can be traced to a corruption of the will by unjust motives that do the work of fixing belief, while reasons are picked out only insofar as they legitimate and sustain the motives. But this must only be done after the fact, after one has practiced the virtues of intellectual charity, humility, and open-mindedness toward the interlocutor and his arguments, and concluded that such vicious ulterior motives are the most reasonable explanation for why they hold the beliefs they hold.

Pride

Intellectual Paternalism. The intellectually paternalistic mind says, "*This particular bit of information that I possess, though true, should be

---

7. Ruse, "Two Cultures Revisited."
8. Ruse, "Two Cultures Revisited."

hidden and never ceded, lest it be used as ammunition by the enemy, who currently does not possess it." Such a habit of mind creates distrust. It further works against open-mindedness by making impossible any *mutually* profitable use of this information by the supposed intellectual enemies. Intellectual paternalism either fails to humbly acknowledge the epistemic peerhood of those whom it paternalizes by doubting their ability to properly assess information, or else it does indeed recognize them as epistemic equals but fails to extend sufficient charity towards them.

Idle Curiosity. Augustine writes of "the malady of curiosity" as "the reason why we proceed to search out the secret powers of nature—those which have nothing to do with our destiny—which do not profit us to know about, and concerning which men desire to know only for the sake of knowing."[9] The root of this vice is arguably pride, since those with idle curiosity, according to Augustine, are not motivated by a love of knowledge but by a hatred of the unknown—that is, they can't stand that there are things out there they don't know—and this response implies a refusal to accept our created natures as limited knowers, to be content with what we are given (and *not* given) to know per our natural ends or "destinies." Refusing to accept creaturely limits (intellectual or otherwise) is, at bottom, a refusal to acknowledge an independent order of goodness, independent from the self, who must bow down before this order.

The morally detached mind. Similar to the curious mind in this respect, the morally detached mind suffers from intellectual pride because it assumes that it can ignore its created nature as a moral agent.[10] It believes that the life of the mind has nothing to do with our moral selves. The attitude of this mindset says, "What's true is true; how I live my life is beside the point." Consider the following hypothetical choice: would you rather know everything, including the morally correct thing to do in every circumstance, but lack the will to act on this knowledge, *or* would you rather be a saintly person but with little knowledge of the world and unable to give a reasoned account of the basis for one's morality? The

---

9. Augustine, *Confessions* 10.35; hereafter *Conf.* in footnotes. For an in-depth discussion of the vice of curiosity, see Griffiths, *Intellectual Appetite*.

10. To be fair, this vice comes into focus only against the backdrop of the following assumptions: that we are created, that we have moral selves, that these moral selves have a certain content, and that this content should bear on how this self behaves.

morally detached mind chooses the first and, wrongly, sees no tension, no contradiction, and no choice between competing goods, in doing so.

The performative mind. The performative mind tends to idolize mental athleticism. In it, the desire for conceptual artistry and shows of mastery trump the desire to make persuasive or populist arguments. What some have called the "vanity trap of footnotes" for scholarly writers becomes, for the performative mind, the vanity trap of every intellectual activity. The performative mind is interested in showing off, not getting at the truth or persuading others. It cares about spectacle, not the independent order of truth and goodness. Valuing performance closes off one's mind from other views by turning its attention away from the reasonableness (or perhaps unreasonableness) of another's views and focusing instead on the usefulness (or uselessness) of another's views in aiding one's personal intellectual performance.

Mental Over-Tidiness. An overly tidy mind is one that over-sorts knowledge. It organizes truths into their appropriate bins, and knows what defines each bin. Over here, biology. Over there, theories of cultural evolution. And so forth. Mental cleanliness requires one to make distinctions, sometimes many. If a newly discovered truth doesn't conform to any of the preexisting categories, the overly tidy mind forces it into a bin that cannot truly accommodate it or, barring this, simply denies the existence of such truth. The latter could be called *intellectual eliminativism* or *Horatioism* ("There are more things on heaven and earth, Horatio, than are dreamt of in your philosophy"). The compulsively organized mind cannot tolerate a bin of truths or possible truths labeled "Don't yet know what to do with these." In a prelapsarian world where intellects are still unfallen, mental tidiness wouldn't be a problem. But in our fallen world, mental hygiene is a virtue of the mean. Too little of it (too few distinctions) makes of the mind a messy garden; too much of it prevents us from recognizing new branches of knowledge and leads to an overly uniform garden lacking in variety. Mental over-tidiness is a species of pride. It fails to humbly acknowledge that we humans are not the sorts of creatures whose minds can apprehend reality with total clarity. When a piece of information fails to fit into our intellectual architecture, it is pride that insists on concluding that it is the supposed information, rather than our minds, that is to blame. The overly tidy mind is given to barricading itself against the challenge—the psychological threat—that new ideas might pose. It is afraid that, if the new ideas are given credence, its neat bins of truths may topple under their weight; worse, the ideas may leave the person unable to construct a new arrangement—a great assault on his or her pride.

Originality/Creativity. Thinking differently for the sake of thinking differently is not a virtue. But the larger problem with considering creativity as a virtue is that creativity is less a habit than an event that happens. As the economist Albert Hirschman first demonstrated, a look at the history of great inventions shows that creativity was more often than not an unexpected occurrence rather than an inborn (or stable) trait that could, in theory, be cultivated in individuals to help foster great inventions. Hirschman writes,

> Creativity always comes as a surprise to us; therefore we can never count on it and we dare not believe in it until it has happened. In other words, we would not consciously engage upon tasks whose success clearly requires that creativity be forthcoming. Hence, the only way in which we can bring our creative resources fully into play is by misjudging the nature of the task, by presenting it to ourselves as more routine, simple, undemanding of genuine creativity than it will turn out to be.[11]

Human pride makes us hesitant to admit what Hirschman observes, because pride pushes us to boast about accomplishments for which we are not responsible. As Hirschman points out, historians tend to speak of stumbling into the more horrible events of history (such as war) but we, historians included, do not like to imagine that our great cultural *achievements* "have come about by stumbling rather than through careful planning, rational behavior, and the successful response to a clearly perceived challenge. Language itself conspires toward this sort of asymmetry: we fall into error, but do not usually speak of falling into truth."[12]

Intellectual Nihilism. The intellectually nihilistic are interested only in preserving their own opinions. Historian Maurice Cowling, a Christian skeptic who put little stock in the process of giving and taking reasons, demonstrated this vice in an exchange with philosopher Bernard Williams: "I find the Provost's dislike of 'parochiality' difficult to understand,"

---

11. Hirschman, "Principle of the Hiding Hand," 13.
12. Hirschman, "Principle of the Hiding Hand," 13.

he says (speaking of Williams). "We may not all be able to be 'acerbically' parochial, but we are all parochial.... Whether a clique, and its claque, becomes conspicuous or not may be related to the quality of its mind and activity, but is equally likely to be related to quite extraneous considerations, like its capacity for self-promotion and mutual admiration, and the contribution that it makes to prevailing fashions."[13] But, says Cowling, that doesn't mean that all cliques and claques are equally true or that we should hold our own views with a sense of irony:

> At various points in his review the Provost states that I am incapable of arguing for my opinions. Given that I have a certain articulateness, it is, it seems to me, quite likely that I *can* argue them. Argument, however, is not what it seems to me suitable to do with opinions. What one does with opinions—all one needs to do with them, having found that one has them—is to enjoy them, display them, use them, develop them, in order to cajole, press, bully, soothe and sneer other people into sharing (or being affronted by) them. To *argue* them is, it seems to me, a very vulgar, debating-society sort of activity.[14]

Cowling's intellectual nihilism goes hand-in-hand with an intellectual might-makes-right attitude long present in the world. In his *History of the Peloponnesian War*, Thucydides reconstructs an exchange between the Melians and Athenians, who are about to subdue the weaker Melians on their march toward Sparta. "For ourselves," the Athenians say,

> we shall not trouble you with specious pretenses—either of how we have a right to our empire because we overthrew the Mede [an Iranian tribe], or are now attacking you because of wrong that you have done us— ... since you know as well as we do that right, as the world goes, is only in question between equals in power, while the strong do what they can and the weak suffer what they must.[15]

Both Cowling and the Athenians exhibit a form of intellectual nihilism that thwarts open-mindedness insofar as it denies the possibility of peaceful, selfless, and profitable intellectual exchange between those who disagree. The intellectually nihilistic lack any desire for intellectual union

---

13. Cowling, "Exchange with Bernard Williams," para. 3.
14. Cowling, "Exchange with Bernard Williams," para. 2.
15. Thucydides, *History of the Peloponnesian War*, 331.

in truth and care only for intellectual domination and the preservation of their own currently held beliefs, regardless of their truth.

Intellectual gluttony. This vice might be thought of as coming in two forms. First, intellectual gourmandizing or, for our purposes, being a connoisseur of rare (i.e., esoteric) ideas to an inordinate degree, and being unable and unwilling to enjoy partaking of more commonly held views is a form of intellectual gluttony. Second, intellectual escapism into a mental world that provides a thrill or removes a person from more real considerations of life is, at bottom, a form of intellectual gluttony as well. Such escapism can occur via certain types of literature, for example. Or via one's own ideas or system of thought, a kind of concupiscence towards the own-ness of one's thoughts, an over-indulgence in one's own ideas, a (blinding) love affair with, perhaps, the inner symmetries and beauties of the intellectual system one has built for oneself.

It's important to distinguish intellectual gluttony, the pursuit of an intellectual high for its own sake, from the sort of intellectual delight enjoyed by those mentally communing with the highest forms of Truth, Beauty, and Goodness. The Platonist mathematician, lost in wonderful thoughts about the Truth of perfect Pi, the artist living out Diotima's call to experience and love Beauty itself, and the monastic meditating on the Goodness of God, are not, I would argue, guilty of the vice of intellectual gluttony; if they are intellectually virtuous, they are not pursuing these things for the sake of intellectual delight but rather pursuing them for their own sakes, with delight naturally following—much in the way that, according to Aristotle, happiness comes to (but is not the proper target of) the person engaged in virtuous activity.

Libido Dominandi. "Lust for rule" or "desire for domination" is Augustine's phrase in *The City of God* for the vice that epitomizes the City of Man. It is to blame for the bloodshed upon which every earthly city is, at bottom, built. But *libido dominandi* has an often-overlooked intellectual manifestation, too, one that fights on the battlefield of the mind rather than at the gates of Rome. As Augustine tells us, it is the content of our loves that determine our citizenship in the cities of God and man. And when we love impressing others and "winning the argument" more than we love goodness and truth (whatever truth turns out to be), we inhabit the City of Man.[16]

16. In more Thomistic terms, renouncing this vice means always praying for

A related, encroaching danger—not a vice, necessarily, but merely a moral hazard—exists when a person is so closely associated with a certain idea (particularly outlier ideas), or so synonymous with a school of thought (perhaps because he or she is its founder), that it can be hard for that person to change his or her position without great loss of face. When one "owns a theory" in the view of others, sticking to one's guns can seem like the only option.

Intellectual paranoia. This vice occurs when the so-called "hermeneutics of suspicion" become debilitating. "Anxiety of influence," a feeling Allan Bloom attributes to Nietzsche, is the worry that someone or something other than myself is influencing my beliefs or actions, which is to say that my beliefs or actions are not *entirely* my own (as Nietzsche desired for himself). The corresponding virtue of docility permits our ideas to be not entirely (or even partially) our own. There is an element of pride in this Nietzschean impulse. But there is also an element of intellectual injustice, which I'll describe later, since the impulse amounts to a refusal to show gratitude to what the past and other influences have contributed to one's intellect. Refusing to give the past any intellectual votes—to recognize the democracy of the dead, to use Chesterton's phrase—is an act of intellectual injustice.

Vices of Omission

The next set of corresponding intellectual vices to open-mindedness can be grouped together because they all entail the lack of certain desires that are appropriate to open-mindedness, particularly the desire for unity of mind (accord) with other people. These are passive vices, as opposed to the active vices of prejudice or pride. They constitute a failure to do something (an under-willing) one should do rather than the doing of something one shouldn't (an over-willing).

Sloth. Aquinas defines sloth as a "weariness of work," and "an oppressive sorrow which so weighs upon a man's mind, that he wants to do nothing."[17] Insofar as sloth entails an unwillingness to do the hard

---

"fraternal correction" if appropriate, no matter what disadvantage or embarrassment it brings with it.

17. *ST* II-II.35.1.

intellectual work that follows from open-mindedness, it is a vice. Declaring that such work is beyond the scope of human abilities is not an instance of humility, importantly.[18] If you identify yourself as a political conservative, ask yourself the following question: "In what sort of society would I be a liberal and why?" If you self-identify as a progressive, ask yourself the opposite question: "In what sort of society would I be a reactionary and why?" For the more slothfully closed-minded among us, the thought experiment is painful in the way a jog is for someone who is out of shape and disorienting in the way a new city can be for a first-time visitor. It forces us to find some merit, however small, in the opposing side's views, rather than arguing in our usual direction. The inclination to remain intellectually comfortable, to surround ourselves with people who confirm us in our views, to avoid the hard labor of seriously and charitably engaging other opinions—this is nothing less than what medievals called the mortal sin of sloth, or what we moderns commonly call "laziness." Aquinas spoke of the *labor addiscendi*[19]—the "labor of learning"—because learning is hard work. For Aquinas, the vice opposing the virtue of studiousness is something close to intellectual apathy. He writes, "the desire to know directly regards knowledge, to which studiousness is directed, whereas the trouble of learning is an obstacle to knowledge, wherefore it is regarded by this virtue indirectly, as by that which removes an obstacle."[20] Studiousness removes the "obstacle" of a lack of intellectual eagerness. Consider, as an example, the following passages from Pascal's *Pensées*:

> 225. Atheism shows strength of mind, but only to a certain degree.

> 226. Infidels, who profess to follow reason, ought to be exceedingly strong in reason. What say they then? "Do we not see," say they, "that the brutes live and die like men, and Turks like Christians? They have their ceremonies, their prophets, their doctors, their saints, their monks, like us," etc. (Is this contrary to Scripture? Does it not say all this?) If you care but little to

---

18. "It is a sign of humility if a man does not think too much of himself, through observing his own faults; but if a man contemns the good things he has received from God, this, far from being a proof of humility, shows him to be ungrateful: and from such like contempt results sloth, because we sorrow for things that we reckon evil and worthless." *ST* II-II.35.1.

19. Augustine, *Of the Morals of the Catholic Church*, 2.

20. *ST* II-II.162.2.

know the truth, here is enough of it to leave you in repose. But if you desire with all your heart to know it, it is not enough; look at it in detail. This would be sufficient for a question in philosophy; but not here, where it concerns your all. And yet, after a trifling reflection of this kind, we go to amuse ourselves, etc. Let us inquire of this same religion whether it does not give a reason for this obscurity; perhaps it will teach it to us.[21]

The reference to "repose" here suggests, in the logic of the original French, something more like *negligence*, or willful (i.e., morally culpable) ignorance. Its connotation is one of passing or superficial repose—that is, not paying enough attention to the details.[22]

Intellectual acedia. This corresponding vice entails the failure to take appropriate pleasure in, or properly delight in, beautiful ideas and the gift of truth. Related to this vice is taking *wrongful* pleasure in making provocative arguments simply to get reactions, not because one actually believes the arguments. This habit, I would argue, often has intellectual boredom at its root. Again, this vice can be traced to pride, for it reveals a deeper dissatisfaction with the created moral order in which it finds itself: that is, its behavior implies that it can imagine a different, preferable order (a counter-creation, in effect) that would not require it to engage the people and ideas it finds itself surrounded by. And in closing itself off to the real world, it closes itself off to this world's ideas as well.

Intellectual sportism. This vice assumes that the purpose of conversing about important matters, especially with those who disagree, is not to achieve intellectual unity, but rather to perpetuate (and enjoy) the conversation. Beliefs and ideas, on this view, are things to be played with like a game. This vice is related to intellectual mercenarism, since, in theory, one could easily switch positions for personal advantage without sacrificing one's goals or values. Doing so requires a certain detachment from one's beliefs the way a baseball player might be amenable to playing a different position in the field or switching teams entirely.

---

21. Pascal, *Pensées*, 51.

22. Special thanks to church historian Elsie McKee for helping me through these French passages.

Reductionism or atomization of knowledge. The atomized mind is something like an encyclopedic mind that cares only for adding to a body of knowledge without regard for synthesizing it. "He who dies with the most pieces of knowledge wins" is the motto of this kind of mind. In addition to the broader corresponding virtue of open-mindedness, the specific corresponding virtue to this vice would be something akin to intellectual holism or hylomorphism—not the belief that mind and body are one, but rather the virtuous habit of mind that believes all knowledge is ultimately one and thus that we can and should work toward unifying it. The hylomorphic intellect desires consilience, a word coined by E. O. Wilson that stands for the unity of knowledge or (translated into a volitional mental habit) the quality of mind that seeks to harmonize one's various pools of knowledge. Consilience is a virtue of the mean, for the same reasons that tidiness (recall the hyper-organized mind) is. While tidiness concerns the number of puzzle pieces that comprise a person's total knowledge, consilience concerns how well they all fit together. Its corresponding vice, the denial of the unity of knowledge and commitment to the plurality of truth, works against open-mindedness. Consider the following example from philosopher Philip Kitcher, who questions the working assumption on the part of philosopher Thomas Nagel that multiple valid truths about our universe must, finally, be reconcilable if they are all valid truths and that a unified explanation can, as matter of logic, be given for both. Kitcher imagines and predicts an alternative future in which,

> [I]t may fall to some neuroscientist to explain the illusion of unity, a last twist on successful accounts of many subspecies of mental processes and functions. Or, perhaps, it will be clear by then that the supposed unity of mind and of value were outgrowths of a philosophical mistake, understandable in the context of a particular stage of scientific development, but an error nonetheless.[23]

Kitcher is not here describing intellectual eliminativism (he recognizes, in the context of the review, the possibility that consciousness is not illusory), or intellectual relativism, or even what I will later call intellectual reductionism. Instead, he is failing to practice the virtue of intellectual consilience (and thus limiting his desire for and the possibility of open-mindedness) by believing that truth is not one, in the end, and/or that

---

23. Kitcher, "Things Fall Apart," para. 13.

human beings simply lack the intellectual capability necessary for complete consilience and therefore should stop trying to achieve it.

Intellectual Loquaciousness. This is not idle curiosity, since there is no hate of the unknown in the intellectually loquacious person's wandering around in the world of ideas. It's more like that person can't help himself. He meanders here and there, his actions and inquiries governed by free association, if anything at all. He does not travel like an intellectual cosmopolitan (to be discussed later), since there's no order to his mental travels, no discipline, and no desire for eventual consilience. Augustine, in criticizing proud philosophers like the Manichees, speaks of a kind of intellectual curiosity that sounds more like mindless intellectual tendency than what has been described above as idle curiosity. He says of the Manicheans that they fail to "slaughter . . . their own curiosities by which, like the fishes of the sea, they wander through the unknown paths of the deep."[24] This is a kind of loquaciousness of ideas that prevents the mind from having the sort of perspective and clarity beneficial to open-mindedness.

Intellectual Cowardice. This vice occurs when one is either afraid that exposure to alternative viewpoints or new information will cause himself intellectual discomfort (picture a dog in open water desperately doggy-paddling back to the safe rock he knows) or, alternatively, when one declines to engage others in open-minded, honest conversation, out of fear that his own ideas will cause others to think ill of him. Related to this vice is what might be called the inclination toward intellectual downsizing, a timidity about being the first to explore new academic terrain rooted in an anxiousness about making mistakes (as is likely to happen) in undertaking such explorations and venturing experimental ideas.

Deference to Truth-Making Processes. Deference, in this context, means not merely handing the decision of what to believe over to a process rather than deciding for oneself, but also making a truth-maker out of a process itself. It means committing oneself to the intellectual equivalent of central planning, with the trusted process functioning as the state. One could, for instance, place his faith in the British common law tradition, a bureaucratic process, or the marketplace of ideas to determine moral

---

24. Augustine, *Conf.* 5.3.

"truths." Insofar as people treat such processes as secular magisterium, without being able to give their own reasons for why they should take such a radical stance, they engage in deference as defined here. This vice of deference, or what might be called "proceduralism," is at odds with the virtue of open-mindedness insofar as it results in a personal recusal from determining one's own beliefs and one's own involvement in the process of settling disagreements. Because we are not involved, we cannot cultivate the virtue of open-mindedness.

It is telling, for instance, that historical evidence suggests that many legal concepts regarded by people today as value-neutral epistemic tools (in other words, rules/steps in the aforementioned truth-making processes) were never designed to be so. Consider the concept of reasonable doubt in legal cases, which holds that defendants must be found innocent if a juror still entertains a degree of doubt about the guilt of the defendant after hearing all the evidence. Legal historian James Whitman explains that the concept of reasonable doubt

> was not primarily [or initially] intended to protect the accused. Instead, it had a significantly different, and distinctly Christian, purpose: The "reasonable doubt" formula was originally concerned with protecting the souls of *the jurors* against damnation. Convicting an innocent defendant was regarded, in the older Christian tradition, as a potential mortal sin. The purpose of the "reasonable doubt" instruction was to address this frightening possibility, reassuring jurors that they could convict the defendant without risking their own salvation, as long as their doubts about guilt were not "reasonable." It is only if we see the rule in this original context that we can grasp its significance: The rule was simply never designed to protect the accused, nor even to serve as a standard of proof in the proper sense of the term.[25]

The concept of reasonable doubt was not proof procedure—it was a moral comfort procedure. It was not an impersonal, value-neutral intellectual choice but a personal, normative intellectual decision.[26] It was

---

25. Whitman, "Origins of 'Reasonable Doubt,'" 4.

26. Whitman draws on work by mathematician James Franklin, who argues, "The relevant sense of reasonable, and the phrase reasonable doubt, [first] appeared in the 16th century Scholastic Saurez," a curious fact, given the pivotal role Saurez plays in histories of modernity and secularization told by modern Thomists. Franklin, *Science of Conjecture*, 63. Franklin, if one follows the trail of footnotes, here cites Deman, "Probabilisme," cols. 417–619, at col. 473; Michalski, *La philosophie au XIVe siècle*, 253.

never meant to be a matter of moral arithmetic if by this is meant a procedure involving calculations of probabilities that are used to determine one's vote. As with notions of "acceptable" margins of error in research, responses to probabilities are unavoidable personal and *moral* decisions. Knowing "enough" is an ethical question just as acceptable probability is an ontological question (i.e., "Do I know enough, given the kind of moral creature I am?").

Legal scholar Mike Paulsen has uncovered a similar history and moral-intellectual pedigree in the legal privilege against self-incrimination.[27] According to Paulsen, "the temptation of the guilty to commit the huge sin of lying under oath to save themselves from temporal punishment, only thereby to incur eternal damnation, initially led not only to the *privilege* not to testify but a (common law) ban on a criminal accused's even being *allowed to* testify in his own defense."[28] The privilege was originally intended to protect souls from damnation.

Accompanying Intellectual Virtues

The virtues I describe below are often found in the same moral ecosystem as open-mindedness and/or are mental habits that strengthen or are themselves strengthened by open-mindedness. Some of them, unsurprisingly, are merely opposite (which is to say, virtuous) versions of corresponding intellectual vices described above.

I won't be talking about intellectual hope, intellectual faith, or intellectual charity in this section, instead saving those discussions for the second, theological half of this book. But here, in the portion of the project focused on natural or acquired virtues, we can speak of intellectual courage (or fortitude), intellectual temperance (including humility), and intellectual justice. I treat these as cardinal intellectual virtues and, below, describe specific subspecies of each.

Intellectual Temperance

Awe/Wonder. These two habits of mind are sometimes considered as feelings or experiences evoked by external events, and as intellectual in character, given that we make judgments about what is worthy of awe or

---

27. Paulsen, email correspondence with the author, April 22, 2016.
28. Paulsen, email correspondence with the author, April 22, 2016.

wonder. If so, they appear to be morally neutral for the person experiencing them. After all, people sometimes find it hard to look away from grotesque visuals that can be psychologically and morally harmful. But this common understanding is, in fact, a common misunderstanding. Instead, awe and wonder, properly understood, can be regarded as moral virtues (though affecting the mind) that tend to accompany the virtue of open-mindedness. The awe of the psalmist is intellectually virtuous, as is the awe of the pagan astronomer, each gazing into the starry heavens with the same humble (that is, intellectually temperate) appreciation. Each, too, is enabled to be more open-minded because of his awe (learning lessons from the heavens), just as pre-existing open-mindedness (a willingness to listen to the skies, so to speak) makes this awe more possible.

Intellectual Meekness/Simplicity. The awed mind is (actively, willfully) inclined to take little for granted, and is, in this way, childlike, though a person with such a disposition may be of any age. This intellectual simplicity is a form of intellectual humility that should not be confused with intellectual cowardice. The child is not afraid, per se. She is unassuming, not given to intellectual pride or presumption. In the spirit of the Sermon on the Mount, blessed are the intellectually meek. G. K. Chesterton exemplified such an intellectual attitude when giving thanks for how the fairytales of his youth taught him that "this world is a wild and startling place, which might have been quite different, but which is quite delightful"—a helpful way for Christians like Chesterton to understand Jesus' remarks in Mark 10:15 about the necessity of childlikeness for admission into God's kingdom.[29]

Regret. Blessed are those who mourn. While seemingly every other intellectual virtue under discussion is either present- or future-oriented, regret orients its possessor toward a past event. It concerns a desire to have chosen, acted, or thought differently in the past,[30] and includes a longing to remedy the injury caused by this past mistake. Its corresponding vice, intellectual pride, prevents a person from experiencing such regret.

---

29. "Truly I tell you, anyone who will not receive the kingdom of God like a little child will never enter it" (Mark 10:15 NIV).

30. It is interesting to note that Nietzsche's "eternal return," in which one wills everything that has ever happened, would preclude the possibility of such profitable regret wherein one learns from past mistakes. See Nietzsche, *Notes on the Eternal Recurrence*.

Regret makes open-mindedness more possible, as it more fully allows us to learn from and be shaped by the past. "Late have I loved thee," declared Augustine, looking back on his life's journey to God, which he finally sees for what it was: a long series of loves all found to be unsatisfying before God who alone satisfies found him.

To be sure, as with other virtues, regret has its own semblances. While genuine regret is born of intellectual temperance, there exists ill-born (which is to say non-virtuous) "regret" motivated by pride, a realization made by Richard Wilbur in these self-reflecting verses:

"A Reckoning"

> At my age, one begins
> To chalk up all his sins,
> Hoping to wipe the slate
> Before it is too late.
> Therefore I call to mind
> All memories of the kind
> That make me wince and sweat
> And tremble with regret.
> What do these prove to be?
> In every one, I see
> Shocked faces that, alas,
> Now know me for an ass.
> Fatuities that I
> Have uttered, drunk or dry,
> Return now in a rush
> And make my old cheek blush.
> But how can I repent
> From mere embarrassment?
> Damn-foolishness can't well
> Entitle me to Hell.
> Well, I shall put the blame
> On the pride that's in my shame.
> Of that I must be shriven
> If I'm to be forgiven.[31]

---

31. Wilbur, *Anterooms*, 45.

When we regret having been duped into believing a false promise, we must ask ourselves: is our regret due to our wishing that we had paid closer attention to the facts or perhaps been less prejudiced in a way that, in hindsight, seems to been partially responsible for us being misled, *or*, instead, do we regret having been duped because it hurt our pride or reputation (as in Wilbur's case, despite his use of the word "sin"), or caused us to feel anger towards the person who misled us? If the former, we are practicing the virtue of intellectual regret, an ally of open-mindedness, but if the latter, we are practicing the sin of pride, disguised (ironically) as its corresponding virtue.

Intellectual Fortitude

Independent Thinking. This is a virtue of the mean between a kind of over-deference to intellectual authorities and an intellectual rebelliousness that is overly suspicious of teaching authorities, while also under-aware of the way in which influences are necessary and sometimes beneficial to the formation of beliefs. Galileo, to take an easy example, was intellectually courageous because he was unafraid to believe or inquire into what others (out of fear) would not and to suffer whatever consequences might result.

Intellectual Justice

The vice of intellectual injustice often has a form of intellectual prejudice at its roots, but it is perhaps more helpful to think of it as a sin against the fifth commandment (honoring one's mother and father) as broadly applied to all of one's intellectual parents (i.e., those who have shaped us in our beliefs). As justice concerns giving to each what each is due by right with a constant and perpetual will (to use Aquinas' language), it includes submitting one's mind to instruction by those whose epistemic status makes them deserving of this relationship.

Docility. It might seem strange to treat outright deference to truth-making processes as morally neutral (or even vicious), as I've done above, while arguing that a prudent form of intellectual docility toward the teaching of some institutions or processes (e.g., church councils) can be virtuous. The difference between the two is not immediately obvious. Docility is the virtue by which a person willingly submits his or her mind to the teaching authority of another person or institution. It is explicitly recognized by Aquinas[32] as a virtue and, implicitly so, by Augustine in his criticism that Platonists are among a certain "elect" who consider themselves never in need of intellectual authority and thus docility, while Christianity, by contrast and to its credit, actually requires it.[33] Augustine writes, "By thy ordinance, O God, discipline is given to restrain the excesses of freedom; this ranges from the ferule of the schoolmaster to the trials of the martyr and has the effect of mingling for us a wholesome bitterness, which calls us back to thee from the poisonous pleasures that first drew us from thee."[34] Docility, rightly practiced, is good for us even if it is painful; within this pain is a "wholesome bitterness," a necessary restraint that our selfish pleasure-seeking impulses instinctively resist and want to flee from.

Imagine a member of Augustine's Carthage church responding in the following way, when asked his position on issue x: "I don't know what my position is on x. I haven't given it much thought. But I *do* know that my position is whatever the position of the church is on x." Suppose, further, that when asked what he would do if, upon giving more thought to issue x, he found himself attracted to a position different than the church's own, the member of Augustine's congregation responded, "I would nevertheless desire to believe as the church does, as the Bishop teaches, about issue x. I would try to make it my own through increased docility towards and trust in the church." While some modern secular thinkers may find such an attitude lacking in epistemic credibility, a more subtle diagnosis of its intellectual virtuousness or viciousness—like that of any ethical analysis of the same attitude towards, say, the rulings of the United States Supreme Court—needs to look at the reasons behind such deference. What has been described as the golden mean of independent thinking (i.e., a docility that avoids gullibility at one end and obstinateness on the other) entails being able to provide reasonable justifications for why one grants (and the degree to which one grants) epistemic authority to a particular teacher or institution. If Augustine's parishioner, when asked this question, answers, "It is to my social advantage to submit to the church in this way," he is not virtuously docile. But if he answers,

---

32. To be fair, Thomas assigns docility to prudence, not justice. In other words, he places it in the practical intellect, whereas I place it in the will by attaching it to justice.

33. Augustine, "Two Ways to Knowledge," *Essential*, 9.26.

34. Augustine, *Conf.* 1.14.

"The church has produced people whom I recognize as true saints and I wish to be like them. If accomplishing this requires, as I am told it does, accepting all the teachings of the church (even those I find hard to accept) while renouncing all prior beliefs that come into conflict with these teachings (even those I find hard to give up), then I am prepared to so"—if he answers with a justification of this kind, the man is virtuously docile.

Intellectual Magnanimity. Giving each his due includes giving oneself one's own due and giving one's own kind what it is rightly due.[35] Intellectual magnanimity concerns the proper recognition of human beings' nature as capable of true knowledge of the world and the acceptance of the attending epistemic responsibilities this nature entails. Aquinas described magnanimity as "a stretching forth of the mind to great things."

It is telling that Aquinas never speaks of the importance of magnanimity outside the context of man's place in the metaphysical landscape, the great chain of being. Per Aquinas, proper intellectual humility must be informed by a metaphysical picture that places man above animals and below angels and God. Man derives from this position both his cognitive limitations *and* cognitive abilities (thus magnanimity). This view of intellectual humility should not be confused with the self-imposed boundaries of human mental capacities argued for by modern philosophy, which may be born of intellectual pride (that man can be his own measure, discovering and determining his own epistemic limits) or of intellectual cowardice (a kind of metaphysical acrophobia). As Joseph Cardinal Ratzinger writes, "That we cannot know God himself, that everything that can be stated and described can only be a symbol: this is nothing short of a fundamental certainty of modern man, which he also understands somehow as his humility in the presence of the infinite."[36]

Because one man's intellectual humility is another man's presumptuousness—the humility of Job[37] vs. the humility of Kant, for instance—it is necessary to dig deeper into what is responsible for such conceptual

---

35. To be fair, Aquinas counts magnanimity as part of courage, which would make intellectual magnanimity part of intellectual courage. This is no doubt partially the case. It is fairer to say, I think, that both courage and justice play a role; I have chosen to accent the latter.

36. Ratzinger, *Introduction to Christianity*, 20.

37. "But where shall wisdom be found? And where is the place of understanding? Mortals do not know the way to it, and it is not found in the land of the living. The deep says, 'It is not in me,' and the sea says, 'It is not with me.'" Job 28:12–14 (NRSV).

confusion and disagreement. Aquinas is again helpful here: "When a man, considering his own failings, assumes the lowest place according to his mode: thus Abraham said to the Lord (Genesis 18:27), 'I will speak to my Lord, whereas I am dust and ashes.' On this way humility is a virtue. Sometimes, however, this may be ill-done, for instance when man, 'not understanding his honor, compares himself to senseless beasts, and becomes like to them' (Psalm 48:13)."[38] The ill-done humility is not a virtue. Notice also how the true variety of intellectual humility described by Aquinas unifies the moral and intellectual dimensions of humility with the inclusion of magnanimity. Also interesting is that Aquinas consciously parts ways with Aristotle by treating humility not as a matter of legal justice between two people (or, translated for our purposes, as the recognition that someone is your intellectual superior), but rather as pertaining to the subjection of man to God, a kind of intellectual piety,[39] where "God" need not be the specific God of Christian theology—were this the case, then true intellectual humility would require theological faith to be practiced or, put differently, intellectual humility would be only a theological virtue and never an acquired one. The previously mentioned natural piety is possible for all people. It need only entail a kind of general "divine reverence," says Aquinas, "which shows that man ought not to ascribe to himself more than is competent to him according to the position in which God has placed him."[40] He later adds, "humility has essentially to do with the appetite, in so far as a man restrains the impetuosity of his soul, from tending inordinately to great things: yet its rule is in the cognitive faculty, in that we should not deem ourselves to be above what we are. Also, the principle and origin of both these things is the reverence we bear to God."[41]

Augustine provides examples of what such a virtuous, magnanimous version of intellectual humility looks like. In the preface to his *Retractions*, he admits, "The following works of Scripture, too, terrify me much: 'In a multitude of words, you shall not avoid sin,' (Proverb 10:19) not because I have written a great deal," which Augustine certainly did—but "because, indeed, without a doubt, many things can be collected from my numerous disputations which, if not false, yet may certainly seem or

38. *ST* II-II.161.
39. *ST* II-II.161.
40. *ST* II-II.161.
41. *ST* II-II.161.

even be proved unnecessary."[42] To concede that many things one has said or written will no doubt be incorrect is not to say that one believes any particular thing he or she has said or written *is* incorrect (more on this in the next chapter). The intellectual humility on display here in Augustine is an admission of his intellectual imperfections—he knows, for the time being, through a glass darkly. Consider his commentary on the Apostle James's words, "Let not many of you become teachers, my brethren, knowing that you will receive a greater judgment. For in many things we all offend. If anyone does not offend in word, he is a perfect man" (Jas 3:1–2). Augustine says, "I do not claim this perfection for myself even when that I am old, and even less when, in early manhood, I had begun to write or to speak to the people."[43] Augustine further demonstrates intellectual humility in scriptural exegesis. There are, he says, two respectable, orthodox ways to interpret the meaning of the words "fire" and "worm" in the following passage about the damned: "Their worm shall not die, neither shall their fire be quenched" (Isa 66:24). Some readers attribute both fire and worm to the spirit and not to the body of the damned (they are burned, then, by a purely spiritual anguish), while other readers, Augustine included, find it more "reasonable" to interpret, at minimum, the reference to the worm as suggesting a physical body, meaning that both the souls and bodies of the damned suffer.[44] Important for the purposes of this project, though, is that Augustine does not deem either interpretation as definitive or binding for the faithful exegete. As he says, "let each one make his own choice, either assigning the fire to the body and the worm to the soul—the one figuratively, the other really—or assigning both really to the body," despite the fact that he personally, he tells us, has "already sufficiently made out" what he believes on the matter and why.[45]

The Fertile Mind. Unlike the preceding virtues, this one is not a virtue *simpliciter* (to use Aquinas's word) and is, in this way, more like the traditional intellectual virtues of wisdom, art, and understanding as described by Aquinas: something it is good to be, all things being equal, and that is beneficial to human flourishing but not morally praiseworthy in the same

---

42. Augustine, *Retractions*.
43. Augustine, *Retractions*.
44. Augustine, *City of God*, Book 21, Chapter 9.
45. Augustine, *City of God*, Book 21, Chapter 9.

way that true, full moral virtues are (imagination, to be discussed in the next chapter on semblances, is alike in this manner).

It is not a sin to be boring. That is, it is not an intellectual vice to have uninteresting thoughts (it is not the fault of the person about whom this is true). If I come to your house and eat at your table, I am not obliged to be interesting and lively. Rather, I am obliged to try to be. Many of us will fail. And we are no further from sainthood because of this failing. Still, it would seem that it is, in fact, an accompanying virtue of open-mindedness to be intellectually interesting, for the fertile mind offers itself more and better opportunities to encounter ideas that expand its intellectual character and that push its practitioner. The fertile mind makes for a better conversation partner with those of different minds. The boring mind must rely on others to provide it with interesting thoughts and connections to entertain.

3

Semblances

Background

A SEMBLANCE, IN THE common use of the term, is a thing that looks like something else but isn't it. The semblance could pass for the other thing, and could easily be mistaken for it, but it lacks some of the essential qualities that would make it the real thing. It is the ethicists' fool's gold. It is the courage of the person so intoxicated that he no longer appreciates the risks he's taking. Virtue ethicists have a particular interest in semblances because human agency (good and bad habits, included) can be such a difficult thing to parse. And if habits are totally unparsable—if we can never truly say which habits are good and bad, if we throw up our hands and say all human actions are psychological and spiritual black boxes— then the project of the virtue ethicist is dead before it can get off the ground. The better we can parse, the stronger the project. Semblances are the tricky test cases, the grey areas that require the keenest examinations. Many books have been written by virtue ethicists, particularly Christian virtue ethicists, on the vexing question of whether some semblances can and should be thought of as good but limited virtues (simply imperfect but not necessarily bad) or whether they are all really vices in disguise. It will be enough, for my purposes, to point out habits of the mind that might be mistaken for open-mindedness (or, put differently, definitions proposed for open-mindedness that, for whatever reason, don't give us the strongest, most relevant, possible definition for it). I categorize some of these habits as moral and others as amoral or immoral. In cataloging these imposters, I hope to help bring open-mindedness into focus.

Amoral Semblances

Mental Non-codification. The non-codified mind is committed to keeping things fluid, its affirmations always tentative and partial, never calcified or resistant to change. Codification can take different forms, among them an allegiance to a set of logical rules. Philosopher Miranda Fricker describes the non-codified mind as "Free from any such dependence on advance rules, . . . able to adapt and rework [its] thinking to the indefinitely diverse contexts liable to confront [it]."[1] Indeed, Fricker considers this kind of intellectual non-codification as the heart of the virtue of open-mindedness, as she understands it. "Virtuous perception," she says, "gives us a moral understanding of experiences, people, situations, and events— . . . and it is part and parcel of this way of seeing that even the morally wisest person remains open to surprises."[2] Put differently, "the fact that [a person] is open-hearted enough to resist the dishonest safety of fixed moral understandings *is* the crowning mark of her moral wisdom."[3] An intellectual disposition that is open to surprises and to being wrong about moral questions is not bad in itself. And yet the expression of this kind of disposition is not a full virtue. Like the semblance of weak cognitive empathy (described below), non-codification (or the kind of open-mindedness Fricker advocates) can be helpful when put in proper balance. But it is liable to mislead in certain circumstances when not balanced out by harder (i.e., calcified) moral commitments, and, moreover (and not unrelatedly), is also of limited ability to help people who disagree strongly on important questions in reaching intellectual accord. As an alternative to this kind of non-codification, chapter 5 will describe the truly and fully open mind as being, like a non-Newtonian fluid, pliable and intellectually accommodating in many ways and at many levels, but able to firm up—to calcify—when certain moral understandings are called into question.

Moderateness. Open-mindedness does not imply moderateness about one's beliefs. Being a more open-minded Muslim who works to make a contribution in an intellectually diverse setting need not require being less Muslim in one's beliefs (i.e., suspending judgment about or temporally forgetting certain truth claims, watering down one's Islamic truth

1. Fricker, *Epistemic Injustice*, 73.
2. Fricker, *Epistemic Injustice*, 73.
3. Fricker, *Epistemic Injustice*, 74.

claims, or lessening the intensity of commitment to the beliefs one has). The same goes for any political or philosophical belief. Open-mindedness requires no compromise since there is no inherent inconsistency in affirming what is, in a given cultural setting, a marginal view while doing so with an open mind. Indeed, there is nothing about moderate opinions that necessitate that *they* be accompanied by open-mindedness since, in theory, an individual could hold a middle-of-the-road (the mathematical mean, median, or mode—it doesn't matter) position on a matter and do so with an unwillingness to entertain arguments that might change that position.

That prejudice-free open-mindedness does not necessarily imply that moderateness is confirmed by sociological data. Political scientist Lilliana Mason, for instance, has shown that the trend towards political and intellectual segregation across the United States (as discussed in chapter 1) and the increased levels of partisanship that have accompanied this segregation have not (as one might assume) been similarly accompanied by an increased radicalism in the actual positions and ideas of the respective cultural camps. Position polarization has not kept up with social polarization. Mason writes, "The partisan-ideological sorting that has occurred in recent decades has caused the nation as a whole to hold more aligned political identities, which has strengthened partisan identity and the activism, bias, and anger that result from strong identities, even though issue positions have not undergone the same degree of polarization."[4] If open-mindedness is akin to moderateness (within a relative range), then it is also compatible with (and does not seem to help prevent) partisanship, a fact that casts serious doubts on its candidacy for a strong intellectual virtue.

The supposed connection between moderateness and non-biasness can be refuted in the opposite causal direction, too. Political scientist Shanto Iyengar has shown that people can hold strong positions (both intensely held and sociologically aberrant) without being guilty of the kind of partyism that distrusts and is malicious towards people ascribing to other schools of thought. The intensity of a person's policy preferences is, it turns out, a poor predictor of their partyism or non-partyism. "Surprisingly," says Iyengar, "the connection between ideological polarization and negative [partisan] affect is relatively weak. It appears that people's partisan attachments are a product of their identity rather than their

---

4. Mason, "I Disrespectfully Agree," 128.

ideology."⁵ Republicans dislike Democratic, and vice versa, not so much because of the views they hold, but because of who they are: the other team.

Imagination. Suppose James fails to appreciate modern sculpture. Moreover, James cannot wrap his mind around what it is that other people like about the stuff. He is particularly dumbfounded by the fame of Richard Serra. When James admits this to his friends, they insist that Serra is a genius, that his sculpture is profound. Listening to their arguments, James is half-convinced (on an intellectual level) that he must be wrong about Serra—that so many smart, well-intentioned people couldn't be wrong about his greatness—so, with new resolve, he returns to Serra's work. As best he can, James tries to overcome any lingering prejudices—that many fans of modern art are only pretending to "get it," that much of it is culturally destructive—and calls to mind the opinions of his friends, focusing on what he is "supposed" to see, as he stares as the sculptures. To his disappointment, nothing happens. He still cannot see and enjoy what others can. To him, it still looks like scrap steel in shapes and configurations that an average nine-year-old could have produced.

Assuming, for the sake of argument, that James's friends are correct about Serra, what are we to say about the limited intellectual imagination that prevents James from appreciating Serra's art? From a virtue ethics standpoint, it is not a moral failing. Nor are James's friends to be admired for their imaginative abilities. Their capacity to appreciate Serra is morally on par with their height and IQ. Likewise for one's ability to think outside the box to solve puzzles, and one's mental plasticity, or the ability to shift with ease between very different activities such as, say, sequencing DNA and choreographing ballet. Many of us struggle to imagine our parents or grandparents as children. Some philosophers have a knack for thinking up wild but useful thought experiments. The "house flipper" who can "see" the potential in a dump, as compared to those who cannot see past the ugliness and structural problems, has intellectual imagination but is no more ethical by virtue of this skill. While the qualities described in these examples may be desirable or undesirable in a non-moral sense, none rise to the level of moral goodness or failure. Therefore, if open-mindedness is to be a virtue, it cannot be synonymous with imagination.⁶

5. Iyengar and Westwood, "Fear and Loathing," supranote 1.

6. Of course, we do speak of moral imagination—the capacity to see and acknowledge the good of others—in terms similar to those I have used for intellectual virtues.

To take another example, it is well-known that professional mathematicians tend to do their best work in their twenties and early thirties, hitting their "prime" around age thirty-five. As British number theorist G. H. Hardy famously remarked, "No mathematician should ever allow himself to forget that mathematics, more than any other art or science, is a young man's game."[7] For whatever reason, young minds seem to be better conduits for creative mathematical inspiration. Mathematician Carl Friedrich Gauss, describing one of his own great insights, wrote, "I succeeded, not on account of my painful efforts, but by the grace of God. I myself cannot say . . . what made my success possible."[8] Should we judge Gauss morally better in light of this, and his older colleagues (and his later-in-life self) worse? Clearly not, provided this difference is, as Gauss himself seems to think, largely the result of some natural intellectual imaginative powers that are stronger at some ages than others.

At times, the ability to "think outside the box" can be vicious. A truly uninhibited "*anything* goes—just throw out ideas—this is a safe space!" brainstorming session is not always harmless even if it gets "results." Take, for example, a group formed to find a creative solution to the problem of mass incarceration. One participant blurts out, "What if bringing back chain gangs would deter potential criminals?" He or she would most likely (and rightfully) be met with astonishment and condemnation. Worse, what if such an idea actually gained traction within the group? Ideas have consequences. The common saying that there are no bad questions is simply untrue. If intellectual imagination is to be prevented from becoming vicious in such circumstances, it needs to be well-chastened with intellectual temperance, among other things.

Weak Cognitive Empathy. To empathize with the mental position of another, in the weak sense, is merely to take into account and try to understand their perspective. Successful teaching requires this kind of empathy. If open-mindedness is akin to weak cognitive empathy, then it is an aspect of the virtue of prudence. It is also, however, of limited value when it comes to questions about how we should view our own beliefs and the views of others who disagree with us. In other words, it

---

However, as made clear in the subsequent example involving uninhibited brainstorming, such moral imagination is no less susceptible to immoral thoughts with harmful effects.

7. Hardy, *Mathematician's Apology*, 6.
8. As quoted in Morse, "Mathematics and the Arts," 57.

is of minimal help in figuring out how we should converse with those who do not, for instance, share our personal philosophical or religious beliefs. Weak cognitive empathy, therefore, is not a leading candidate for the definition of open-mindedness this project seeks. It is important to note, however, that weak cognitive empathy is necessary to achieve real intellectual diversity as I've defined it. It helps us understand and "see" disagreements, even if it is of limited help to us in overcoming them.

Psychological Openness. This semblance entails a kind of psychological willingness to allow one's inner identity and purposes to remain undefined, even ultimately unknowable. Philosopher Jonathan Lear, in a book entitled *Open Minded*, argues that such an intellectual disposition goes back to the original spirit of philosophy as it emerged in the Greek world. According to Lear, we must never pretend to have good answers to the questions "Who am I?" or "In what does my purpose or fulfillment consist?" The dilemma "How shall I live?" should always remain an open question, says Lear, who recommends a Socratic way of life in which "human living consists in living openly with this question. Any fixed set of norms . . . presents itself as already having answered the question. . . . For Socrates, this is an evasion of life."[9] This makes open-mindedness equivalent to "the capacity to live non-defensively with the question of how to live."[10] Honesty requires as much, since we are not transparent to ourselves, according to Lear, who sees in the battle within the academy over Freud's legacy nothing less than a battle "over our culture's image of the human soul."[11] If there is something there that we cannot see, that remains unknown and intrinsically irrational to us—if, in other words, our modern academic culture is wrong to dismiss Freud as passé—then we have not only betrayed our philosophical forefathers of Socrates and Plato, but we have lied to ourselves by pretending we know more about the human soul than we actually do.[12]

Lear sees in Greek myth a now-lost capacity to live with this uncertainty. In an original interpretation of the Oedipus myth, Lear notes that while

9. Lear, *Open Minded*, 4.
10. Lear, *Open Minded*, 8.
11. Lear, *Open Minded*, 8.
12. To be fair, there is a religious version of this line of thought that can be found in Augustine, which I am not here engaging. "I had become to myself a great question" (*Factus eram ipse mihi magna question*), writes Augustine in *Conf.* 4.9.

> Oedipus was abandoned by his parents, . . . he and his [Athenian] audience were surrounded by the Gods [who were still in control and could give meanings to outcomes]. And there is profound comfort in being able to move almost automatically from hubristic overconfidence in human "knowingness" into humble religious submission.[13]

The problem for modern seculars like Lear is that that path is now blocked; there is "no obvious retreat from 'knowingness,' for there is nothing clear to submit to. We have been abandoned by our parents *and abandoned by the gods*."[14] As a result of the Enlightenment, he says, we have come to believe that "the most basic categories of [existence] like family, fate, nation, etc., must be legitimated before the tribunal of human reason, and cannot simply be handed down as part of the basic moral order of the universe."[15] Freud, then, is the alternative and the true heir to Socrates and the model of open-mindedness. To think, as Aristotle did, that collective discussion among virtuous people could help us set standards for what constitutes a good life is to fail to accept that the individual psyche can be the only final arbiter on these matters.[16]

For the purposes of this project, however, Lear's Freud-inspired variety of open-mindedness cannot be the truly virtuous variety we are looking for. First, by its own admission—indeed, one of its main contentions—it assumes no known or knowable collective human nature or corresponding notions of human flourishing, thereby leaving no room for any kind of virtue ethics logic. In effect, it denies that there can be any kind of intentionally cultivated good habits as described by Aristotle. Second, to the degree that Freud could be salvaged for virtue ethics purposes in a manner different than Lear's, it would result in making a virtue out of psychological well-being that can only be individual, therapeutic, and hedonic—not actual eudemonia, in other words. This, for instance, is the alternative offered by sociologist Phillip Rieff in his book *Freud: The Mind of the Moralist*, an interpretation and recommendation of Freud that proceeds by uncovering the latent normative assumptions of Freud

---

13. Lear, *Open Minded*, 53.
14. Lear, *Open Minded*, 53.
15. Lear, *Open Minded*, 53.
16. Lear, *Open Minded*, 189. Note, too, how this Freudian view limits the possibility for agreement and thus friendship within already intellectually diverse environments, to return to a subject discussed in chapter 1.

in his analysis of the human psyche, assumptions that constitute answers to the very question Lear wishes to leave unanswered: "How shall I live?"[17]

Potentially Vicious Semblances

Reluctance. The semblance of reluctance is something like *principled* noncommittalness, for lack of a better phrase. It includes the conviction that not committing is good, and a will to act upon that belief. Reluctant minds admire the resistance to closure in themselves and others. From this perspective, hazarding beliefs (and accepting their attendant responsibilities) is seen as a moral danger.[18]

We sometimes speak of open-mindedness as though it were an instance of reluctance (i.e., "I watched the debate with an open mind, not having decided which of the candidates I'll support"). But this usage can mislead. Would we be right suddenly to think less of this voter once she makes up her mind? Clearly not. Such reluctance does not belong in a lineup of virtues. Though listed here as a semblance, *principled* noncommittalness is more accurately categorized as a *vice*, since it is an act of self-abnegation, a shirking of the moral duties that befall us as agents trying to make sense of the world around us.

Reluctance should not be mistaken for intellectual cowardice in which one shirks from taking a stance (that is, self-consciously and in practice through discourse) for lack of courage. Reluctant minds may even be intellectually brave. They admire the refusal of intellectual closure (or position-taking) in themselves and others, perhaps because reality, particularly to the well-read student, looks too nuanced to allow for certain, definite judgments. Honesty requires intellectual reluctance. Columnist David Brooks, for instance, has joked that the morality of America's educated elites "doesn't seem compatible with something as

---

17. Rieff, *Freud.*

18. Whether thoroughgoing reluctance of this kind is even possible is disputable. If we refrain from judgment on a matter, we do so for reasons that are no less "positions" than the options declined. As philosopher Charles Taylor points out, "It is the claim of a certain trendy 'post-modernism' that the age of Grand Narratives is over, that we cannot believe in these any more. But their demise is the more obviously exaggerated in that the post-modern writers themselves are making use of the same trope in declaring the reign of narrative ended: *Once* we were into grand stories, but *Now* we have realized their emptiness and we proceed to the next stage." Taylor, *Secular Age,* 717. I will talk more about this charge of false self-consciousness in the next chapter on the semblance of fallibilism.

final and complete as heaven or hell. Maybe instead of a Last Judgment, there will just be a Last Discussion."[19]

Arguably, then, there are two kinds of intellectual reluctance. The first kind thinks that the course of historical change recommends something like an intentional reluctance to take strong positions. The second kind fears the consequences of the intolerance that is thought to go hand-in-hand with confident belief.

Novelist Robert Musil, in describing a man who desires "to live without qualities" (in a book by this name), for whom nothing can ever be final or complete, put his finger on this first kind of reluctance. Such a man, Musil writes, "suspects that the given order of things is not as solid as it pretends to be; no thing, no self, no form, no principle, is safe, everything is undergoing an invisible but ceaseless transformation, the unsettled holds more of the future than the settled, and the present is nothing but a hypothesis that has not yet been surmounted."[20] In light of this, such a man can do no better "than hold himself apart from the world, in the good sense exemplified by the scientist's guarded attitude toward facts that might be tempting him to premature conclusions." And the same goes for any kind of personal values or the setting of personal goals: "Hence he hesitates in trying to make something of himself; a character, a profession, a fixed mode of being."[21] No doubt, there is a certain darkness and sadness to the psychological life of the man described by Musil, but that is not the important point here. From the perspective of the virtue ethics tradition, the habit of intellectual reluctance cannot be a virtue because it refuses to fully intellectually assent to and practically work toward habits considered "good"; it considers the qualities and goals implicit in all normative claims to be untrustworthy, like all other truth claims in a world where there is no given order of things.

Reluctant minds that are motivated less by the kind of worldview Musil describes and more by a fear (one, no doubt, grounded in historical evidence) that beliefs regarded as fixed, final, or absolute tend to respond to disagreement (internally or externally) with violence, a scenario made all the more possible in a pluralist society. Literary critic George Steiner, for instance, speaks of today's liberal imagination as "more or less at ease with the manifold discourse of uncertainties. It perceives in this

---

19. Brooks, *Bobos in Paradise*, 250.
20. Musil, *Man Without Qualities*, 132.
21. Musil, *Man Without Qualities*, 132.

multiplicity and indeterminacy of possible discourses and metaphoric modelings a guarantor of tolerance. It suspects in any thirst for absolutes not only an infantile simplicity but the old, cruel demons of dogma."[22]

Likewise, consider the words of literary theorist Hans Gumbrecht, as he reflected on a book he wrote out of a desire for "an alternative to the endlessness of interpretation and of narrating the past in ever-different ways"[23]—something with which literary theorists are well-acquainted. Gumbrecht found himself longing for a form of "being that . . . refers to things of the world before they become part of a culture,"[24] "tangible things, seen independently of their culturally specific situations."[25] And yet, despite these longings, Gumbrecht understood (perhaps in part even agreed with) the kind of principled reluctance of the liberal imagination described by Steiner:

> Given where the trajectory of Western thought has led us, given also the devastating political impact, during the past few centuries, of philosophies and ideologies based on ontological premises and on claims to absolute truth, we may indeed have no real alternative—for most practical purposes—to the range of worldviews that we subsume under names like "constructivism" or "pragmatism." But inhabiting worlds (and the plural is of essence here) that we want to be shaped and "constructed" by changing sets of concepts, discourse, and narratives obviously produces a desire for what these concepts, discourses, and narratives—at least seen from a constructivist or pragmatic perspective—no longer even pretend to touch.[26]

Lord Russell uttered a similar sentiment:

> It remains deeply ingrained in the modern mind—as I find even in my own mind—that though doubt may become nihilistic and imperil thereby all freedom of thought, to refrain from belief is always an act of intellectual probity as compared with the resolve to hold a belief which we could abandon if we decided to do so. To accept a belief by yielding to a voluntary impulse, be it my own or that of others placed in a position of Arians and Catholics, Crusaders and Muslims, Protestants and adherents of

22. Steiner, *Real Presences*, 199–200.
23. Gumbrecht, *Production of Presence*, 7.
24. Gumbrecht, *Production of Presence*, 70.
25. Gumbrecht, *Production of Presence*, 76.
26. Gumbrecht, *Production of Presence*, 141.

the Pope, Communists and Fascists, have filled large parts of the last 1600 years with futile strife, when a little philosophy would have shown both sides in all these disputes that neither had any good reason to believe itself in the right. Dogmatism . . . in the present age as in former times, is the greatest of the mental obstacles to human happiness.[27]

However commendable these tolerance-motivated attitudes may be, such a self-understanding is finally philosophically ambiguous in ways that call into question its ability to be authentically intellectually virtuous. Unlike the fully virtuous version of open-mindedness that will be described in chapter 5, an open-mindedness with this kind of principled non-committalness at its core is context-dependent, and has "value" for utilitarian purposes, whereas virtues *simpliciter* are non-context-dependent, being good habits, full stop, at any place and any time. While history can teach us much, from the standpoint of virtue ethics it cannot tell us what are acquired virtues and what are vices. It is only through observation, practice, and philosophical reflection that we can make these distinctions. Another example makes this point nicely. Writing about the need for advocating certain positions—and only certain positions—in the college classroom, philosopher of religion Mark C. Taylor describes his work as a kind of social corrective. "For years," he says,

> I have begun my classes by telling students that if they are not more confused and uncertain at the end of the course than they were at the beginning, I will have failed. A growing number of religiously correct students consider this challenge a direct assault on their faith. Yet the task of thinking and teaching, especially in an age of emergent fundamentalisms, is to cultivate a faith in doubt that calls into question every certainty.[28]

This is a telling admission, for Taylor is concerned and seemingly motivated by the religious fundamentalism (religious correctness being a counterpart to political correctness) he sees in the society around him. It is fair to ask Taylor, as I asked of the partisan mind in chapter 2, "In what sort of society would you consider it your objective to make students less skeptical, more willing to take hard positions?"

---

27. As quoted in Polanyi, *Personal Knowledge*, 285.
28. Taylor, "Devoted Student," para. 7.

Intentional Ignorance. It might seem odd to include ignorance among the semblances of open-mindedness—amoral or vicious—since this project aims to find a virtuous version of open-mindedness, and ignorance is clearly a *bad* thing. How could anyone confuse the two? Yet we frequently do. What could be called "voluntary ignorance" is, in some contexts and by some people, treated as a virtue. This, ostensibly, is why wine is served "blind" (i.e., unlabeled) at wine competitions, why authors' names and institutions are omitted from peer-reviewed papers, and why some argue for race- and gender-blind admissions procedures at colleges and universities. Such intentional ignorance is meant to protect us from ourselves, from prejudices that must be controlled lest they control us.

John Rawls exploited this belief in ignorance's usefulness in his famous "veil of ignorance," his guarantor of impartiality (and thus his basis for justice) in the construction of an ideal society. Whether or not Rawls's political philosophy is prudent or workable is not my concern here. Even if, for the sake of argument, Rawls's philosophy is correct, this fact would not impart any virtue to the act of stepping behind his veil. As virtue ethics teaches us, only an agent's habits and actions, not their consequences, can be properly called "virtuous" or "vicious." Furthermore, in the case of the initial voluntary ignorance, the agent's virtue is questionable, because he is engaged in removing the human struggle implicit in all moral acts, thereby stripping the ethical dimension from subsequent decisions made from behind the veil. It would not be an exaggeration to say that such efforts aspire to *transcend* human nature. Thus, if open-mindedness is a virtue (i.e., a contributor to *human* flourishing), it cannot be synonymous with this kind of intentional ignorance. Placing one's faith in a decision-making process like Rawls's removes the opportunity to act virtuously on the part of the participants. Moreover, reliance on such a system removes the arduousness or struggle that are key ingredients in the performance of virtue. Indeed, such reliance assumes a tension between competing virtues—a red flag to virtue ethicists—insofar as it assumes that justice or impartiality are best assessed and enacted when we forget our basic assumptions about, say, what temperance entails (or, in this case, how our understanding of it should inform the ways in which we organize society). From the standpoint of virtue ethics, the truly virtuous—indeed, the truly just—person is the one who, with no veil in front of him, and sensing all the temptations towards serving his own interests and towards partisanship that go along with being born a particular person with certain experiences, nevertheless treats all people with the dignity they deserve and gives to each what is rightfully owed him, even if this means acting against one's own interests as regards power or wealth.

"Voluntary ignorance" should not be confused with the Catholic obligation to avoid situations known to tempt one to sin (i.e., "occasions of sin"). Avoidance is not amnesia. Moreover, Catholics are free to affirm that obstacles to virtue have a proper place in the created order. On the question of whether women should have been made (in light of Eve's sin), Aquinas offers the following hypothetical objection: "[O]ccasions of sin should be cut off. But God foresaw that the woman would be an occasion of sin to man. Therefore He should not have made woman." He replies, "If God had deprived the world of all those things which proved an occasion of sin, the universe would have been imperfect. Nor was it fitting for the common good to be destroyed in order that individual evil might be avoided; especially as God is so powerful that He can direct any evil to a good end."[29]

Strong Cognitive Empathy. Unlike weak cognitive empathy, strong cognitive empathy asks us to enter into the minds of others, to walk around in their mental shoes, feeling what it would be like for their thoughts and views to be ours and, assuming it were possible, to imagine that these views were *true*. The problem with considering strong cognitive empathy as a candidate for a virtuous definition of open-mindedness, however, is that engaging in it can prove to be non-edifying at times.

As philosopher Roger Scruton notes, describing an assumption that all virtue ethicists share,

> A teacher who sought to induce moral principles in his pupils by asking them to explore the various "alternatives" would be engaged in a self-defeating task. We do not discover the moral reality of murder by giving it a try, nor do we come to a better understanding of the evil of rape or torture by experimenting with a variety of points of view upon them, or by trial and error. . . . Children, as Aristotle put it, enter the palace of reason through the courtyard of habit, and in morality and religion it is the habit, not the reason, which counts.[30]

Few if any would counsel sexually curious youth to read the Marquis de Sade. Adult readers of Nabokov's *Lolita* have been known to wind up

---

29. *ST* I.92.
30. Scruton, *Education and Indoctrination*, 54.

unconsciously sympathizing with the narrator, sometimes despite their own conscious disapproval. To be fair, the person who wants to understand better the lives of traditional Muslim women, and who, as a result, spends a year behind the veil and sequestered from men, may or may not suffer moral harm. But because she very well *might* suffer harm, the habit of strong cognitive empathy that made it possible cannot be a full-fledged virtue. The same goes for, say, a secular liberal woman trying to find an imaginative entry into the lives of religiously conservative women; if such empathy passes from the weak to the strong form, it has the ability to lead her into moral and intellectual error—something a true virtue cannot do.

Even in cases where conversions born of such empathy are socially respectable, there remains the question of causal attribution. Suppose a non-religious Bach enthusiast wishes to experience, just once, the Saint Matthew Passion in all its glory and affect by listening to it as a convinced Christian, believing through sheer force of mental will that the story it tells is true. Now suppose this person is suddenly convinced of the gospel's truth as a result of his listening experience. It is fair to ask, first, what values led him to will belief in this manner, and second, what reasons or values he now has that lead him to affirm the gospel as true. The answers to these questions should reveal that the strong cognitive empathy in question was merely an enabling, not a sufficient, factor in the process, thereby limiting its moral importance as habit in the example.

There are many acts of the imagination or acts of strong cognitive empathy we might like to have but cannot—time or history acting as obstacles—that parallel the Bach example. I wish I had experienced the excitement of the 1960s before so many of the era's intellectual hopes were dashed. As Wordsworth said of the French Revolution and the excitement and hope it created, "Bliss it was in that dawn to be alive / But to be young was very heaven."[31] I wish I could, just once, listen to the Beatles without knowing of the harmful effects of the sexual revolution. But why should I trust any conclusions I came to in the event that such a listening were possible? "Nobody born after 1914 knows what a childhood could be like," an anonymous writer born in the nineteenth century once remarked. The world lost its innocence with the World Wars and the Holocaust. Would trying to imagine such a childhood, assuming it were possible, give a person credible insights?

---

31. Wordsworth, *Complete Poetical Works*.

Strong cognitive empathy is an unreliable moral guide and habit of character. Intentionally catching the mental contagion of a partygoer enjoying ecstasy on a dance floor would be pleasurable, no doubt, but not conducive to human flourishing. In short, strong cognitive empathy is not a habit "of which no one can make bad use" per Aquinas; ask the POW being tortured by a guard with a sick talent for getting inside the heads of captives. In Jorge Luis Borges's short story *Deutsches Requiem*, for example, the narrator, a Nazi, tortures a Jewish intellectual (whom he calls David Jerusalem), to the point of psychological breakdown. The narrator remarks, "I do not know whether Jerusalem understood that if I destroyed him, it was in order to destroy my own compassion. In my eyes, he was not a man, not even a Jew; he had become a symbol of a detested region of my soul. I suffered with him, I died with him, I somehow have been lost with him; that was why I was implacable [in torturing him]."[32] In other words, the Nazi narrator engaged in a kind of strong cognitive empathy, as I've been calling it here, for vicious reasons and with heinous results.

Consider another example from Nazi Germany. Writer Primo Levi recounts an instance in a concentration camp in which a Nazi guard was cruel to a prisoner for no apparent reason. When the prisoner asked him why he had acted as he did, the guard responded, "Here there is no why." Levi goes on to implicitly resist the desire for a kind of strong cognitive empathy in situations of great evil. He writes,

> Perhaps one cannot, what is more one must not, understand what happened, because to understand is almost to justify. Let me explain: "understanding" a proposal or human behavior means to "contain" it, contain its author, put oneself in his place, identify with him. Now, no normal human being will ever be able to identify with Hitler, Himmler, Goebbels, Eichmann, and endless others.[33]

Levi goes on to say that to understand this cruelty, or to empathize with it, might cause it to occur again. To engage in strong cognitive empathy in these situations, in other words, is not only not a virtue, it is actually dangerous. We should let incomprehensible evil remain just that. If Levi is right, then we should resist reading books like August Kubizek's *The*

---

32. Borges, *Collected Fictions*, 232. Special thanks to Stefan McDaniel for suggesting this book to me.

33. Levi, *If This Is a Man*, 395–96.

Young Hitler I Knew,[34] a firsthand account of the adolescent Hitler from a boyhood friend that claims to shed light on some of the early events and motivations that formed Hitler. To find biographical patterns in the lives of Eric Harris and Dylan Klebold may be prudent in trying to prevent future Columbines, but we cannot and ought not enter their minds to the degree that we come to regard their actions as in any way reasonable or human. That Germanwings pilot Andreas Lubitz suffered from psychological depression does not explain how he could fly a passenger plane into a mountainside with unchanged breathing throughout (as heard on the recovered black box recorder). No psychological or scientific explanations are available for the genocide in Rwanda in 1994.[35] We should not try to feel or relive the evil mental wave in the minds of the Hutu using recounted testimonies.

As a possible counterexample, though, consider the seemingly humane realizations of novelist George Orwell as he recounts an experience he had during the Spanish Civil War. He was a soldier in the field when he spotted a half-dressed enemy soldier,

> holding up his trousers with both hands as he ran. I refrained from shooting at him. . . . I did not shoot partly because of that detail about the trousers. I had here to shoot at "Fascists"; but a man who is holding up his trousers isn't a "Fascist," he is visibly a fellow-creature, similar to yourself, and you don't feel like shooting at him.[36]

Again, there is something seemingly humane (and humorous) about Orwell's reaction and non-action. But this, I think, is mostly due to the fact that the Spanish Civil War was such a morally ambiguous conflict. Tweak Orwell's example a bit and we can see how the strong cognitive empathy it implies becomes problematic. Instead of a Spanish Fascist with his pants down, suppose Orwell had seen a Boko Haram leader, a trainer of child soldiers, who was trying to shake a pebble out of one of his shoes, jumping around on one foot to do so. For Orwell (or any of us), does or should the Boko Haram leader shed part of his identity in our eyes at that moment, when he is shown to be human in a mundane, somewhat funny, way? Many would say no.

---

34. Kubizek, *Young Hitler I Knew*.
35. See Graham, *Evil and Christian Ethics*, 192–94.
36. Orwell, *Collection of Essays*, 193–94.

Strong cognitive empathy should be distinguished from *sympathy*. "Suppose," says philosopher Jesse Prinz, "I feel outraged for someone who has been brainwashed into thinking she should follow a cult leader who is urging mass suicide. That would not necessarily qualify as empathy." We feel sorry for that person. We don't come to share their distorted ideas, or at least we ought not. But neither is it enough to simply *imagine* what another feels, says Prinz, for imagination is more akin to *self*-projection, "a kind of mental act that requires effort on the part of the imaginer," whereas "in its simplest form empathy is just emotional contagion: catching the emotion that another person feels."[37] Further, empathy does not involve imagining what another *should* be feeling, a definition that is already morally loaded. To return to Prinz's example, "Suppose I encounter a member of a cult who is delighted by the cult leader's nefarious plans. The cult member *should* be afraid, but is not. If I feel fear on the cult member's behalf, that is not putting myself in the cult member's shoes."[38] We are already making other normative assumptions that determine how we view the situation, assumptions not based in or enabled by any kind of strong cognitive empathy.

That strong cognitive empathy is an unreliable (i.e., lacking in constancy) habit of the mind when it comes to causing more actions or conclusions is also supported by recent research in the social and cognitive sciences. Empathy, it turns out, can sway moral opinions in harmful ways. Even in cases where empathy is followed by concern for the wellbeing of another, it is prone to bias. Long before social science demonstrated this fact with empirical data, David Hume, while championing empathy (or what he called "sympathy"), recognized,

> Where there is similarity in our manners, or character, or country, or language, it facilitates . . . sympathy. The stronger the relation is betwixt ourselves and any object, the more easily does the imagination make the transition.[39]

For example, empathy is prone to "similarity bias," in which we feel greater empathy for others most similar to ourselves. Data from brain imaging scans suggests that Caucasians are more empathetic to the pain of other Caucasians than they are to people who look Chinese, and vice

---

37. Prinz, "Against Empathy," 214.
38. Prinz, "Against Empathy," 230.
39. Hume, *Philosophical Works of David Hume*, 54.

versa.[40] In this particular experiment, participants (some Chinese, some Caucasian) watched as others were touched by a Q-Tip (painless) or a needle (painful) and then rated the other's level of pain and their own personal pain.

Empathy is also liable to lead to unequal, which is to say unjust, treatment of some people by others, especially in the form of disproportionate allocations of charitable resources. When we empathize with a single individual or a small group of people, we are liable to show them preferential treatment at the expense of others who are equally or perhaps *more* needy. In one study, subjects were asked to decide the fate of a sick girl named Sheri, who was awaiting medical treatment.[41] The subjects were given the opportunity to move Sheri up a "waitlist" of sick people (past individuals who were said to be "more needy") waiting for a drug in scarce supply. In the first round of the experiment, a majority of the subjects moved Sheri up the list. In the second round, when subjects were asked to empathize with Sheri, an even greater majority moved her up the list.

Other social scientific evidence suggests that we are also more likely to feel empathy (and feel it to a greater degree) with those who live

---

40. Xu, "Do You Feel My Pain?," 8525. Xu writes, "Using functional magnetic resonance imaging we demonstrate that, whereas painful stimulations applied to racial in-group faces induced increased activations in the ACC and inferior frontal/insula cortex in both Caucasians and Chinese, the empathic neural response in the ACC decreased significantly when participants viewed faces of other races." See also, for an updated defense of Xu's study with the added element of group identifications that cut across races, Contreras-Huerta et al., "Racial Bias in Neural Empathic Responses." They conclude: "we have shown a racial bias in neural empathic responses to pain in the left insula cortex, . . . confirming findings from a number of previous studies regarding racial biases in affective-motivational aspects of empathy. Furthermore, we found that this racial bias persists and is not influenced by in-group bias in a minimal group context, even though participants clearly showed implicit and explicit identification with their minimal in-group rather than their racial group behaviorally. These results are consistent with an early and automatic brain response to observed pain that is modulated by race."

41. Batson et al., "Immorality From Empathy-Induced Altruism." Batson et al. write, "Results of two experiments supported the proposal that empathy-induced altruism can lead one to act in a way that violates the moral principle of justice. In each experiment, participants were asked to make an allocation decision that affected the welfare of other individuals. Participants who were not induced to feel empathy tended to act in accord with a principle of justice; participants who were induced to feel empathy were significantly more likely to violate this principle, allocating resources preferentially to the person for whom empathy was felt." Batson et al., "Immorality From Empathy-Induced Altruism," 104.

nearby, the so-called proximity effect. Hurricane Katrina claimed 1,836 lives—a tragedy, no doubt—but one that pales in comparison to the loss of 315,000 lives in the Indian Ocean Tsunami that struck a year before Katrina, and yet compared with Katrina, the Tsunami garnered little media coverage and yielded fewer financial contributions in America.

In the context of strong cognitive empathy, the criticism above does not deny that even true virtue can, at times, lead to an intellectual error. Situations occur in which the knower does "everything right" (i.e., is morally upright as regards intellectual habits) and yet arrives at the wrong conclusion, perhaps because of the context in which he or she has practiced virtue (consider, for example, the non-heliocentric views of the universe held by thinkers such as Aristotle, who was blamelessly ignorant of what modern science would later discover). This is a fair charge as regards arriving at incorrect beliefs but if, as has been argued in this book, the true purpose of intellectual virtues is to make knowers *good*, then it is the potential to lead a person into moral error—not intellectual error—that is the telltale sign of a purported virtue being a false virtue. And such is the case with a strong form of intellectual empathy: it has the ability to harm its practitioners morally and thus cannot be a part of open-mindedness, if open-mindedness is to be a virtue.

Existential Openness. What might be called open-*being*ness or existential openness is the psychological disposition by which a person makes herself vulnerable to the forces of the natural world (as opposed to the propositional content of ideas). Philosophers Hubert Dreyfus and Sean Dorrance Kelly advocate this way of life in their book *All Things Shining*. Whereas Jonathan Lear wants to found such humility on the uncertainty of our inner lives, Dreyfus and Kelly wish to found a kind of intellectual humility on man's helplessness in the face of nature and its meanings. The proper response to this realization is to be "open to the manifold truths our moods reveal."[42] Note, however, how Lear, Dreyfus, and Kelly all generate their "humility" from prior metaphysical pictures of human beings and nature (to return to a point made in chapter 2), despite locating the uncertainty that grounds it in different places (the first in the inner soul, the second in the outer world).

Dreyfus and Kelly are fans of *Moby Dick*. They pit the character of Ahab—who, they say, desires and searches for transcendent meaning

---

42. Dreyfus and Kelly, *All Things Shining*, 157.

and final, ultimate metaphysical truths in the natural world through conceptual violence and mastery (the hunt for the whale being the relevant symbol)—against his wiser, pagan crewmember Queequeg, who seems to know that there are no such truths or meanings to be found by mere humans and that the best we can do is to not despair or hope for them. That Queequeg is a pagan in the story is not incidental, according to Dreyfus and Kelly; like the classic Homeric hero, he stands in contrast to the monotheistic and medieval picture of the world in which God is the first and final basis for the world's meaning, sitting atop the Great Chain of Being that puts to rest any existential uncertainties. Ahab still longs for this old picture and its promises, while the modern world has abandoned it. Dreyfus and Kelly quote Ishmael as remarking, "man must eventually lower, or at least shift, his conceit of attainable felicity; not placing it anywhere in the intellect or the fancy; but in the wife, the heart, the bed, the table, the saddle, the fire-side, the country."[43]

And it's here that Dreyfus and Kelly, in dismissing questions of propositional content in order to remove the specter of monotheism and capital "T" truth, end up with a way of being in the world and an open-mindedness that, for the purposes of this project, cannot be virtuous. They so demote the capacity of man's intellect to know right from wrong, while so advocating vulnerability to collective, emotional whims that "whoosh" (their word) over crowds, that they are finally unable to distinguish between even the most extreme forms of virtuousness and viciousness made possible by such existential openness. *What* it is that captivates and energizes audiences at churches, soccer games, public executions, and fascist rallies is beside the point—the ideas and ideology make no difference. The important thing is that we be Queequegs and not Ahabs. More, this kind of open-mindedness is liable to the same kinds of abuses mentioned in relation to the semblance of strong cognitive empathy.

The semblance of intellectual fallibilism, to be discussed next, will receive a chapter unto itself.

---

43. Dreyfus and Kelly, *All Things Shining*, 157.

4

The Semblance of Strong Fallibilism

Context

THE SEMBLANCE OF STRONG fallibilism deserves, indeed requires, a chapter unto itself because it would likely be the most popular answer given for what grounds and shapes a proper form of open-mindedness. And understandably so, since it is the most philosophically formidable of the semblances I describe. I call it "strong" to distinguish it from what was described in chapter 2 as a "virtuous, magnanimous version of intellectual humility" (recall Augustine's exegesis of the worm and the fire), or "weak fallibilism." As a reminder of what that form of admirable humility looked like, consider Augustine's closing prayer in *De Trinitate*: "Before you [Lord] lies my knowledge and my ignorance.... O Lord the one God, God the Trinity, whatsoever I have said in these books [that] is [true] of you, may those that are yours acknowledge; whatsoever of myself alone, do you and yours forgive. Amen."[1] In the same vein, George Orwell displays such virtuous intellectual humility in the epilogue of *Homage to Catalonia* when reflecting on his description of the Spanish Civil War:

> I hope the account I have given is not too misleading. I believe that on such an issue as this no one is or can be completely truthful. It is difficult to be certain about anything except what you have seen with your own eyes, and consciously or unconsciously everyone writes as a partisan. In case I have not said this somewhere earlier in the book I will say it now: beware of

---

1. Augustine, *Trinity*, 443–44.

my partisanship, my mistakes of fact, and the distortion inevitably caused by my having seen only one corner of events.[2]

Note that neither Augustine or Orwell evince a belief that they *are* wrong, or are even *most likely* wrong. They simply admit their epistemic finitude, that is that they are imperfect knowers who do not have a God's-eye view of the subject matters or events in question. But, crucially, this recognition does not alter the content or character of the beliefs they have relayed, nor does it prevent them from writing and circulating them—after all, both works were published. This form of weak fallibilism is perfectly reasonable, no different in kind than the recognition that one has green eyes or was born in Seattle. Unlike its stronger counterpart, weak fallibilism is fully compatible with and even complements the virtue of open-mindedness.

Strong Fallibilism

Judge for yourself the truthfulness and virtuousness of the following three apparent instances of intellectual humility:

(1) Henry Sidgwick: "the denial by another of a proposition that I have affirmed has a tendency to impair my confidence in its validity.... And it will be easily seen that the absence of such disagreement must remain an indispensable negative condition of the certainty of our beliefs. For if I find any of my judgments, intuitive or inferential, in direct conflict with a judgment of some other mind, there must be error somewhere: and if I have no more reason to suspect error in the other mind than in my own, reflective comparison between the two judgments necessarily reduces me . . . to a state of neutrality."[3]

(2) Robert Nozik: "the usual manner of presenting philosophical work puzzles me. Works of philosophy are written as though their authors believe them to be the absolutely final word on their subject. But it's not, surely, that each philosopher thinks that he finally, thank God, has found the truth and built an impregnable fortress around it. We [philosophers] are all actually much more modest than that. For good reason. Having thought long and hard about the view he proposes, a philosopher has a

---

2. Orwell, *Homage to Catalonia*, 228.
3. Sidgwick, *The Methods of Ethics*, 342.

reasonably good idea about its weak points; the places where great intellectual weight is placed upon something perhaps too fragile to bear it, the places where the unraveling of the view might begin, the unprobed assumptions he feels uneasy about."[4]

(3) Julian Barnes: "How can we be sure that we [non-believers] know enough to know [that God doesn't exist]? As twenty-first-century neo-Darwinian materialists, convinced that the meaning and mechanism of life have only been fully clear since the year 1859, we hold ourselves categorically wiser than those credulous knee-benders who, a speck of time away, believed in divine purpose, an ordered world, resurrection and a Last Judgment. But although we are more informed, we are no more evolved, and certainly no more intelligent than them. What convinces us that our knowledge is so final?"[5]

It is natural, almost intuitive to find yourself nodding along with Sedgwick, Nozik, and Barnes, sensing in them a laudable honesty, an intellectual modesty and self-deprecation worthy of respect and all too rare in our current cultural climate. And yet such a reaction is mistaken. Sedgwick, Nozik, and Barnes are reasoning under the influence of a version of fallibilism that is not only *not* virtuous but also philosophically confused and flawed. This fallibilism, which I call strong fallibilism, is recognizable by its ironic, skeptical stance towards its own beliefs or convictions—the sense or meta-belief that one can and should regard one's beliefs as less epistemically credible (in other words, less likely to be true) for various reasons such as: the apparently contingent biographical factors responsible for the formation of one's beliefs; the relatively small scales of time and place (vs., say, geological scales) in which these beliefs have evolved (within ourselves as individuals or as a species); or the fact that there are other (or even many) intelligent, well-intentioned people who disagree with one's own beliefs about certain matters.[6] The moral of the strong

---

4. Nozick, *Anarchy, State, and Utopia*, xii, as quoted in Whitcomb et al., "Intellectual Humility," 1.

5. Barnes, *Nothing to Be Frightened Of*, 22.

6. Purely as a matter of intellectual history, I have never encountered this form of strong fallibilism in any major author in antiquity up through the Middle Ages in Western thought. Neither Plato, Socrates, Aristotle, Augustine, nor Aquinas seem to evince it, though I welcome correction on this point. Why (again, if true) such fallibilism did not emerge in Western thought until the advent of the modern period (as late as the eighteenth century, perhaps) is a question that merits investigation.

fallibilist story about our beliefs is that we should take them with a grain of salt, and that doing so is the philosophically respectable and virtuous response to the factors in the previous sentence. This chapter will argue that it is, in fact, neither philosophically coherent nor morally admirable to do so.

Ethical Critique

According to the version of strong fallibilism I critique here, any and all beliefs are potentially revocable. Not necessarily at the very moment in question and not all at once, to be sure, but, in theory, given sufficient time and enough gradual change to less fundamental beliefs, no plank on our personal ships (or worldviews) is immune from possible replacement.

Such a theory of truth, for instance, is given in the popular description of a holism from the fallibilist W. V. Quine.[7] In denying as Quine does that there are such things as self-evident facts (forever untouchable planks)—such as, say, that every event has a cause, or the principle of non-contradiction, or that it is better to suffer harm than inflict it—all our moral commitments, no matter how basic and unquestionable they may seem, are, in theory, live questions for discussion and targets for reversals. In short, there are no moral brute facts or moral absolutes in the universe. From the virtue ethics standpoint, such a worldview is potentially harmful to us as normative creatures.

It is telling that most of Quine's examples are scientific, not ethical, since it is when moral questions arise, especially extreme ones, that strong fallibilism is revealed as a worldview that requires its adherents to regard as possibly true even the most unethical of propositions. Strong fallibilism is thus harmful to us as normative creatures by preventing in us the confidence to pursue and achieve human excellence.[8] To believe

7. With reference to his metaphor of the web, Quine remarks, "the lore of our fathers is a fabric of sentences [which] develops and changes, through more or less arbitrary and deliberate revisions and additions of our own, more or less directly occasioned by the continuing stimulation of our sense organs. It is a pale grey lore, black with fact and white with convention. But I have found no substantial reasons for concluding that there are any quite black threads in it, or any white ones." Quine, "Carnap and Logical Truth," 132.

8. Quine: "Self-evidence is sometimes ascribed to judgments of moral value. Instances of such ascription in the Declaration of Independence come to mind; but surely those commendable sentiments have been less universally shared, early and late, than self-evidence would require. A moral precept that perhaps has more of a claim

in the possibility that, for instance, we or perhaps future generations will come to regard support for the forced sterilization of certain groups of human beings considered to be polluters to our collective gene pool as naïve or simplistic—and to look down on our current views on this issue as laughable and on the wrong side of history—is more than morally offensive to those who hear it; it is also morally harmful to those who believe it. Furthermore, it is false intellectual humility. Yes, moral platitudes about the basic injustice of slavery or about the equality of women would have been considered impossible to believe (and yes, morally offensive) by many of our recent ancestors. They considered these claims indubitably false. And they were wrong. But it was not their confidence that was wrong or harmful; it was the beliefs. Likewise, if it turns out to be the case that we, today, are wrong about our confidence that they were wrong to hold such views, it will, again, be the views and not the (inevitable) confidence with which we hold them that are to blame.

What, though, motivates Quine to adopt such a view of certainty and justification given the uncomfortable if not undesirable moral (philosophical) consequences that follow from it? In a paragraph that could have been written by John Stuart Mill (whom I will discuss in greater depth shortly), Quine states,

> we must recognize that there are almost certain to be many items of today's so-called common knowledge . . . that will illustrate the follies of our age in the next century's textbooks. We like to believe that much of what we hold in common is firmly established and will stand as long as there are people to believe it. Probably we are justified in such confidence. But almost certainly too, if the intellectual history of our species be any guide at all, much of what we hold in common will come to be repudiated.[9]

Don't, however, confuse this with despair, says Quine. It's humility, on his view.

---

to self-evidence is 'One should not inflict needless pain.' Mostly, however, what the ascription of self-evidence to a moral precept is apt to reflect is just a resolution that the precept is to be regarded as basic and hence as exempt from discussion. We resolve to treat such a maxim as a starting point rather than as standing in need of support itself. *But even here, should several principles be advanced, questions of their consistency might very well arise."* Quine, Web of Belief, 30, emphasis added.

9. Quine, Web of Belief, 36.

Philosophical Critique

Doubt

The role of doubt in the strong fallibilist's imagination is the place to begin a philosophical correction of the semblance of virtue that is strong fallibilism. Doubt, I will argue in this chapter, is always principled, always advantaged. It is a conclusion, not a premise. It is epistemically derivative, as opposed to generative. Ludwig Wittgenstein's work *On Certainty* offers several insights into why this is the case. "Whether a proposition can turn out false," he observes, "depends on what I make count as determinants for that proposition."[10] In other words, one must already have in place certain criteria for what would disprove a proposition—criteria about which one must be confident—before one can get as far as doubting a belief.[11] As Wittgenstein says, "If you tried to doubt everything you would not get as far as doubting anything. The game of doubting itself presupposes certainty."[12] Total doubt is an impossibility. It is confidence in some beliefs that give doubt its traction, its bite, or as Wittgenstein puts it, "The *questions* that we raise and our *doubts* depend on the fact that some propositions are exempt from doubt, are as it were like hinges on which those turn."[13] Again, commenting on the form of intellectual confidence put forth by G. E. Moore in his example of there being a hand in front of him, Wittgenstein sees that, "It's not a matter of Moore's knowing that there's a hand there, but rather we should not understand him if he were to say 'Of course I may be wrong about this.' We should ask 'What is it like to make such a mistake as that?'—e.g., what's it like to discover that it was a mistake?"[14] The first-person use of the verb "mistaken" (to be mistaken) can only properly be used in the past-tense ("I was mistaken")

---

10. Wittgenstein, *On Certainty*, §115.

11. Michael Polanyi makes a similar point: "Yet even though . . . the agnostic suspension of belief in respect to a particular statement says nothing about its credibility, it still has a fiduciary content. It implies the acceptance of certain beliefs concerning the possibilities of proof. Kant's demand that, in pure mathematics, unless we *know*, we must abstain from all acts of judgment, would therefore make agnostic doubt itself untenable. For this demand is based on affirming 'I believe *p* is not proven' or 'not provable', which implies the acceptance of some not strictly indubitable framework within which *p* can be said to be proven or not-proven, provable or not-provable." Polanyi, *Personal Knowledge*, 288.

12. Wittgenstein, *On Certainty*, §115.

13. Wittgenstein, *On Certainty*, §341.

14. Wittgenstein, *On Certainty*, §32.

never in the present tense ("I am mistaken"), for as soon as we come to believe we are mistaken we simultaneously cease to regard ourselves as presently mistaken, our mistaken beliefs now regarded as things which have been left behind, existing in our previous mental biographies.

The partial doubt towards one's own beliefs prescribed by strong fallibilism suffers from an incorrect anthropology as well. "My *life*," says Wittgenstein with his own italics, "consists in my being content to accept many things."[15] The original German here is instructive.[16] "My being content to accept" is more literally "to give myself." It is perhaps not a coincidence that, shortly after these remarks in section 344 of *On Certainty*, Wittgenstein makes reference to his famous notion of a "way of life," which could also be translated as "life form." Contrary to the self-understanding and implied anthropology of fallibilists, for humans the act of believing—wholeheartedly—is essential to our natures, in the same fashion as Aristotle would say that humans are moral, rational animals, or as Augustine would say that we are creatures who must love things (the question not being whether but what we love), or as Aquinas would say that we are the sort of creatures who desire to know the causes of things. Just as sports scientists often describe the act of running as a "controlled fall," our human ontology, our nature, pushes us in the back at every moment, forcing us to hazard confident beliefs. Whether we wish to be or not—whether we understand ourselves to be or not—we are agents because we are believers, just as we are believers because we are agents. No matter how much we value doubt or regard ourselves as "doubters," we are forced to live intentionally with goals, some of us deciding to take up croquet (Hume) or cigar smoking (Freud) or to forgo drinking alcohol (Nietzsche), and others to go looking for certainty after the cruel, surprising death of a young child (Descartes).[17] Those who consider themselves cautious in assenting to beliefs are, like the rest of us, intellectual riverboat-gamblers, forced to play their chips.

15. Wittgenstein, *On Certainty*, §344.

16. "Mein Leben besteht darin, daß ich mich mit manchem zufriedengebe."

17. David Hume, on dealing with feelings of depression: "Most fortunately it happens that, since reason is incapable of dispelling these clouds, nature herself suffices to that purpose, and cures me of this philosophical melancholy and delirium, either by relaxing this bent of mind, or by some avocation and lively impression of my senses which obliterate all these chimeras. I dine, I play a game of back-gammon, I converse and I am merry with my friends; and when after three or four hours' amusement, I would return to these speculations, they appear so cold and strain'd, and ridiculous, that I cannot find in my heart to enter into them any further." Hume, *Treatise*, 175.

Admittedly, this can sound counterintuitive. After all, aren't some people, well, lazy, while others engage in more activity? Aren't some people full of confident beliefs and others apparently unwilling to believe anything? Much like the examples of supposed intellectual humility from Sedgwick, Nozik, and Barnes, this realization can be difficult to accept until the clear-eyed philosophical work is confronted, until we see that the choice to stay at home, sit in a chair, and stare at the wall is as much a choice and expression of beliefs as the decision to travel to the third world to fight preventable diseases. No doubt, some choices are more arduous or admirable than others. All are choices, however. The same goes for beliefs. Martin Luther's famous proclamation, "Here I stand. I can do no other" is not the exception as regards the character of human beliefs and actions; it is, instead, merely the most emphatic and honest verbal summation of it.[18] We are confident creatures.[19]

A belief in strong fallibilism can similarly confuse one's picture of knowledge. While Wittgenstein's oft-quoted sentences at the end of his *Tractatus* concerning subjects that "must be passed over silence" are usually taken as a prohibition against metaphysical language and speculation (or at least a recommended silence on these matters), they are arguably, instead, about his view of supposed learned ignorance or Socratic wisdom.[20] Following upon these remarks, he writes, "The book will ... draw a limit to Thinking, or rather—not to Thinking, but to the expression of thoughts; for in order to draw a limit to Thinking, we should have to be able to think both sides of this limit (we should therefore have to be able to think what cannot be thought)."[21] On the other side of the limit is

18. Roman Catholic readers can take comfort in knowing that, in accord with the (preferable) weak fallibilism described in this chapter, it is nevertheless entirely possible that Luther was mistaken in his theological beliefs.

19. Along these lines, Leo Strauss critiques Isaiah Berlin for not recognizing the false consciousness entailed in Berlin's distinction between the barbarian and the civilized man, the later, he says, being the person who realizes the relative validity of his beliefs, valid only for a time, there being no eternal truths. This distinction, says Strauss, was meant and used by Berlin as "final and not to be subject to revision in light of future experience." Strauss writes: "Berlin cannot escape the necessity to which every thinking being is subject: to take a final stand, an absolute stand in accordance with what he regards as the nature of man or as the nature of the human condition or as the decisive truth and hence to assert the absolute validity of his fundamental conviction. . . . [If Berlin were right], Plato and Kant would be barbarians." Strauss, "Relativism," 140.

20. Wittgenstein, *Tractatus*, 27.

21. Wittgenstein, *Tractatus*, 27.

nonsense. Knowledge, in this view, is not a count-noun, on the boundary of which are things we can speak of as unknown or up for debate. The frontier is being created as it is explored. It is interesting to compare this last sentence from Wittgenstein with the comment, much beloved by strong fallibilists, from physicist John Archibald Wheeler, that "[w]e live on an island surrounded by a sea of ignorance. As our island of knowledge grows, so does the shore of our ignorance."[22] The island is the wrong metaphor, for, as Wittgenstein correctly observes, we cannot speak of a boundary to our knowledge because doing so (much like speaking of the boundaries of the universe—what's it expanding *into*?) requires us to know what's on the other side.[23]

Immanuel Kant, too, establishes the limits of human reason as arrived at by the powers of human reason, offering what was described in chapter 2 as a false, magnanimity-lacking form of intellectual humility. It should be added that this Kantian humility also suffers from a false consciousness about the quality of its own doubts. As Michael Polanyi points out, Kant's systematization of regulative principles is "the typical device of modern intellectual prevarication,"[24] for his "as-if" approach to ethical questions actually requires values and normative commitments we must take for granted without any hedging or "as-if" caveat or qualification. Polanyi writes that, if we are to be Kantians,

> Knowledge that we hold to be true and also vital to us is made light of, because we cannot account for its acceptance in terms of a critical philosophy. We then feel entitled to continue using that knowledge, even while flattering our sense of intellectual superiority by disparaging it. And we actually go on, firmly relying on this despised knowledge to guide and lend meaning

---

22. Horgan, "Gravity Quantized," 18–19.

23. For this same reason, the distinction between constructive and deconstructive academic projects is misleading, for we are all knowledge builders, even when we think we are only in the demolition business. Apophatic theologians, for instance, set the boundaries of human reason at the point at which human reason (their own) delimits itself. The hubris of apophaticism is not that it is confident about this boundary, since we all set one in our own minds with confidence, but that it sees itself as exempt from the kind of anthropocentrism of human reason that would be responsible for it. This also helps explain why, in debates over the relationship between nature and grace among theologians, it is possible for one side to see in the other side's views a degree of epistemological Pelagianism, while the opposing side sees epistemological extrinsicism (an inability to get outside of itself) in their opponent's views.

24. Polanyi, *Personal Knowledge*, 373.

to our more exact inquiries, while pretending that these alone come up to our standards of scientific stringency.²⁵

Kant, uncharacteristically, admits as much in the section of his *Critique of Pure Reason* entitled "Of the Transcendental Faculty of Judgment in General," but otherwise almost never acknowledges this fact.²⁶ While modern thinkers, says Polanyi, may regard our understanding of scientific truths as "mere working hypotheses or interpretive policies" akin to "generalizations of the Kantian regulative principles to the whole of science," the fact remains (though it goes unacknowledged by strong fallibilists because it is philosophically damaging) that "we would never use a hypothesis which we believe to be false, nor a policy which we believe to be wrong."²⁷ Denying this or forgetting this while still employing a belief amounts to evasiveness of commitment, absolving us of the responsibility for our truth claims or the "universal intent" of our convictions. Polanyi notes that the operating principle of "innocent until proven guilty" is the legal equivalent to this regulative principle, functioning the same way and suffering from the same false self-consciousness:

> To take into consideration any matter which the court must not notice, or to form beliefs that are contrary to the proper legal presumptions, or quite generally, to form any legally unreasonable beliefs, is condemned as bias or caprice [according to this principle]. In so far as these rules exclude the forming of certain beliefs to which we would normally be prone, they enforce a doubt or a state of agnosticism in respect to these beliefs. But once more, as in the scientific interpretation of experience, the

---

25. Polanyi, *Personal Knowledge*, 373.
26. "If the understanding is explained as the faculty of rules, the faculty of judgment consists in performing the subsumption under these rules, that is, in determining whether anything falls under a given rule (*casus datæ legis*) or not. General logic contains no precepts for the faculty of judgment and cannot contain them. For as it takes no account of the contents of our knowledge, it has only to explain analytically the mere form of knowledge in concepts, judgments, and syllogisms, and thus to establish formal rules for the proper employment of the understanding. If it were to attempt to show in general how anything should be arranged under these rules, and how we should determine whether something falls under them or not, this could only take place by means of a new rule. This, because it is a new rule, requires a new precept for the faculty of judgment, and we thus learn that, *though the understanding is capable of being improved and instructed by means of rules, the faculty of judgment is a special talent which cannot be taught, but must be practiced.* . . . [G]*eneral logic can give no precepts to the faculty of judgment.*" Kant, *Critique of Pure Reason*, 108–9, emphasis added.
27. Polanyi, *Personal Knowledge*, 307.

> system of beliefs which displaces here the beliefs of the man-in-the-street *is no less definite and comprehensive than that which would be held otherwise*. The law which orders that a man be presumed innocent until he is found guilty, *does not impose an open mind on the court*, but tells it on the contrary what to believe at the start: namely that the man is innocent. Even the legal exclusion of normally relevant matter may be interpreted as the prescription of specific beliefs, namely that they are in fact irrelevant to the issue. In all these respects the supposedly open mind of an unbiased court can be sustained only by a much *stronger* will to believe than the usual beliefs of a person discharging no judicial responsibility. The former beliefs are much less plausible than the latter, and to this extent they may be said to be dogmatically imposed for the occasion.[28]

The supposed epistemic, value-free neutrality of such a regulative principle is (once philosophically scrutinized) revealed as anything but. Indeed, it is no less epistemically confident and value-laden than the very opinions it wishes to relegate. The same can be said for the philosophical question about whether one should hold (or is warranted in holding) beliefs false until they are proven true or, alternatively, trusting beliefs as true until they are proven false, as the two supposed strategies are (epistemically) qualitatively identical once all the doubts and supporting beliefs are sorted out and seen in full light.

Why we doubt what we doubt, why we treat things "as if" rather than simply "as," is always rooted in more fundamental beliefs. Dig deep enough and long enough, and one will find reasons for a person's skepticism. This is also why discussions about Pascal-like wagers about important issues like religious faith so often occur at too a high level, for the question must first be: why was the faith doubted in the first place?

Indeed, the form of strong fallibilism I critique here would be unlivable even if it were philosophically viable. We cannot flourish as human beings in the way virtue ethics recommends when we are unable to make and keep promises, as strong fallibilism, properly thought through, would prevent us from doing, given that it would prevent us from having confidence about and a commitment to the sort of person we will be in the future. Getting married requires promising one's spouse that one will continue in one's commitment to the bond. Having children requires that one commit oneself (in a way and to a degree that strong fallibism

---

28. Polanyi, *Personal Knowledge*, 294, emphasis added.

could not approve of) to the raising of one's children for the entirety of one's life. Strong falliblism prevents us from living out the central ethical obligations that define us as human beings and, without which, we cannot fully flourish.

Thus, there can be no such thing as the ignorance-based ethics that some modern philosophers have tried to advance. Consider, as found in this genre, the following statement from philosopher Joe Marocco, who wishes to shift the environmentalist argument regarding climate change away from trying to *prove* climate change to admitting that we are unable to do so. This admission of ignorance and accompanying ethic, he says, "posits that scientific proof of the existence and the potential harmful effects of climate change should not be a prerequisite for action.... [W]e proceed from a position of ignorance."[29] Consider also philosopher Anna Peterson's remarks about what she sees as the problem with the style of ethics shared by different kinds of Christians. Catholics, she notes, tend to use natural law to ground their ethics while Protestants use knowledge of Jesus. Nevertheless, despite these differences, both approaches require "certainty about human knowledge." And this is their common mistake, because "basing morality on knowledge claims generates a host of political and indeed ethical problems, including denial of moral diversity, the premature closure of possibilities."[30] Call this mistaken approach "knowledge-based ethics" as opposed to ignorance-based. Peterson favors the second because it is not guilty of the epistemic hubris that presumes moral progress that culminates in our own ethical positions. Such hubris, she says, is only possible when we begin by denying "the possibility that smart, knowledgeable, and well-meaning people might have different values from our own."[31] Peterson argues that knowledge-based ethics of the kind offered by natural law Catholics, Jesus-following Protestants, or even Kantians (Peterson includes them in her list) fails to recognize that we simply do not know what human nature *is* or what people will *do* in a given situation, adding, "It is more than likely that our assumptions and

---

29. Marocco, "Climate Change and the Limits of Knowledge," 316. Anecdotally, many of my students at a seminar in the fall of 2018, when the Marocco text was assigned, reacted by reexamining their preference for an ignorance-based approach to ethics. Surrendering a science-based argument for the reality of climate change proved too great a cost to them.

30. Peterson, "Ignorance and Ethics," 123.

31. Peterson, "Ignorance and Ethics," 123.

predictions are wrong, ... our ethics will be better if we take seriously the likelihood of error from the very beginning."[32]

The case studies from Marocco and Peterson are instructive not because they are unusual but because they are typical. They appear to many to be sensible, ethically sensitive, and to gel nicely with the spirit of our increasingly globalized, pluralist world. And yet, Marocco and Peterson, too, reason and labor under the misleading philosophical premises of the strong fallibilism I describe in this chapter. To begin with, Marocco fails to acknowledge that, at the root of his avocations for curbing fossil fuels is an implicit and confident valuing of the environment—of its instrumental if not intrinsic worth, in his view—and the knowledge (not ignorance) that, while climate change cannot be proven in a way acceptable to the determined skeptic, there are nevertheless good scientific reasons (which Marocco regards as knowledge and about which he is presumably confident) to think that climate change could be or likely is occurring (e.g., models of greenhouse gas cycles). In short, Marocco offers us a knowledge-based worldview and ethic, just like everyone else. The same goes for Peterson. Among other things underexplored or simply unexplored in her essay are the reasons why we should decline a knowledge-based ethic on the grounds that other equally intelligent people hold different views (a philosophical issue that I explore below)—reasons that she presumably regards as true and as forms of knowledge.

The Contingency of Beliefs

In 1859, John Stuart Mill lamented that,

> [W]hile every one well knows himself to be fallible, few think it necessary to take any precautions against their own fallibility, or admit the supposition that any opinion, of which they feel very certain, may be one of the examples of the error to which they acknowledge themselves to be liable.... And the world, to each individual, means the part of it with which he comes in contact; his party, his sect, his church, his class of society.... [The average man's] faith in this collective authority is not at all shaken by his being aware that other ages, countries, sects, churches, classes, and parties have thought, and even now think, the exact reverse.... [I]t never troubles him that mere accident has

---

32. Peterson, "Ignorance and Ethics," 124.

decided which of these numerous worlds is the object of his reliance.[33]

Depending on how one interprets Mill's thought there are two ways to attack this sentiment philosophically. The first, and more common way, is to note that Mill's reading of history is itself immune from doubt within his own system. That is, in order to identify "reversals" in history—stronger, to identify *prudent* reversals in the history of thought—is to already assert a form of confidence in one's interpretation of history (after all, it is not hard to imagine someone disputing Mill's history here). Hand-in-hand with this goes Mill's progressiveness as regards the unfolding of history: As various truths are tried and put to the test by other conflicting truths, there will emerge, over time and given sufficient freedom and liberty to express different views, beliefs that constitute progress being made in history as regards the acquisition of true beliefs. The ideal system of political freedoms and societal arrangements that naturally follow from this view of history and view of how truth is best ascertained are, for Mill, similarly not called into question.[34]

On Mill's view, then, the biographical contingencies that influence (and can typically predict) the worldviews we will later hold should, if we are honest and mature, lead us to distance ourselves from our current beliefs, to view them with a sense of irony. However, if you or I or Mill were not born the person we were, we would not be the person we are. This is not a pointless tautology. There is, as the axiom goes, no view from nowhere. Robert Musil, for instance, notes that a thought, any thought, be it about what we should make for dinner or about what Mill's man in Peking believes, "is not something that observes an inner event, but,

---

33. Mill, *On Liberty and Other Writings*, 21.

34. As Polanyi says of Mill's supposed skepticism: "No proclamation of intellectual integrity could be more sincere; yet its words are devoid of any definite meaning, and their ambiguity conceals precisely the kind of personal convictions which they so loudly repudiate. For we know that J. S. Mill and other writers standing in the Liberal tradition of philosophic doubt held—and hold today—a wide range of beliefs in science, ethics, politics, etc., which are by no means unquestioned. If they regard these as not having been 'proved unfounded,' this merely reflects their decision to reject the arguments which are or were advanced against them. At no time could the beliefs of Liberalism be regarded as irrefutable in any other sense. But in this sense all fundamental beliefs are irrefutable as well as unprovable. The test of proof or disproof is in fact irrelevant for the acceptance or rejection of fundamental beliefs, and to claim that you strictly refrain from believing anything that could be disproved is merely to cloak your own will to believe your beliefs behind a false pretense of self-critical severity." Polanyi, *Personal Knowledge*, 285.

rather, it is this inner event itself. We do not reflect on something, but, rather, something thinks itself in us."[35] Put another way, in any person belief has "to be there before they themselves could be there; if one did not look at the world with the world's eyes, the world already in one's own gaze, it [would fall] apart into meaningless details."[36] The same goes for hypotheticals or philosophical thought experiments in which we are asked to, for instance, imagine we were born in a different place and time, and thus to derive a philosophical and ethical lesson from this possibility. A number of background assumptions need already be in place, and remain in place, for such worlds to be imagined and such ethics to be derived—assumptions that we carry with us and that result from the very factors of specific biography we are trying to forget and transcend by way of these meta-reflections and thought experiments.[37]

Mill is also guilty of an intellectual version of what is sometimes called the genetic fallacy. The fact that someone is likely to be a socialist because they were raised by socialist parents, or the fact that someone is likely to ascribe to a classical humanist model of education because they attended such a school, does not therefore damage the epistemic credibility of their beliefs on these matters. In other words, it is not merely unjust but philosophically sloppy to respond to these biographical facts by saying, "Well, of course you're a socialist. Your parents gave you *The Daily Worker* to read when you were young," etc. This fact is not a philosophical defeater (or even damager) to whatever arguments such a person might be putting forth for the rightness of the socialist outlook. As is important for the second half of this book, religious belief is no exception to this standard of fairness and philosophical coherence, though it is often a victim of such a double standard. Beliefs cannot be (and typically are not taken to be) disproved once their casual origins are uncovered. Likewise for social forces that cause our beliefs. That children are Christians because parents "coerce" them into attending church at a young age does not, by itself, debunk the children's resulting faith or knowledge of God—why should it? For disproof to occur, we would need to look more closely at the actual character and knowledge produced by the parenting in question. These factors, among other things, are what distinguish, say,

---

35. See "Tonka" in Musil, *Five Women*, 110.
36. See "Tonka" in Musil, *Five Women*, 110.
37. On this point, see Wilkes, *Real People*.

Presbyterian catechesis from North Korean brainwashing, the latter being politically and epistemically repressive.[38]

Pragmatist Critique

Pragmatists, who, like virtue ethicists, look first and last to human action when analyzing human beliefs, note that strong fallibilism has an inert quality. Philosopher Akeel Bilgrami, for instance, asks how, given its philosophical incoherence, strong fallibilism (or what he calls Millsian philosophy) nevertheless animates our "law, philosophy, and even our everyday understanding of the justifications for academic freedom."[39] His answer is that Mill works with a fallibilist epistemology that nicely gels with the popular classical and orthodox liberal mentalities. Bilgrami's problem with strong fallibilism is that it makes no practical difference in the lives of its adherents and thus, from a pragmatist standpoint, can be of no epistemic difference either. "The doubt expressed by the thought 'for all one knows even our strongest convictions as to what is true might be false' is an idle form of doubt."[40] Thus, we needn't hedge our bets with a kind of strong fallibilism. "In our own pursuits towards the truth," writes Bilgrami, "we may be as confident in the truth of the deliverances of our investigations as is merited by the evidence in our possession, and we need feel no unnecessary urge to display balance in the classroom, if we have shown balance and scruple in our survey of the evidence on which our convictions are based, the only place where balance is relevant in the first place."[41]

---

38. On the matter of singling out religious beliefs as epistemically suspicious, I submit the following observation from my time spent in institutions of higher education: namely, that professors of religion within secular institutions who are themselves religious (that is, personally believe in the belief systems they explain to their students) are the only kind of teachers who are viewed by some (not by all, to be fair, but clearly and nonetheless by some) as being less objective about their subject matter—as having beliefs that are somewhat epistemically suspect—by virtue of their being adherents to that belief system. No one, for instance, would regard as more biased a chemist who believed that chemistry described real processes—indeed, we would find strange and suspicious any chemist who did not think their science corresponded to reality. A historian who believed that the history he taught was fabricated, that it is impossible to truly know the past, would not be seen as "more objective" by fellow historians.

39. Bilgrami, "Truth, Balance, and Freedom," 12.

40. Bilgrami, "Truth, Balance, and Freedom," 15.

41. Bilgrami, *Secularism, Identity, and Enchantment*.

There is a natural, understandable reaction to Bilgrami's conclusion on the part of those who continue to think that fallibilism is not an idle belief. Consider an author who has written a book and is convinced it contains no errors. He is, in other words, decidedly *unfallibilistic* about his claims. Imagine a friend emails him to say that she has discovered an error in one passage. Now, if he is truly certain that his book contains no errors, it would seem that he has no reason to spend time investigating his friend's claim. If, on the other hand, our author is *confident* but not *fully certain* about the claims of his book (i.e., he's a good fallibilist), he would appear to have good warrant for looking into his friend's claim: he acknowledges the possibility that his book could contain errors. Thus, Bilgrami must be mistaken, since the author behaves *differently* than if he had lacked strong fallibilism. Again, this all seems quite sensible. And yet it is philosophically flawed.

From the standpoint of an alternative, preferable psychology, the deeper reason (i.e., the belief doing the "real philosophical work") the author takes seriously his friend's claim that something in his manuscript is wrong—and the reason I would take seriously a reader's contention that something in this essay is off-kilter—is not because he has any particular belief that it is wrong or likely to be wrong (as strong fallibilism would argue) but because the author never excludes the possibility that, as a finite creature with limited perspective, there is always more for him to learn, perhaps from unexpected sources, that may force him to revise his views. But, contrary to the self-understanding of our fallibilist interlocutor, it is not *doubt* per se or any sense of strong fallibilism that functions as the psycho-philosophical engine behind his action. Such fallibilism, as Bilgrami argues, is indeed inert. A real "know-it-all" is, rather, someone who, contrary to the spirit of true and virtuous open-mindedness as defined and argued for in this project, lacks studiousness and wonder, the openness to the world of teachers.

Defensive Irony

There is an intriguing, generally unremarked upon, connection between comedic irony and the kind of irony being here associated with strong fallibilism and John Stuart Mill. Both are parasitic upon "how things ought to be." That's the foil, usually unstated, that makes comedic irony work, and it is the view of how the world ought to work, again usually unstated, that gives intellectual irony its bite. Christy Wampole has taken note of this strange parallel in her works that act as a kind of negative reaction to the ironicization—personified in the hipster—of so much in modern society. Consider, she says, an advertisement that pokes fun at itself by making fun of its own advertising format. In so doing, that advertisement "pre-emptively acknowledges its own failure to accomplish anything meaningful. No attack can be set against it, as it has already conquered itself."[42] According to Wampole, this seemingly harmless and funny habit of modern culture actually springs from something deeper, darker, and potentially more harmful in the collective psyche of society. "The ironic frame," she notes, "functions as a shield against criticism," a kind of defense mechanism. "The same goes for ironic living. Irony is the most self-defensive mode, as it allows a person to dodge responsibility for his or her choices, aesthetic and otherwise. To live ironically is to hide in public. It is flagrantly indirect, a form of subterfuge, which means etymologically to 'secretly flee' (subter + fuge)."[43]

How and why has irony become so dominant, particularly among Western society's younger generations? Here the connection between ironic living and the kind of intellectual irony found in Millian strong fallibilism becomes clearer. As Wampole suggests, this trend toward defensive living stems from a belief that "serious commitment to any belief will eventually be subsumed by an opposing belief, rendering the first laughable at best and contemptible at worst."[44] In other words, there is a Millian-like view of history hovering in the background that makes us fearful to hazard confident beliefs of our own. Interestingly, Wampole observes that we find the clearest examples of *non*ironic living among some of the segments of our population who lack advantages, a fact that ought to give pause to those implicitly advocating the ironic lifestyle. Wampole lists "very young children, elderly people, deeply religious people, people with severe mental or physical disabilities, people who have suffered, and those from economically or politically challenged places" as examples of those whose minds are characterized by seriousness rather than irony. Quoting her friend Robert Pogue Harrison, Wampole states, "Wherever

---

42. Wampole, "How to Live Without Irony," para. 4.
43. Wampole, "How to Live Without Irony," para. 4.
44. Wampole, "How to Live Without Irony." Interestingly, in a visit to my seminar in the fall of 2018, Wampole remarked that, due in part to Trump's presidency, there has been a noticeable revival of "seriousness" among the younger generation.

the real imposes itself, it tends to dissipate the fogs of irony."[45] Many strong fallibilists (or those who have unknowingly been influenced by the doctrine of strong fallibilism) can be found in wealthy countries and among the socioeconomically privileged generation Xers, but they are hard to find in refugee camps or among those working in hospice care.

The Conciliarist vs. Steadfaster Debate

I have already alluded to the belief, responsible for some people's adherence to what I call strong fallibilism, that the undeniable reality of there being other (perhaps many) equally smart and apparently well-intentioned people who disagree with one on a given issue ought to cause one to think twice about (or be somewhat ironic or skeptical about) one's own particular belief on the matter. Among philosophers today, there is a lively running debate concerning whether or not this logic makes good philosophical sense. The two sides are sometimes called conciliarists and steadfasters (the latter, as one might guess, are those who double down and stick to their guns or beliefs in spite of intellectual pluralism). At other times, the two camps are called conformists and nonconformists, though the definitions remain the same.

Nonconformist Thomas Kelly, for instance, argues that even if there are good reasons to call into question one's views when confronted by damaging evidence (something that, empirically, happens all the time), it is not (as conformists wish to say) disagreement from epistemic peers that motivates a changed mind or is even capable of motivating the change. Kelly points out that, in such cases, "the reasons that we have for [new] skepticism are provided by the state of the evidence itself, and our own judgments about the probative force of that evidence. The role of disagreement, whether possible or actual, ultimately proves superfluous or inessential with respect to the case for such skepticism."[46]

Second, strong fallibilism (if it is to withstand philosophical scrutiny) must always privilege its own truth in the face of disagreement from epistemic peers over the question of whether conciliarism itself is a prudent belief, something it can only do on pain of self-contradiction. As Nicholas Wolterstorff notes, "I assume that the conformists regard at least some of the nonconformists as epistemic peers. Conformists hold

---

45. Wampole, "How to Live Without Irony."
46. Kelly, "Epistemic Significance of Disagreement," 19.

that, in this situation, both parties ought to change their view in some way. But they, the conformists, have not done this: they continue vigorously to espouse their conformist position"[47]—meaning, conformism is effectively baked in from the start for its adherents.

Philosopher Philip Pettit, interestingly, gives us another option: to be a conformist on peripheral matters (recall Quine's web) while being nonconformists on core matters.[48] That is, we can and should be conformists about whether or not we saw a car go through a red light (we should go with the majority view, if there is one) but not about our views about the morality of war, a presumably core issue in our personal web of beliefs. Pettit's reasons for trying to articulate a third way (a compromise between the comprehensive compromisers and comprehensive non-compromisers, so to speak) is that the alternatives are hard to live by. Majoritarian and testimonial deference works well for the "who caused the traffic accident?" example, but not for things like the plausibility of intelligent design theory or conviction that abortion is immoral, assuming you strongly believe in such things. Here, you have to decide on your own. "You should not be prepared to shift your ground just because a majority of those you regard as equally intelligent, informed and impartial take a different view."[49] If you do, you'll end up in epistemic no man's land. While Pettit's is an interesting proposal, it is finally flawed, for its basis and selling point, so to speak, concerns what forms of philosophy are livable rather than what points of view are philosophically coherent. If conformism is the first (in some cases) but not the second, it is perhaps worth asking, instead, how it is that people come to change their minds at all on issues of great importance. Particularly interesting are those case studies in which the person in question is someone who is deeply involved—intellectually and actively—in a cause or worldview before undergoing a profound transformation in which they come to switch teams, as it were, becoming deeply invested intellectually and vocationally in their new, opposite, set of views.

Historian Daniel Oppenheimer, for instance, has written a book about major intellectual or political figures who, during the twentieth century, experienced a profound shift in their political views.[50] Oppenheimer

47. Wolterstorff, "Significance of Inexplicable Disagreement," 319.
48. Pettit, "When to Defer to Majority Testimony," 185.
49. Pettit, "When to Defer to Majority Testimony," 185.
50. While Oppenheimer focuses on people who transitioned from the far left to the far right end of the political spectrum, this feature of his book is incidental for

notes that we all believe what we do largely because of how we were raised, or the professors we had in college, or who we married, and so on. "We know belief is complicated, contingent, multi-determined," he writes. "But do we really know it? Do we feel it? Do we act as though it's true, with the humility that such an acknowledgement would entail?"[51] Few of us do, and even then rarely, he answers. His argument is that the people he profiles did live this way. And he admires them for their courage, even if he doesn't share their eventual political views. What fascinates him is the intellectually painful and thus unsustainable period of time in which these figures found themselves caught between worldviews: no longer able to identify with their previous world, not yet ready to enter their next world, or as Oppenheimer describes it, when "the bones of one's belief system are broken and poking out through the skin," and when the frailness and contingency of our beliefs show themselves.[52]

Most relevant for the purposes of this chapter is the metaphor Oppenheimer chooses for characterizing how the transition between worlds takes place. Our worldviews are like coats, he says. Over time, they can get harder and harder to put on (a tad too tight in the shoulder, etc.) until, one day, we can't stand it anymore and are forced to find a new coat. As uncomfortable as it has become, it's hard to part with the old coat. This metaphor is intuitive but also misleading, for the profiles of change Oppenheimer offers suggest, instead, that our personal coats are always being patched and re-sewn to adapt to and incorporate new evidence; that is, that they are never fully replaced. Thus, Oppenheimer's interest in whether the big conversions of famous political apostates would have been different or perhaps never have happened if not for the contingencies of their lives is misplaced. For instance, he examines the life of the Communist-spy-turned-Christian and sworn enemy of Communism Whittaker Chambers, who went from one extreme to the other with the same zeal. He was a traitor to his cause. Oppenheimer reflects, "[And] what about us? Could we be wrong about everything?" Summoning Mill, "Would we believe differently if we were born twenty years earlier, or later? Could we be as frail and fallible as apostates [like Chambers] so

---

the purposes of this chapter: what matters is simply how such transformations are possible, no matter the subject matter or direction of shift.

51. Oppenheimer, *Exit Right*, 2.
52. Oppenheimer, *Exit Right*, 2.

visibly are, only without the courage or bad judgment to put it all out there for the world to see?"[53]

How, though, did Chambers come to change his mind? Not, it turns out, as a result of a realization that, had he been born at a different time and place, he would not have been a Soviet sympathizer and spy (again, the Millian take). Rather, his reasons were rooted in prior commitments. In the context of looking for "truths . . . fixed in [Chambers] when he was young," Oppenheimer notes that, early on, Chambers (perhaps because of his socialist parents or perhaps not—it doesn't matter) felt that "[t]here was a deep pain in the world. He [felt] called to sacrifice himself in the cause of healing or excising it." These convictions, says Oppenheimer, preceded reason and politics. "They were the raw ore he spent his life trying to forge into authentic and correct political beliefs and commitments."[54] He learned that he was in the wrong system based on his true, unswerving commitments (a tacit reply to Meno's puzzle regarding how we grow in knowledge). Some of these commitments were so violated by communism as Chambers experienced it that he had to choose between them and his communist faith. Chambers himself wondered what finally caused his break with the party in his autobiography. He gave two answers. The first was metaphysical. As Oppenheimer interprets it, "the spark of the divine in his soul, the ineradicable immanence of God, enabled him to eventually recognize that communism wasn't a solution to the crisis of modernity, but in fact its most terrible manifestation."[55]

The second answer, though, was more biographical. Oppenheimer points to "the menagerie of grotesque characters [Chambers] met in the underground, people whose vulgarity . . . made him wonder, despite himself, at the worth of a cause that could hand authority to such types." More, "there were the astounding facts of Soviet cruelty, which were lying in wait for him, in plain sight, if ever he proved unflinching enough to look at them."[56] It was consistency, not contingency, that led to Chambers's transition. He became, as it were, a better and fuller version of who/what he already was.[57] Indeed, Oppenheimer finally seems

---

53. Oppenheimer, *Exit Right*, 3.
54. Oppenheimer, *Exit Right*, 212.
55. Oppenheimer, *Exit Right*, 59.
56. Oppenheimer, *Exit Right*, 59.
57. One is reminded here of the literary critic Terry Eagleton (a minor apostate in his own right) who spent his many years as an atheist Marxist before rediscovering Catholicism later in life, as a result of coming to see that Marxism and Catholicism

to realize as much himself, despite his initial thesis that the realization of the causal contingency of one's beliefs is what distinguishes these men and their supposedly unusual intellectual stories. Ultimately, Chambers "achieved a kind of grace not because he had the right answers, or chose the right side, or knew himself perfectly, but because he persisted in trying to become himself more fully."[58] Such a sentiment, as will become more evident in the next chapter, is a blueprint for true open-mindedness for us all.

The Challenge of Temporalism

How should one's sense of intellectual humility be affected by the recognition of the long stretches of time that have preceded one's life, the long stretches of time that will follow upon one's death, and the relatively small amount of time each of our lives occupy in the timeline of history? Consider a few examples of how one might reply to such a question, even if only implicitly. A person might say (sarcastically), "Why on earth would we think that any book written by people over two thousand years ago is of relevance to our lives today?" Or a person might say that such-and-such feature of society "has been the norm in Western civilization for over two thousand years and has never been questioned—why, then, should we put any stock in public opinion, a mere decade long, that would change this feature of society?" Or, again, consider the words of biologist Konrad Lorenz:

> Being biologists we are modest regarding man's position in the totality of nature, but more demanding in regard to what the future may yet bring us in the way of knowledge. To declare man absolute, to assert that any imaginable rational being, even angels, would have to be limited to the laws of thought of Homo sapiens, appears to us to be incomprehensible arrogance.... For the lost illusion of a unique lawfulness for man, we exchange the conviction that in his openness to the world he is basically capable of outgrowing his science and the [perhaps Kantian] a priori formulations of his thought.[59]

---

shared a premise: namely, that the world is broken, that it is not as it should be, as it was intended to be. But, as Eagleton came to realize, only God and Christianity has the ability to make such change possible.

58. Oppenheimer, *Exit Right*, 211–12.

59. Lorenz, "Kant's Doctrine of the A Priori," 246.

Each of these three reactions is understandable and yet all three, on the view of this project, make the mistake of misconstruing the proper philosophical relationship between relative scales of time and intellectual humility. Alternatively, consider the response of Pope John Paul II when asked whether or not he thought we were living in what Christians call "end time." After a long pause, he answered "No. . . . I think some day future Christians may refer to us as the 'early church.'" And, though of a different theological persuasion, neo-Barthian theologian Robert Jenson evinced a similarly proper form of intellectual humility with respect to time—a sufficiently long view of history that does not commit the errors of strong fallibilist thinking—when observing that "[i]t took two centuries to correct Marcionism and Montanism, three centuries to defeat Adoptionism, four centuries to defeat Arianism, and five centuries to defeat Nestorianism," in light of which he asks rhetorically, "Why not think it could take twenty-one centuries for the church to correct its understanding of divine impassibility?"

More than any other philosopher today, J. L. Schellenberg has argued for the position that a proper view of time and our relatively small place in it should instill in us a humility—by which he means a lesser degree of confidence—in our currently held views. He calls this position "temporalism." Schellenberg asks, "Should we not expect that our ideas about [ultimate] things may well seem to an enlightened human of the year 4000 or 40,000 CE as antiquated or inadequate as many of the ideas of the ancient Egyptians or Babylonians or Greeks appear to us today?"[60] We are, from the standpoint of the evolutionary biologist, a young species who have only just begun our investigations into reality. We should be intellectual, modest, and humble, says Schellenberg, "given the Great Disparity between the time already devoted to inquiry on our planet and the time that may yet be devoted to it" in the future.[61]

While apparently sensible, Schellenberg's temporalism has philosophical problems. To begin with, it is unclear, given his view, how any humans (living our future) could ever know when he or she (or we,

---

60. Schellenberg, *Wisdom to Doubt*, 95.

61. Schellenberg, *Wisdom to Doubt*, 26. It is interesting to compare Schellenberg's temporal humility to the respect paid tradition by G. K. Chesterton, who in many ways presents the other, balancing, side of Schellenberg's coin (a side Schellenberg nowhere acknowledges) when remarking, "Tradition means giving a vote to most obscure of all classes, our ancestors. It is the democracy of the dead. . . . Tradition refuses to submit to the small and arrogant oligarchy of those who merely happen to be walking about." Chesterton, *Orthodoxy*, 43.

collectively as a species) had reached a level of intellectual maturity that would warrant the kind of confidence and closure that Schellenberg warns us against claiming today. In the spirit of Wittgenstein, one could ask, "What would it be like to know that you or I had not reached such maturity?"

Second, Schellenberg makes a key admission in opening himself up to the possibility that the best future ideas (or those regarded as best by future generations) might actually be old ideas reconsidered. "Realizing," he says, "that our enquiry into the fundamental nature of the world is just beginning, we might have to say that, for all we know, some of the new ideas of the future will be old ideas, whose time has finally come."[62] Perhaps, then, the ultimate truths about the world were revealed in the past, truths by which we must judge all future truths, even if we believe in the evolutionary progress of our species—as many religious people wish to believe. Insofar as people today fail to acknowledge these truths, there is an occurrence of what might be called "lost knowledge."

Third, Schellenberg's temporalism suffers from a deficiency of certain virtues described by Aquinas (though, to be fair, never in connection with anything like temporalism). For instance, Aquinas argues that patience is not the same as longanimity (sometimes called forbearance). For our purposes, let it be argued that intellectual patience (waiting for the truth to finally be revealed) is not the same as intellectual longanimity (or virtuously enduring the unfortunate fact that we don't have all the answers at this present moment). Aquinas writes,

> Just as by magnanimity a man has a mind to tend to great things, so by longanimity a man has a mind to tend to something a long way off. Wherefore as magnanimity regards hope, which tends to good, rather than daring, fear, or sorrow, which have evil as their object, so also does longanimity. Hence longanimity has more in common with magnanimity than with patience.[63]

Note the connection Aquinas makes between longanimity and magnanimity, the latter being an ingredient lacking in false forms of intellectual humility such as that found in Schellenberg's temporalism, in which a form of supposed intellectual patience is motivated by apprehensiveness about the future.

---

62. Schellenberg, "Time Out of Mind."
63. Schellenberg, "Time Out of Mind."

Aquinas offers us a corrective to any kind of temporalist intellectual anxiety or fear. Tellingly, in his discussion of fear generally, Aquinas never speaks about fear of being wrong (what might be called intellectual fear); instead, he always speaks about fear as fear of sin or punishment, or of offending God (a kind of fear that Aquinas, as well as Augustine in following Paul, calls servile and filial fear). As concerns effects, he says, the beginning of wisdom is found in fear.[64]

Finally, Aquinas's remarks about solicitude, when applied to the more modern debate about intellectual humility and time, suggest that it is wrong (i.e., not virtuous) for us to be solicitous about earthly truth or knowledge. In the spirit of Matthew 6, we are told to not be anxious about what we shall eat or drink. Knowledge, if considered a temporal good, should be counted by Christians among the temporal goods that we should trust will be, as Aquinas says, "granted us according to our needs, if we do what we ought to do," and are not solicitous about the future.[65]

---

64. *ST* II-II.19.7.
65. *ST* II-II.19.7.

5

The Virtue of Open-Mindedness

HAVING NOW SPENT SEVERAL chapters arguing what open-mindedness cannot be, if it is to be virtuous, it is now time to say more, constructively, about what virtuous open-minded *could* in fact be. This chapter, therefore, will offer some metaphorical descriptions of open-mindedness, followed by multiple real examples of it in action, before turning to the question of what, at bottom, motivates open-mindedness in those who practice it. Admittedly, this is an unusual way to proceed for a virtue ethics project, and intentionally so. A more traditional path would describe open-mindedness's acts, ends, and circumstances. Virtuous open-mindedness has all those things (as do all habits), but focusing on them would, I believe, come at the cost of turning some readers off from this project. If my sole purpose were to persuade an academic audience of a certain argument, then the traditional path mentioned above would be appropriate. But since this project is equally concerned with appealing to the hearts and thus changing the moral character of readers both academic *and* lay, then proceeding by example is arguably a more effective strategy.

The Open Mind Is Like . . .

To use a chemical analogy, the open mind is like a sprawling, complex, multidimensional compound with many chains, each different, but with exterior rings to which it is easy to bond. Its open chains extend here and there like unfinished thoughts or gropings just waiting for the right compound to come along and couple with them. The edges of the open mind have highly positive valences (combining power); they are chemically gregarious, intellectually amiable.

The thoughts of the open mind are not completely fungible, but neither is the open mind unable to entertain new thoughts. Pushed too far, as when asked to keep as live options the moral rightness of horrific wrongs, the open mind firms up. In this way, the open mind behaves like what chemists call non-Newtonian fluids, or pressure-dependent substances such as Oobleck (the cornstarch and water concoction beloved by children), which, unlike standard materials, become harder instead of weaker when great pressure is applied.

To draw an analogy from a different discipline, the open mind is like an energetic living system. As biologist James Miller wrote in his seminal book on information theory and architecture, *Living Systems*, "information" does not exist until there is a living system, which is, by definition, a self-organizing system that exchanges material and information with its surrounding environment for the purposes of maintaining itself and developing.[1] The essence of life, simply put, is information processing, which makes open minds more alive.

Interestingly, Heraclitus drew a similar conclusion to Miller's without any need for biology, contrasting the sleeping mind, which is shut inside its own private thoughts, with the awake mind, open to the thoughts of others, writing, "Those who are asleep are fellow-workers in what goes on in the Cosmos,"[2] and later, "that the waking have one Cosmos, but the sleeping turn aside, each into a world of his own."[3] Indeed, Heraclitus goes so far as to say that, by this logic, God is most alive and those completely trapped in their own thoughts are most dead. We living mortals live in between and must choose in which direction we want to strive.

Meteorologically speaking, the open mind is like a cyclonic storm, drawing in warm air from surrounding events on the ground, gaining in size and strength as it incorporates this material—foreign and sometimes conflicting ideas—before processing them to produce weather in the sky that emits its product outward. By contrast, closed minds are like anticyclone storms, spreading their fair (i.e., boring) weather on the ground by way of surface divergence instead of surface convergence.

---

1. Miller, *Living Systems*.
2. Heraclitus, *Fragments*, Fragment DK22b75.
3. Heraclitus, *Fragments*, Fragment DK22b89.

Agriculturally speaking, the open mind is less like a cattle roper (of ideas) than a sheepdog (this, I propose, being a superior animal analogy to Isaiah Berlin's fox and hedgehog metaphor). For the sheepdog is always circling, and, like the good shepherd, goes in search of the lost sheep and brings him back to the fold.

For the sports enthusiast, picture the open mind as a wise free safety playing defense on a football team. He sees the whole field, and never lets the play get behind him, always keeping the action in front of him, because these are his assignments. The open-minded person may or may not be a fisher of men, but he is certainly a fisher of ideas, brave and adventurous enough "to put out a little way from the land," perhaps in familiar parts, and "out into the deep water" (Luke 5:3–4), perhaps (even especially) when he has gone all day without catching anything.

The open mind has a large taxonomic tree of knowledge, having given a good deal of thought to where all the fields and subfields of knowledge belong in its mental flowchart. Blindfolded and dropped off in what is to it (at least initially) strange intellectual territory (perhaps behind enemy lines, so to speak), it does not panic but instead quickly regains its bearings using its intellectual GPS. No matter how far from his intellectual home he finds himself, the open-minded person learns how to speak the native language and navigate the different world or worldview. Indeed, he *seeks out* those who speak a different tongue. He intentionally reads the columnist with whom he disagrees deeply, hoping to learn from him; he attends conferences on disciplines other than his own; and, if possible, he tries to befriend and learn from people of different persuasions. The open mind allows its thoughts and ideas to be proofread and edited by others. No doubt, such a gregarious, intellectual omnivore runs the risk of being a dilettante, acquainted with all but grasping nothing, a kind of intellectual dandy, fun to have around (and perhaps a good conversationalist) but not all that serious. But this concern is less worrisome when it is remembered that integral to open-mindedness is a healthy studiousness that should prevent such shallowness.

To borrow an analogy from travel literature, the open mind is a real traveler, as opposed to a "tourist." It is ideologically cosmopolitan without sacrificing its own beliefs. Its intellectual passport is well-stamped, because it is gregarious with respect to ideas. But the open mind (unlike the strong fallibilist mind described in the previous chapter) never forgets where it's coming from. It is not, intellectually, a rootless cosmopolitan.[4]

---

4. I am not unaware of the unfortunate origins of this phrase. I can only say that

In this way, the biography of thoughts in the open mind is like the adventures, observations, and reflections of travel literature prior to the eighteenth century, albeit without prejudicial colonial tendencies. As Alain de Botton notes in *The Art of Travel*, "The value we ascribe to traveling [today], to wandering without reference to a destination, connects us . . . to a broad shift in sensibilities dating back to some two hundred years ago, whereby the outsider came to seem morally superior to the insider."[5] De Botton refers his readers to the observation made by Raymond Williams in his influential work *The Country and the City* about English city and country life. "From the late eighteenth century onwards, it is no longer from the practice of community but from being a wanderer that the instinct of fellow-feeling is derived."[6] How this came to be is a story unto itself. For the purposes of this chapter it is enough to say that the open mind should not travel as Williams's subject matter might, as strong fallibilists are likely to. Done correctly, intellectual travel contributes to human flourishing, the cultivation of the virtue being called open-mindedness in this project. The service stations, the motels, the airports, and the train stations of the mind ought to excite the open mind in the same way these places, in their physical instantiations, excite the avid traveler.[7]

Three real examples of such open-mindedness will serve as helpful illustrations. When asked why so many physicists do their most creative work at a young age, the celebrated scientist Subramanyan Chandrasekhar replied,

> [T]here seems to be a certain arrogance toward nature which people develop. These people have had great insights and made profound discoveries. They imagine afterwards that the fact that

---

what the Soviets were accusing the Jews of—refusing to forget their story, where they came from—is precisely what I'm *praising* here as essential to a healthy intellectual cosmopolitanism.

5. de Botton, *Art of Travel*, 57.

6. As quoted in de Botton, *Art of Travel*, 57.

7. If this is the case, then single-minded focus on a particular intellectual question or topic over a portion of one's allotted time on earth, though perhaps the best (or only) way to achieve certain intellectual accomplishments, is not actually conducive to human flourishing. Closing off all mental paths but one and strictly prohibiting oneself from any intellectual wanderings may result in works like the acclaimed biographies (e.g., of Lyndon B. Johnson) by Robert Caro, but such behavior makes open-mindedness and other intellectual virtues nearly impossible. I realize that it is unusual to claim that the mental life of someone like Caro is unhealthy but, according to the logic of this project, it appears to be so.

they succeeded so triumphantly in one area means they have a special way of looking at science which must therefore be right.[8]

But they are closed-minded for doing so and, further, they are mistaken about science, as the history of discipline reveals.[9]

Consider, too, the reflections of Father Joseph McSorley, a New York priest in the early 1900s, who wrote of open-mindedness,

> To see light, that is to react against the stimulus of rays, which fall upon the retina, is less a virtue than a mechanical, or physiological, necessity. But to hold the eyes open when they are tired, to strain our sight when the light is dim, to peer about and search eagerly for the truth which we are aware will make us uncomfortable—this is to serve the cause of virtue and to obey the law of God.[10]

But many and natural are the temptations that prevent people from serving this worthy cause. "The example of the crowd, the wish to preserve reputation, the love of personal comfort, the affection of friends, the traditions of race and family, the revolt of judgment and temper"—all of these work against open-mindedness. "*And finally there is the inevitable temptation to defer action and to re-examine arguments endlessly.* If, despite these obstacles, a man becomes a convert from genuine conviction; if he withstands the influence of disposition, training, and habit; *if he overcomes that last foe of duty, self-distrust*; then we may regard him as a noble example of open-mindedness."[11]

---

8. Chandresekhar, as quoted in Roberts and Wood, *Intellectual Virtues*, 253.

9. Roberts and Wood, *Intellectual Virtues*, 253.

10. McSorley, "Open-Mindedness," 231, emphases added.

11. A mistake commonly made by contemporary philosophers applying virtue ethics techniques to inherited problems in epistemology is to begin by defining open-mindedness (and assessing its value) in terms of its reliability in leading to the acquisition of truth. If today's "virtue epistemologists" adopted the starting-point of the normative (implicit in McSorley's distinction between mechanical and virtuous sight), it would reframe their self-imposed problem of how to relate "low-" and "high-level" types of knowledge, or (in what amounts to the same) how to relate "reliabilist" and "responsibilist" approaches to intellectual virtues. This difficulty is created by defining epistemic virtues in terms of their truth-generating tendencies, as per the standards of modern philosophy. If logical priority is given to "low-level knowledge" like acute hearing, it's unclear how to accommodate apparent virtues like inquisitiveness, which may or may not lead to knowledge. If, however, logical priority is given to cognitive character (the "responsible" mind) and "high-level" knowledge that requires inquiry, it's unclear how to accommodate characterless faculties of sensation.

Consider, too, the admirable words from a counselor of King Edwin of Northumbria. When the first Christian missionaries visited what would eventually become England in the seventh century, King Edwin, the local authority, was advised by the counselor as follows:

> When we compare the present life of man on earth with that time of which we have no knowledge, it seems to me like the swift flight of a single sparrow through the banquet-hall . . . on a winter's day. In the midst there is a comforting fire to warm the hall; outside the storms of winter rain or snow are raging. This sparrow flies swiftly in through one door of the hall, and out through another. . . . Even so, man appears on earth for a little while; but of what went before this life or of what follows, we know nothing. Therefore, if this new teaching has brought any more certain knowledge, it seems only right that we should follow it.[12]

Consider, likewise, the noble words of Simmias in Plato's dialogue *Phaedo*:

> For I dare say that you, Socrates, feel as I do, how very hard or almost impossible is the attainment of any certainty about questions such as these in the present life. And yet I should deem him a coward who did not prove what is said about them to the uttermost, or whose heart failed him before he had examined them on every side. For he should persevere until he has attained one of two things: either he should discover or learn the truth about them; or, if this is impossible, I would have him take the best and most irrefragable of human notions, and let this be the raft upon which he sails through life—not without risk, as I admit, if he cannot find some word of God which will more surely and safely carry him.[13]

Noble sentiments and wise words to be lived by, without a trace of the strong fallibilism described earlier in this book.

Mental Unrest

It is natural to ask what would motivate the open-mindedness on display in the previous examples. As already suggested, the proposed answer of

---

12. From Bede, *Ecclesiastical History of the English People*, as quoted in Placher, *History of Christian Theology*, 122.

13. Plato, *Five Dialogues*, 85c–d.

this paper is kind of a healthy curiosity, wonder, and studiousness, born of a non-ironic, non-Millian, premodern form of intellectual humility. At the heart of open-mindedness is, more generally, mental unrest. In Thomistic terms, we are motivated by a natural desire to know the cause of things; we are by nature curious critters, to which the appropriate response (or correct training of the will) is a kind of virtuous wonder and studiousness. As the beginning of all philosophy (according to the ancients), wonder is a virtue that does not require the kind of mistaken humility found in strong fallibilism or self-doubt.

Though wonder begins and ends in what philosopher Jacques Maritain calls an "avowal of ignorance," it is not an avowal of self-doubt. Instead, it is the recognition that there is more to be known, and that as-yet-unknown things might call into question or force us to revise some of what we currently hold to be true. Yet, if this is so, it is for reasons we do not currently possess and therefore should not motivate us to become skeptical about that which we currently believe, to repeat a point made in the previous chapter. Theologian Josef Pieper writes, "To wonder is not merely not to know; it means . . . that one understands oneself in not knowing. And yet it is not the ignorance of resignation. On the contrary, to wonder is to be on the way, in via."[14] Wonder, unlike the kind of epistemic pessimism critiqued by Bilgrami in chapter 4, begets a kind of human action, specifically the mental habits of studiousness and inquisitiveness. Notably absent from current literature on intellectual virtues or virtue epistemology is talk of the role that wonder plays in human flourishing. Just as surveying the vast cosmos or the tiny intricacies of the nervous systems in fish should evoke wonder in us, so should our encounters with people of different cultures and worldviews. Intellectual humility that accompanies wonder—the *genuine* variety of intellectual humility—draws us intellectually outwards rather than into ourselves.

For Christians who believe that all people are made in the image of God, and thus that all people are of interest to him, wonder presents the added challenge of seeing people's mental lives through the eyes of God. Christians must wager that if we were to know everything about a person's life, i.e., to know a person—even the most apparently boring—as God knows him or her, we would then possess the material of a novel greater than any that has ever been written. Call this the intellectual equivalent of the story of Saint Francis's decision (perhaps apocryphal,

---

14. Pieper, *Leisure*, 136.

THE VIRTUE OF OPEN-MINDEDNESS   113

but it matters not) to eat the pus of a leper after he is disgusted by his own initial revulsion at the poor man, and his determination to see the leper and love him as Christ would—indeed, to see Christ in him.

Short of possessing Saint Francis's faith, there is still a nontheological intuition that such wonder befits human nature. Novelist Gustave Flaubert left us travel literature replete with this kind of wonder. He recalls, for instance, while travelling on a riverboat from Du Camp to Marseilles, seeing a woman to whom he reacted with great wonder. After describing her in detail in his travel journal, he goes on to say,

> I'm obsessed with inventing stories for people I come across. An overwhelming curiosity makes me ask myself what their lives might be like. I want to know what they do, where they're from, their names, what they're thinking about at that moment, what they regret, what they hope for, whom they've loved, what they dream of. . . . How quickly you would want to see [a person] naked through to her heart.[15]

De Botton is taken with this passage from Flaubert and rightly so, since it exemplifies the restless, open mind here being advocated. Likewise, de Botton admires the appreciation for detail in the travel literature of explorer Alexander von Humboldt, who, in 1802, climbed what was at the time believed to be the tallest mountain in the world, in Peru. He documented the physical surroundings every step of the way in his journal. At one point, Humboldt mentions that he is climbing next to a great abyss roughly eight hundred feet deep; and yet, somehow he still has the composure of mind and the studiousness to continue to describe his surroundings: "A few rock lichens were seen above the snow lines, at a height of 16,920 feet. The last green moss we noticed about 2,600 feet lower down. A butterfly was captured by M. Bonpland [Humboldt's travelling companion] at a height of 15,000 feet and a fly was seen 1,600 feet higher."[16] De Botton, like many of us, is amazed that a person in such great danger could still appreciate the precise height at which he sees a butterfly, asking himself, "How does [one] begin to care about a piece of moss growing on a volcanic ridge ten inches wide?"[17] De Botton's answer, which is his theory of how curiosity (as he calls it, though his description better fits studiousness) comes to be and grows, is to look at the longer

---

15. As quoted in de Botton, *Art of Travel*, 90.
16. de Botton, *Art of Travel*, 114.
17. de Botton, *Art of Travel*, 116.

history of questions that preceded this question—for Humboldt or for anyone else:

> Curiosity might be pictured as being made up of chains of small questions extending outwards, sometimes over huge distances, from a central hub composed of a few blunt, large questions. In childhood we ask: "Why is there good and evil?" "How does nature work?" "Why am I me?" If circumstances and temperament allow, we then build on these questions during adulthood, our curiosity encompassing more and more of the world until, at some point, we may reach that elusive stage where we are bored by nothing. The blunt large questions become connected to smaller, esoteric ones.[18]

De Botton's description of "curiosity" (again, better labeled studiousness) captures part of the motivation for the kind of open-mindedness being described in this chapter, and is in keeping with Aquinas's notion of the natural desire on the part of humans to know the causes of effects, as well as the unrest that characterizes the believing mind for Aquinas.

Here, more than other places in this project, I will depart from what has been called "Thomism of the strict observance" by borrowing from Aquinas and reappropriating what he says about the quality of theological faith for what I wish to say about all belief.

In *Light of Faith*, Aquinas remarks that "[N]o matter how much we may advance in this kind of understanding, whereby we derive knowledge from the senses, there still remains a natural desire to know other objects. For many things are quite beyond the reach of the senses."[19] This natural desire is the mental unrest that makes a mind open, lost in wonder, and (in the healthy way) curious. Concerning things that can be experienced by our senses, Aquinas says that "there are many whose nature we cannot know with any certainty. Some of them, indeed, elude our knowledge altogether; others we can know but vaguely. Hence our natural desire for more perfect knowledge ever remains."[20] More perfect knowledge means, among other things, knowing the causes of things observed. "So great," says Aquinas, "is the desire for knowledge within us that, once we apprehend an effect, we wish to know its cause."[21] To wonder is to not know

---

18. de Botton, *Art of Travel*, 116.
19. Aquinas, *Light of Faith*, 116–17.
20. Aquinas, *Light of Faith*, 116–17.
21. Aquinas, *Light of Faith*, 116–17.

in full—indeed, Aquinas defined wonder as the desire for knowledge or *desiderium sciendi*.[22]

For Aquinas, faith (as well as the beliefs of the open mind, according to this project) is both perfect and imperfect. The firmness that pertains to the assent, he says, "is a perfection, but the lack of sight, because of which the movement of discursive thought still remains in the mind of one who believes, is an imperfection."[23] In other words, a mind can be open, restless, and curious without questioning what it already believes, as the strong fallibilist would have us do. It is not a contradiction for someone to be intellectually restless without being intellectually ironic about their truth claims. Regarding the knowledge brought by faith, Aquinas writes that it "does not bring rest to desire but rather sets it aflame, since every man desires to see what he believes."[24] The same, it could be argued, is true of all beliefs about the world. In claiming this, I am aware that I am locating all beliefs somewhere between what Aquinas calls *scientia* and *opinio*, precisely where he happens to locate faith. All beliefs are like faith in that they are served by "a certain keenness of interest in seeking knowledge of things" or what Aquinas calls studiousness, resulting from the imperfection of all knowledge.[25] All beliefs are like faith, as described by Aquinas, in that they entail a movement of the mind that is both discursive and deliberating while not questioning what it already believes to be true.[26]

Aquinas's notion of mental unrest—"*Motus cogitationis in ipso remanet inquietas*"[27]—can be expanded beyond supernatural faith insofar as the open mind "still think[s] discursively and inquires about the things which it believes, even though its assent to [these things] is unwavering." Aquinas explains that when it comes to supernatural faith, "a movement directly opposite to what the believer holds most firmly can arise in him, although this cannot happen to one who understands or has scientific knowledge."[28]

---

22. Pieper, *Leisure*, 130–31.
23. Aquinas, *Summa Contra Gentiles*, 14, 1 ad 5.
24. Aquinas, *Summa Contra Gentiles*, III, c. 40, n. 5.
25. *ST* II-II.166.2.
26. *ST* II-II.2.1.
27. Aquinas, *Disputed Questions on Truth*, 14, 1, 5.
28. Aquinas, *Disputed Questions on Truth*, 14, 1, 5.

Aquinas's reasons for thinking differently about scientific knowledge can be traced back to his clean distinction between *scientia* and *opinio*, a distinction that this project not only does not make but also implicitly challenges. Aquinas regards scientific knowledge as somehow self-evident and its acquisition as requiring no moral virtues, let alone faith. You either understand the mathematical proof or you don't; there's no subjective attitude toward it. As he says of scientific knowledge, "For by the very act of relating the principles to the conclusions he assents to the conclusions by reducing them to the principles. There, the movement of the one who is thinking is halted and brought to rest."[29] Arriving at scientific knowledge is a matter of logic and (apparently) intellectual determinism. "For in scientific knowledge the movement of reason begins from the understanding of principles and ends there after it has gone through the process of reduction. Thus, its assent and discursive thought are not parallel"—as they are in faith—"but the discursive thought leads to assent, and the assent brings thought to rest."[30] It would require a book unto itself to give an adequate explanation for why Aquinas is wrong about this distinction (between the human, contingent truths of opinion and the necessary, metaphysical truths of science) and why, it could be argued, all knowledge and beliefs fit the description he reserved for supernatural faith, including his description of its assenting and discursive dimensions. For now, let it simply be said that, once this distinction is set aside, and once Aquinas's notion of mental unrest is applied to belief as a whole, an ideal basis within Thomism is provided for the virtue of open-mindedness spoken of in this chapter.

---

29. Aquinas, *Disputed Questions on Truth*, 14, 1, 5.
30. Aquinas, *Disputed Questions on Truth*, 14, 1, 5.

6

The Value of Intellectual Diversity

CHAPTERS 2–5 OF THIS book concern the habit of open-mindedness. The present chapter will return to a related theme, first raised in chapter 1 in a discussion of the relevance of this project: intellectual diversity. As with chapters 2–5, this chapter will approach the topic through a philosophical lens, reserving its theological—explicitly Christian—analysis for Part II of the book, which begins with the next chapter.

The central question taken up in this chapter is "What, if anything, is the value of intellectual diversity?" Among the forms of diversity that could conceivably characterize a group of people, an institution, or a syllabus, the diversity of thought (in which a variety of sometimes conflicting ideas and beliefs are communicated and argued for) is the most poorly understood when it comes to its value. It is often assumed to have value, but people find it hard to explain why.

The first thing to notice about intellectual diversity is that it is context relative. Our modern world is more pluralist than medieval Europe, if by this we mean that the average twenty-first-century person has greater exposure to foreign peoples and ways of life and thinking than the average citizen of, say, twelfth-century France. But both people lived in intellectually *diverse* times—for there are always disagreements to be found (this side of heaven), and different perspectives to be had, if only we pay attention or, better yet, go looking for them. The question is not whether there is intellectual diversity in the water but how we should think about it and handle it.

The second thing to note about intellectual diversity, before getting into the body of this chapter, is that the open-minded person will naturally find him or herself surrounded by it, routinely exposed to it, as a consequence of being open-minded. You might say that intellectual diversity naturally supervenes upon the open-minded person, even when the open-minded agent isn't aiming for it, not unlike the way in which a virtuous person achieves happiness, according to Aristotle. If a person or a society does not find himself or itself surrounded by intellectual diversity, something has gone wrong. To put it simply, where open-mindedness as a virtue is not being practiced, society's fabric is strained and at risk, and the possibility for human friendship is limited.

As mentioned in chapter 1, Aristotle rightly noted that friendship is the basis of justice, and justice is the foundation of society. In other words, if friendship (or even healthy intellectual collaboration) is made difficult or even impossible because the relevant parties do not have enough in common, then a healthy society is impossible to attain. Note, interestingly, how this Aristotelian notion of justice differs from a more modern Rawlsian understanding that would, according to its theory, make possible justice without friendship. "Friendship," says Aristotle, "seems to hold states together," and, conversely, when society is intellectually fragmented, when its citizens live in ideological silos, society breaks down.[1] When we cease to be what Aristotle calls "fellow-voyagers" with our neighbors in the great conversation, especially those with whom we disagree, our common polis, and its shared ends, are put in jeopardy.[2] In sum, it is the argument of this chapter that the lives of individual minds and the activity of collective societies should find themselves in the business of intellectual diversity *not* because we are committed to any kind of strong fallibilism (as discussed in chapter 4) and *not* because, as will be argued below, intellectual diversity has any intrinsic *or* instrumental worth; rather, intellectual diversity matters because it is found where virtue is being practiced and where friendship (something possible only between virtuous people, as Aristotle claims) is flourishing.

Arguments for Intellectual Diversity's Intrinsic Value

Cases for the instrumental value of intellectual diversity outnumber those for its intrinsic worth, but there do exist a few of the latter. I'll address those first, subjecting them (as has been the thread of this project) to a

---

1. Aristotle, *NE* VIII.1.
2. Aristotle, *NE* VIII.1.

philosophical and virtue ethics analysis. Arguments for the instrumental value of intellectual diversity tend to be secular and unrelated to any talk of virtue or friendship, as opposed to the kind of arguments proposed above. Nevertheless, some of the cases are worth considering:

a. Perhaps intellectual diversity might be seen to have intrinsic value in the way that sampling a variety of cuisines is enjoyable. The person who lives his whole life on a single diet is missing out on something in much the same way that the person who never experiences other ways of looking at things is missing out on something of value, and living a less than fully enjoyable intellectual life. The problem, however, with this justification (and analogy) for the value of intellectual diversity is that human beings do not ingest ideas the way we ingest food. Variety may be the spice of life when it comes to food, but it is not so for ideas that we hold. In moving from one to another with regularity and rapidity, we are either not fully committing to the ideas (a sort of false ingestion, perhaps like spitting out bourbon at a tasting) or apt to suffer from psychological fatigue after all of our changes of position. We as humans are not meant for, and cannot endure, this kind of intellectual life.

b. Perhaps intellectual diversity can be seen as having intrinsic value (i.e., unrelated to its supposed truth conduciveness) because it prevents things from becoming boring. While it may sound glib or shallow, it is not entirely absurd to point out that, when there is total intellectual homogeneity within a group, the intellectual life of the group *is* less interesting. This justification, however, is problematic in that it remains purely at the level of the aesthetic and doesn't touch upon the moral sphere, which guides the assumptions and principles of this project.

c. Perhaps a non-instrumentalist, nature-based analogy could be made for the value of intellectual diversity by adapting the language used by environmental preservationists to argue that over-homogenization makes natural/intellectual environments less interesting and aesthetically poorer, as too many species (of arguments) go extinct or survive only in zoos or seedbanks (libraries). This way of thinking, however, suffers from the same shortcomings as the rationale found in example b.

Arguments for Intellectual Diversity's Instrumentalist Value

a. Perhaps ways of looking at the world—political, religious, philosophical traditions of thought—can and should be viewed the way some people view endangered languages in our world today, those tongues that are dying out or have died out as a result of languages merging or population shifts. The linguist Ken Hale, who mourns this loss of languages, has argued that "[l]anguages embody the intellectual wealth of the people that speak them. Every language lost is like dropping a bomb on the Louvre."[3] Are ways of thinking (not just styles but actual propositions believed in) akin to languages in this respect—assuming Hale is right about languages—and thus deserving of our efforts to preserve them? I explore the logic of such an argument in a later candidate for justification of intellectual diversity's value.

b. Perhaps intellectual diversity can be thought of as something akin to open source programming, whose proponents argue that more coders make for a better final product. Open source communities, interestingly, oppose propriety standards and rights, which, for our purposes, might translate into something like an intellectual tradition being unwilling to let other traditions modify itself. Open source programming (and open source intellectual traditions as well?) tends to have few "bugs" and, when there are bugs, fixes or patches emerge more quickly, as the bugs are brought to the attention of programmers more readily and solutions are effectively crowd-sourced. The problem with this open source model is that it lacks the potential to fully respect the essence, the structural integrity, of a tradition or school of thought—a possible problem that will be discussed more in the next chapter.

c. Perhaps intellectual diversity is valuable simply because it increases our options. Just as a larger pool of people on a dating website is preferable to the "single and looking" user, and multiple bids from contractors on a home remodel are advantageous to the homeowner, it could be argued that intellectual diversity affords people a wider selection of ideas, increasing the chances of the right answer being accessible to them at a given time and place.

What this rationale overlooks, however, is that time and energy are scarce human resources. If knowledge is going to be advanced, we have to begin by taking many things for granted—in other words, we must *eliminate* in advance many ideas from possible consideration, so as to prevent unaffordable distraction or, worse, intellectual paralysis. Thus, there is a purely pragmatic problem to reading everything, and there is a necessary limit to this kind of justification for the value of intellectual

---

3. As quoted in Abley, *Spoken Here*, 9.

diversity. It is an uncomfortable reality (one academics are reluctant to admit) that far too many books have been written and published over the last thirty years, for instance. More is not always better. Too many books clog the system, presenting an obstacle to the young student who must first figure out what is *worth* reading, a sizable task in our contemporary world. And when attempted, it is most likely done with many mistakes, since students are not in a position to know best, and their teachers, who should guide them, are increasingly products of this same overabundance of texts and unable to have a firm and full grasp of what is worth reading, or what is, as Matthew Arnold famously put, "the best which has been thought and said in the world." At some point, negative returns (not diminishing returns) set in on the production of texts representing different interpretations and claims.

Data support the claim that academic books have reached a level of oversaturation. A 2013 study at Seton Hall University found that only 21.5 percent of its collection circulated between 2005 and 2009.[4] Another study of a university library in Illinois found that 55 percent of print monographs purchased after 1990 have never circulated, a number typical for institutions of its kind.[5] A much larger study of a consortium of colleges in Ohio found that of the 5,899,520 titles in the shared collection that could have been circulated in a given year, only 1,041,405 (or 17.7 percent) actually did.[6] The numbers get worse when viewed from the standpoint of the humanities, and this despite the fact that it is in the humanities that the most texts are published. The most recent data on the publication of academic titles by discipline, for instance, shows that the humanities represent a large and growing share of the new academic titles published, over 54,000 in the year 2013 alone, or 44 percent of all titles published—even in the face of a declining readership.[7]

d. Perhaps, instead, a case can be made for the instrumentalist value of intellectual diversity on the basis that sometimes truth is, as it were, behind in the game, and the "powers that be" are maintaining and disseminating views that are simply incorrect, maybe even immoral, such that some degree of intellectual diversity should always be tolerated within

4. Rose-Wiles, "Are Print Books Dead?," 129–52.
5. Stewart, "Overview of ACRLMetrics," 73–76.
6. O'Neill, "Consortial Book Circulation Patterns," 791–807.
7. Developed from a compilation by Stephen Bosch, University of Arizona, of data provided by Ingram Content Group (Coutts Information Services) and YBP Library Services.

society—and inscribed into its laws—as a form of insurance, guaranteeing the freedom and space for the dissenting view (the true one, in this hypothetical) to call out incorrect views and gain ascendency. Such an argument is present in the work of legal scholar Michael Paulsen, whose logic offers a helpful case study into this way of thinking.

Paulsen begins by pointing out that elite law schools suffer from a dearth of intellectual diversity (by which he means the political variety). This is a loss, he says, because intellectual diversity has an instrumentalist value (he dismisses any arguments for its absolute, intrinsic value).[8] But, says Paulsen, only when a diversity of ideas serves the cause of Truth—and sometimes such diversity does *not*—do minority views deserve a place at the table. Racists, holocaust-deniers, phrenologists, and the like should not be admitted to the conversation, no matter how impressive their credentials—just as their social segregation is not a loss to society as a whole. These are the easy cases. The question isn't whether to draw a line but *where*. Given sufficient clout, some liberals would, for instance, exclude views in opposition to same-sex marriage; Paulsen, a traditional Catholic, would exclude opinions in support of abortion rights. Both sides may prefer to avoid cultural (perhaps even brick-and-mortar) neighborhoods in which the other side predominates. Paulsen is aware of the irony that, currently, not a single member of the faculty of Yale Law School (his alma mater) identifies him- or herself as pro-life.[9] In spite of this, Paulsen goes so far as to describe the pro-choice position as a "flat earth view" that "does not deserve to be taken seriously."[10] He maintains that, when stakes are sufficiently high, it can be rational "to seek to exclude from the debate views one regards as so deeply erroneous, misleading, and pernicious that they cannot function as anything other than a threat to Truth. The argument for intellectual diversity can only carry one so far."[11] Consider climate change, for example.[12] It can seem understandable, perhaps morally obligatory, for those convinced

---

8. Paulsen, "Uneasy Case for Intellectual Diversity."

9. By comparison, the latest poll I could find has 41 percent of Americans describing themselves as pro-life, with 43 percent self-identifying as pro-choice. This chapter has assumed that it is detrimental—to Yale and to our society—that the school's faculty is so unrepresentative of the wider public, just as it would be if the faculty's makeup were unanimously pro-life.

10. Paulsen, "Uneasy Case for Intellectual Diversity," 158.

11. Paulsen, "Uneasy Case for Intellectual Diversity," 153.

12. This is my example and I do not know whether Paulsen would endorse it.

by its claims to squelch skeptics. When the sustainability of life seems to hang in the balance, a combative no-holds-barred intellectual style is warranted.[13]

But then comes a turn in the path of Paulsen's argument. Though it is "reasonable" to act in the previous ways, it is nevertheless imprudent to do so when the opposition has sufficient numbers. Thus, the pro-choice position must be taken seriously, given its popularity. Pro-lifers and pro-choicers cannot simply ignore each other's arguments if they are committed to persuading one another, given that shaming or guilt-tripping someone into agreement is generally an ineffective strategy. An attitude that says "I can't believe we even need to have this conversation" tends to offend, polarize, and galvanize.

Thus, Paulsen's strategy for handling abortion-like disputes is to give such "repugnant" ideas the *temporary* respect of a real hearing until they are defeated. He cites the Lincoln-Douglas debates as an example. Had Lincoln offered only condemnation of slavery (as did some abolitionists at the time, and as we should do today) while refusing, on principal, to engage the pro-slavery voices, the anti-slavery cause might have failed. Paulsen casts Yale Law School's lopsided support for the pro-choice position in the same light: Truth is behind in the game, making intellectual diversity of highest value. If those with influence welcome dissenting voices, Truth still stands a fighting chance.

But again comes a caveat from Paulsen. We should tolerate such intellectual diversity only when the opposition appears to be tolerant of dissent themselves, i.e., when we can trust them to return the favor. "[O]ne should never tolerate intolerable ideas when those who advance them will simply seize on your foolishness to try to suppress your own (True) views and drive them out of the marketplace of ideas."[14] Paulsen's solution is, in effect, an answer to game-theory's "prisoner's dilemma" in which it pays for participants to sell each other out rather than cooperate. *Long*-term, he reminds us, you never know when you (and those who are likeminded) are going to be on the other side (i.e., out of power), so you had better now set the precedent you want to be in place when this role reversal happens, as it inevitably will given enough time (a veil of *historical* ignorance, to put a spin on the traditional Rawlsian metaphor).

---

13. I.e., the intellectual equivalent (for those in power) of Carl Schmitt's "state of exception" in political rule. Scee Schmitt, *Dictatorship* and *Political Theology*.

14. Paulsen, "Uneasy Case for Intellectual Diversity," 155.

And yet Paulsen's scheme overreaches because its moral resources are limited to cost-benefit analysis. By his own admission, the abortion question belongs in the exception category for *both sides*, at least when the opposition appears unwilling to tolerate intellectual diversity (and is this not the *status quo* in some cultural pockets today?). Given the opportunity, it makes sense for both parties to subvert, censor, and bully each other, which leads to the startling conclusion that—to the extent that Paulsen sees pro-choice and pro-life contingents as unwilling to show tolerance towards opposing arguments—he does not think it reasonable for today's Yale Law School to hire pro-life applicants, nor, given the chance, would he think it unreasonable or uncharitable of him to behave likewise toward pro-choice applicants.

Surely something has gone wrong here. Paulsen accepts as logical what should be rejected as a *reductio ad adbsurdum*. Tellingly absent from his argument is any virtue-talk; the justification for our actions is ultimately a question of whether they serve the cause of Truth rather than whether they are virtuous. He also says nothing of friendship being the basis for society, as has been argued for in this chapter.

e. Paulsen's oblique reference to the marketplace of ideas is revealing, for it signals support for yet another argument for intellectual diversity's instrumentalist worth: that it permits and encourages competition among ideas, and that this phenomenon promotes the discovery of truth, or at least progress toward the destination of truth. Like others, Paulsen seems to think that Truth will ultimately prevail, given enough time and a fighting chance. This assumption, which has been woven into US jurisprudence on free speech, has its origins in John Stuart Mill's claim that free competition of ideas advances the cause of knowledge:

> As mankind improves, the number of doctrines which are no longer disputed or doubted will be constantly on the increase; and the well-being of mankind may almost be measured by the number and gravity of the truths which have reached the point of being uncontested. The cessation, on one question after another, of serious controversy, is one of the necessary incidents of the consolidation of opinion.[15]

Like financial markets, the unregulated exchange of ideas in society can result in monopolies, or at least oligopolies (there being no intellectual trustbusters, no Teddy Roosevelts of faculty sentiment). Intellectual markets can become overleveraged, they can form bubbles and burst, and

---

15. Mill, *On Liberty and Other Writings*, 45.

they require bears and bulls to function properly—or so the trajectory of this logic seems to go. Mill acknowledges the problem of monopoly in his own way, noting that, despite the natural tendency toward collective opinion to form powers that discourage dissent, the result is still a plus on the whole, though not, admittedly, an unmixed good:

> [T]hough this gradual narrowing of the bounds of diversity of opinion is necessary in both senses of the term, being at once inevitable and indispensable, we are not therefore obliged to conclude that all its consequences must be beneficial. The loss of so important an aid to the intelligent and living apprehension of a truth, as is afforded by the necessity of explaining it to, or defending it against, opponents, though not sufficient to outweigh, is no trifling drawback from the benefit of its universal recognition.[16]

There are various problems with the financial metaphors employed by Mill and others to illustrate the value of intellectual diversity in leading us, as a people, toward truth. Consider, to take an example not given by Mill but consistent with his logic, treating ideas like holdings in an index fund. According to proponents of this investment strategy, we should hedge our bets in the market by buying (assenting to?) a tiny bit of all the major stocks (worldviews?) available and by both shorting and buying a sector at the same time (not unlike strong fallibilism). This might make for sound investing, but in the realm of ideas it is called cognitive dissonance and is unlivable. We are not, intellectually, the sorts of creatures who can approach our beliefs about reality like financial advisors.

Next, ideas are not produced, marketed, and consumed like goods and services. It is now even up for debate among scholars whether markets for goods actually behave the way Mill assumes. Economist Clayton Christensen and entrepreneur Peter Thiel, among others, argue that big advances in businesses and technologies are seldom made by companies or individuals who "compete" in the traditional capitalist sense.[17] Well-run companies frequently fail because they make incremental changes to improve their already successful product, while paying close attention to customerss's opinions. True innovators excel at creating a market where there once was none. They often have the liberty to try out apparently imprudent ideas precisely because they are not beholden to stockholders or consumers. Thiel insinuates that this holds true for academic innovations

---

16. Mill, *On Liberty and Other Writings*, 45.
17. See Christensen, *Innovator's Dilemma*; Thiel, *Zero to One*.

as well. Thinkers who "compete" too much—who pay too much attention to financial pressures, to getting tenure, or to the reception of their work by peers—are less free to explore uncharted intellectual waters. The Silicon Valley inclination towards "disruptive innovation" aimed ultimately at bringing about the best, most clever results turns out to be a better source of good ideas than a Millian state of nature in which sword sharpens sword and the intellectual equivalent of the *libido dominandi* (mentioned in chapter 3) is celebrated as a kind of invisible hand over intellectual history.

Second, few people shop worldviews the way they shop cars (perhaps employing cost-benefit analysis) and it is safe to assume that most people would not admire ideology shoppers. It is also unclear whether people can, even if they desire to, switch their belief systems the way they switch cable packages. There is good reason to think that humans cannot will themselves to inwardly embrace a belief simply because it serves their interests to do so. Consider, for instance, how mispaired the analogy appears between compromises reached in the writing of congressional bills and our decisions about what to believe. Political parties will sacrifice certain goals in exchange for achieving others. Imagine, though, the following intellectual negotiation: "I (person 1) am willing to be wrong about x if you (person 2) are willing to be wrong about y"—absent, of course, any pre-existing doubts about x (on the part of person 1) and any pre-existing attraction to y's truthfulness (on the part of person 2). Whatever the trade advantages of conceding x to get person 2 to "believe" in y, which presumably would be of lesser intellectual comparative worth to person 1, human psychology does not appear to permit such free trade within intellectual markets.

Another problem with the way in which Mill justifies the value of intellectual diversity relates to his remark that, as certain points of view inevitably die out, we (those of present opinion) should make mention of their ideas by trying to recount them ourselves, even though we disagree with them. As Mill admits,

> Nor is it enough that he should hear the arguments of adversaries from his own teachers, presented as they state them, and accompanied by what they offer as refutations. That is not the way to do justice to the arguments or bring them into real contact with his own mind. He must be able to hear them from persons who actually believe them, who defend them in earnest and do

their very utmost for them. He must know them in their most plausible and persuasive form.[18]

Mill describes this as the next-best option and admits that a disinterested person can never make an argument as well as somebody who actually holds the point of view the disinterested person is arguing for. It is fair to ask, however, whether a tradition can even be *poorly* represented by someone who does not belong to it, someone who does not actually live by its code. T. S. Eliot makes this point as regards the practice of reading poetry, though it is reasonable to apply his remarks to *all* schools of thought or "opinions," to use Mill's word. All great poets, says Eliot, have something in common, seeming to be "like parts of one Mind, [despite] working under different conditions and at different times."[19] They are part of a single tradition. Arguably, all traditions work this way, and Mill's consolation of speaking up for dead worldviews proves to be of little consolation at all. Eliot goes on to imagine a hypothetical event in which, suddenly, no one is able to produce poetry. If this were to happen, says Eliot, there would be an interesting consequence: no one would be able to truly appreciate the poetry *previously* written either, it becoming "meaningless" and "flat." This is so, explains Eliot, because "the capacity of appreciating poetry is inseparable from the power of producing it, it is poets themselves who can best appreciate poetry. Life is always turned toward creation; the present only, keeps the past alive."[20]

Last, the argument for the value of intellectual diversity using the "marketplace of ideas" rationale bears on a current debate within higher education itself, and highlights the limits of this logic. Some conservative professors claim that universities are violating the rights of their students, and not fulfilling their pedagogical duties, by failing to have sufficient political diversity within the ranks of their faculties and in their classrooms.

This debate leads to the question of whether higher education cannot help but be partial and selective in what it does and does not tolerate in the way of intellectual diversity. Professor David Horowitz has proposed an "Academic Bill of Rights" that argues that students have rights to things like exposure to a variety of viewpoints, and that "plurality of serious scholarly methodologies and perspectives should be a significant

---

18. Mill, *On Liberty and Other Writings*, 38.

19. See "Modern Tendencies in Poetry" in Eliot, *Complete Prose*, 214. Special thanks to Thomas Pfau recommending these remarks by Eliot.

20. Eliot, *Complete Prose*, 214.

institutional purpose."[21] The response to the proposed bill on the part of the Academic Association of University Professors shows that what constitutes tolerable forms of intellectual diversity can never be neutral.[22] On the question of the student's right to be free of indoctrination on the part of their professors (one of the bill's proposed rights), the AAUP took exception as to how one would distinguish between proper pedagogy and improper "indoctrination."[23] This distinction, said the AAUP, should not be drawn by the students, but rather "determined by reference to scholarly and professional standards, as interpreted and applied by the faculty itself."[24] The bill's stipulation that "curricula and reading lists in the humanities and social sciences respect all human knowledge in these areas and provide students with dissenting sources and viewpoints," was met by the AAUP's questioning of who, if not the teacher, is in a position to fairly assess what is and what isn't deserving of being included in the "the quality and range of pluralism deemed reasonable"?[25]

In the end, the AAUP condemned the bill as a potential infringement on academic freedom and welcoming of too much intellectual diversity, as "no department of political theory ought to be obligated to establish a plurality of methodologies and perspectives by appointing a professor of Nazi political philosophy."[26] Clearly, Mills's "marketplace" must outlaw certain points of view.

Chapter 4 of this book, "The Semblance of Strong Fallibilism," discussed the limits of what propositions an individual can keep as live options, and (in what amounts to the same) the limits of what current beliefs one can regard as possibly false, without doing moral harm to oneself. In

---

21. "Florida House Bill 837," 123–24. Consistent with Horowitz's project, New York University social psychologist Jonathan Haidt has established "Heterodox Academy," a collection of professors who recognize the lack of political diversity in the academy and regard it as a weakness that needs addressing. The group's mission statement quotes Mill's *On Liberty and Other Writings* at length (http://www.heterodoxacademy.org).

22. These developments are understandable in light of Winnifred Sullivan's arguments about religious liberty and Eldon Eisenach's arguments about the American establishment, as discussed in chapter 2.

23. Academic Association of University Professors, "Academic Bill of Rights," para. 5.

24. Academic Association of University Professors, "Academic Bill of Rights," para. 9.

25. Academic Association of University Professors, "Academic Bill of Rights," para. 4.

26. Academic Association of University Professors, "Academic Bill of Rights," para. 3.

the context of intellectual diversity, a similar question can be raised: what are the limits of intellectual diversity that an individual or group should tolerate or even welcome (if there are any such limits)? Or, to create a historical thought experiment, how many, and which, influential books in history would you, if you could—should we, if we could—eliminate (not just mothball), removing them as though they were never written? *Das Kapital*? Imagine one could go back in time and put a lethal bullet, so to speak, in the manuscript of *Mein Kampf*—would you do it? And would doing so represent any loss?

It is not difficult to think of "hard cases" in which the toleration, let alone welcoming or even *celebration*, of intellectual diversity comes up against its limits. It does not "add to the conversation" in a beneficial way, or enrich a community of learning, to show respect for the idea of forced female circumcision on the part of cultures, even though, according to the logic of particular cultures (say, for example, Muslims in Kenya) the practice "makes sense," internally.

Or, consider a historical example of the limits of intellectual and cultural tolerance. In the 1840s, Hindu priests in India challenged Charles James Napier, at the time the commander-in-chief of British forces, about the outlawing by the British of the custom of burning widows alive on the funeral pyre of their husbands (a practice called "suttee"). Napier responded with no tolerance for the intellectual diversity entailed in tolerating the suttee tradition: "Be it so. This burning of widows is your custom; prepare the funeral pile. But my nation has also a custom. When men burn women alive we hang them. . . . Let us all act according to national customs."[27] Even those of us who do not condone capital punishment may nevertheless admire the moral and intellectual integrity of Napier's response. He placed a limit on intellectual diversity, and rightfully so.

Those of a more modern liberal persuasion are likely to do so as well, when pushed, if a particular belief or practice has the consequence of violating another person's freedom; if this line is crossed, the intellectual diversity added by the belief or argument should not be tolerated. Leonard Swidler, mentioned in chapter 2, takes such a liberal stand in response to the question of when true opposition to another's viewpoint (rather than the open dialogue he otherwise recommends) is warranted. The answer, he says, is when doctrines or customs "are perceived as hostile to an authentically full human life."[28] But what is such a "life"?

27. Napier, *History Of General Sir Charles*, 35.
28. Swidler, "Understanding Dialogue," 19.

Swidler tells us that in this century peoples around the world have come to a general consensus that "the foundation of being human is that humans ought to be autonomous in their decisions."[29] From this perspective, those who refuse to join this consensus—and there continue to be many such cultures and peoples with such views—are simply wrong (full stop) about what constitutes an authentically full human life.

Given that there seem to be cases where true opposition to sets of ideas is warranted, and perhaps even morally obligatory, what kinds or levels of coercion are acceptable in such situations? What, for instance, would "intellectual just war" look like, if there were such a thing?

Augustine famously condemned lying or deception in any form but, like Aquinas, made an exception for military ambushes in just wars.[30] We cannot break promises or contracts (this would be lying), says Aquinas, but we can "deceive by what we say or do, because we do not declare our purpose or meaning to [our enemy]."[31] Extending this logic, sometimes it is acceptable to use duplicitous intellectual methods to subdue or convert an intellectual opponent, and sometimes not.[32] And, assuming that the generally accepted criteria for a war to be just are in place, the cause must not only be just, but the effort must, among other things, be plausibly "winnable," which, in this context would mean that it is plausible that the dissenting individuals or parties could be persuaded to change their minds, or, at minimum, that their ideas could be quarantined and their harm reduced, thereby justifying the use of intellectual force. Similarly, the cause must be waged by a legitimate authority for it to be just, according to Aquinas and the wider just-war tradition, which leads to the puzzling question of who or what would constitute the equivalent of a sovereign state in an intellectual just war, it being unclear whether individuals could rightfully claim such authority.[33]

What, then, of intellectual entrapment? We often do this by getting an opponent to agree to something, seemingly uncontroversial to him, and then showing him how, in doing so, he by extension undermines

---

29. Swidler, "Understanding Dialogue," 19.

30. See *ST* II-II.40.3.

31. *ST* II-II.40.3.

32. To be fair, Aquinas elsewhere describes as sinful (and not proper to the virtue of prudence, though resembling it) the habits of "craftiness" and "guile," or the adoption of ways "that are not true but counterfeit and apparently true, in order to attain some end either good or evil" (*ST* II-II.55.4).

33. The possibility of pacifism as regards intellectual warfare will be discussed in the next chapter.

other parts of his way of thinking that he had not before realized. Socrates was the master of this strategy, of course. The aforementioned morality of ambush would seem to apply here, with the caveat that the entrapment not be of such a kind or degree that it produces enmity that prevents the possibility of friendship between the parties once agreement is achieved, if it is achieved.

A Darwinian Justification?

Scientific overtones are present in Mill's writing, as history obeys its own laws of nature: given the diversity of ideas as an initial condition, things will, on their own, eventually lead to a reduction of intellectual diversity and progress towards truth. To be sure, it comes with a loss: you can never represent an opposing argument as well as somebody who (*ceteris paribus*) actually believes it, as mentioned above. Speaking up for passé positions is at times necessary to prevent intellectual complacency and sloppiness, says Mill.

Mill's assertion that the best ideas survive the trial of history nicely fits together with the concurrent work of social Darwinist Herbert Spencer. Together, they influenced the later Supreme Court justice Oliver Wendell Holmes, whose 1919 dissent in *Abrams vs. the U.S.* firmly planted Mill's philosophy in American jurisprudence:

> When men have realized that time has upset many fighting faiths, they may come to believe even more than they believe the very foundations of their own conduct that the ultimate good desired is better reached by free trade in ideas—that the best test of truth is the power of the thought to get itself accepted in the competition of the market.[34]

Economic analogy replaces biological metaphor here. There are problems with this Darwinian justification for the instrumentalist value of intellectual diversity, however.

On this point, it should be recalled that Darwin begins his *Origin of Species* with his own analogy for evolution: the practice of breeding pigeons for certain traits. The analogy was, at the time, and more so today, false to the vast majority of agricultural breeding practices since it assumed a version of artificial selection in which breeders simply bred the best specimens (e.g., horse breeding), relying on small chance variations

---

34. Holmes, *Selections from the Letters*, 320.

to accumulate over time. This fact does not hurt the credibility of Darwin's general theory in the minds of biologists today, which raises the question of what purpose such analogies are designed to serve in the first place, an argument well made by historian of science Bert Theunissen.[35]

The same holds true of analogies for intellectual diversity. Why, in other words, should we expect the behavior of nature (or commerce) to reflect the behavior of human ideas and why should such metaphors be seen as standing in a position of mutual credibility with theories for the behavior of human ideas (and, by extension, the value of intellectual diversity)? Theunissen maintains that Darwin's understanding of breeding practices (wrongly) influenced his understanding of how natural selection worked in nature, while other historians of science (citing some of Darwin's personal correspondence) argue the reverse: that it was Darwin's understanding of horticulture that shaped his understanding of natural section. Whatever the actual case, there is often an un-interrogated philosophical assumption at work in these debates: that these two systems of behavior should mirror one another, a subsummation of human ideas into the realm of (purely instinctive) animal behavior. (And yet, as Darwin himself famously worried, "Would anyone trust the convictions of a monkey's mind?") If, however, such metaphors are being used only for pedagogical purposes, then their persuasive powers are much diminished. There is, lastly, the fact that ideas, unlike corn and cows, are united with human persons, which raises the discomforting feeling that those willing and able to manipulate the lives of ideas by means of the artificial selection of others' ideas (that is, sterilizing the unpromising, arranging marriages between the attractive, etc.) are engaging in something akin to intellectual eugenics, bearing resemblances to the moral hazards this label connotes, inasmuch as specific ideas are synonymous with particular people or peoples and *vice versa*.

The evolutionary metaphor has other weaknesses, too. As is now thought by many biologists about natural evolution itself, the selection of ideas likely involves *multiple* causal levels. Whether an idea survives can have as much to do with the kind of natural environment in which it emerged and with the kinds of authorities that held power during its lifespan as it does with an idea's intrinsic qualities or fitness. Second, by implicitly equating adaptability with "truth," the biological metaphor takes on the duty of explaining why an idea's fitness is evidence of its truth, a task it can attempt only on pain of circularity.

---

35. On this point, see Theunissen, "Darwin and His Pigeons," 179–212.

Another intriguing nature-based analogy for the value of intellectual diversity—unpursued in the relevant literature—is *heterosis*, or hybrid vigor, in which new and superior variations are produced by crossbreeding parents with diverse, non-overlapping, often inbred pedigrees (i.e., effects that are opposite of those caused by inbreeding in plants and animals). On an intellectual level, this "breeding" would look like conversation partners from very distinct (perhaps "inbred") pools of intellectual DNA collaborating with open minds and yielding novel results. But while this justification may be true of corn and other forms of animal or plant breeding, it is empirically not true when it comes to human ideas and beliefs. There is, moreover, no reason to initially think that ideas and their cross-pollination work in similar fashion.

Questioning Whether Intellectual Diversity Is Actually Fruitful

Theologian Paul Griffiths has questioned, fairly I think, whether great intellectual diversity (where this is sizable space between viewpoints, assumptions, and concerns) is actually fruitful rather than detrimental to the advance of knowledge. Though the context for his thoughts concerned how theologians should disagree, the gift of grace (the topic of the next chapter) is not required to see and be persuaded by his observations about intellectual diversity and his resulting recommendations.

Griffiths offers an interesting analogy: when academics of a particular field come together or dialogue across too great a distance of intellectual diversity, it is akin to two parties showing up to play different games. Perhaps one comes with shin guards and soccer balls, the others with shoulder pads and helmets, and each has learned and is assuming different sets of rules for their respective games.[36] The result is that neither game came be played well or perhaps at all.[37]

This is not to discount entirely the potential value of intellectual diversity. Rather, such diversity is most effective where there is already

36. It should be said, in fairness, that this project, in possible tension with Griffiths's analogy here, places a bet (in keeping with the virtue ethics tradition) that whether we immediately realize it or not, we are all in some sense playing the same game—that of being human, this nature being universal and objective, and of human flourishing, its standards being universal and objective—and have the requisite equipment to play the game (the practice of virtue). Indeed, part of the bet is that we can get people to see this and realize they are already playing the game.

37. Griffiths, "Theological Disagreement."

ample agreement between the viewpoints or parties in dialogue. As Griffiths reminds us, "the principal engine of thought . . . is the making of perspicuous and provocative distinctions, and doing that is always a matter of the *agon*."[38] Thus, says Griffiths, "Spending too much time with the like-minded damages speculative thought, and eventually kills it."[39] What we need, then, if we want to do fine speculative work, is to place ourselves in situations where there is deep-seated disagreement between parties. Griffiths lists as good examples of such a situation Augustine's arguments with Jerome over the correct interpretation of Galatians 2 and human sexuality, Pascal's argument with the Jesuits about human agency, John Henry Newman's argument with Pusey over the possibility of Anglo-Catholicism, and so on, adding that the very structure of the *quaestio* in scholasticism is effectively argumentative.[40]

That all of these examples are theological is incidental and simply the result of the particular occasion for Griffiths's reflections. Non-theological examples could easily be given as well. What is not incidental, however, is that all of the examples include parties who already agree about much. Pascal, it is important to keep in mind, had much more in common with the Jesuits than, say, Voltaire, just as Augustine had more in common with Jerome than he did the pagans. And that commonality is what gave their disagreements the necessary traction to make them possibly interesting.[41] As Griffiths says, more is at stake in such disagreements because

38. Griffiths, "Theological Disagreement," 30.

39. Griffiths, "Theological Disagreement," 30.

40. Though Griffiths doesn't consider it, his argument about the need for mostly shared concerns and contexts on the part of conversation partners would (if correct) imply that imaginary meetings or debates between great minds separated by expanses of time, were they to actually happen, would be much less interesting and productive than one might naturally assume. If Augustine were, say, transported to mid-nineteenth-century England with the help of a time machine and brought up to speed on what had been learned about evolutionary biology since his own time, any discussion he could have with Charles Darwin about, for example, the consequences of natural selection for human nature (or the great chain of being) would surely disappoint our natural expectations, for the two men did not share enough concerns and context for their minds to fully profit from one another.

41. There is, interestingly, increasing evidence for the truth of an argument analogous to Griffiths's concerning not distance in terms of disagreement but rather actual physical distance. Too much distance makes a collaboration *less* fruitful: "Articles published by Harvard investigators from 1993 to 2003 with at least two authors were identified in the domain of biomedical science. Each collaboration was geocoded to the precise three-dimensional location of its authors. Physical distances between any two coauthors were calculated and associated with corresponding citations. Relationship between distance of coauthors and citations for four author relationships

the parties already care deeply about some of the same things. The "let-a-thousand-flowers-bloom approach" to a field of inquiry sounds nice in theory, and its logic is at play in Mill's justification for liberty in inquiry and exchange, but, in practice, it doesn't seem to work. "Only with bracingly severe formal constraints in place," says Griffiths, can intellectual productivity occur.[42] The best tools of thought—the ability to make clear distinctions, thought experiments that expose the underlying structure of a position, genuine passion of the part of both parties—are what allow us to advance a field of thought. And, for all these reasons, says Griffiths, "there is nothing half as effective as a good opponent," the sort of person "who agrees with you about almost everything and yet who disagrees with you deeply about the particular matter at hand."[43] Intellectuals should, therefore, actually seek out conversation partners who fit this description, and, what's more, such people and disagreements, when found, should be embraced (intellectually and emotionally) with delight, as with a gift, which is exactly what they are, for "the gift of an argument is what gives you thought as capable itself of offering arguments. For the intellectual life, there's nothing better."[44]

Arriving at similar conclusions, John Garvey, president of the Catholic University of America, commented on the priority of hiring Catholic professors at self-understood Catholic institutions, such as the one he presides over. His reasoning, though outlined in the context of a discussion about the identity of a religious institution, applies equally well to questions about the value of intellectual diversity generally in any community of learning. Garvey knows well the arguments for the value of intellectual diversity offered by John Stuart Mill and his intellectual heirs but is not persuaded by them. After rehashing Mills's arguments, Garvey writes,

> You can probably see where this leads, in the discussion about *Ex corde ecclesiae* and building a great Catholic university. Some

(first-last, first-middle, last-middle, and middle-middle) were investigated at different spatial scales. At all sizes of collaborations (from two authors to dozens of authors), geographical proximity between first and last author is highly informative of impact at the microscale (i.e., within building) and beyond. The mean citation for first-last author relationship decreased as the distance between them increased." Lee et al., "Does Collocation Inform the Impact?," e14279.

42. Griffiths, "Theological Disagreement," 33.
43. Griffiths, "Theological Disagreement," 35.
44. Griffiths, "Theological Disagreement," 35.

people draw from Mill and his disciples the conclusion that a great Catholic university is a contradiction in terms. If we hire a majority of Catholics (instead of a multitude of tongues), we will have a harder time discovering truth than schools that reject "orthodoxy" and "authoritative selection."[45]

Garvey, however, isn't convinced by this Millian way of thinking and claims that the theory does not accurately describe how things work in reality. As he says, there are a number of success stories in universities or their departments that contradict Mills's way of thinking. The Chicago School of Economics, built around Milton Friedman and George Stigler during the 1950s, is a prime example. Keynesian ways of thinking, popular elsewhere, were not welcomed in the department. Instead, the department went out of its way to hire faculty who believed in the neoclassical approach. Ironically, Chicago promoted free-market economics, "yet it did not seek a multitude of tongues for its faculty." Garvey lists other examples—the Yale School of Literary Criticism, the Cambridge School of Political Thought, the Frankfurt School of Critical Theory—to support his point. What they share, he writes, "is a dedication to a common project, usually a departure from some academic orthodoxy, and a sense that the group is working on its own to build something new." In this, they "seem inconsistent with Mill's idea of academic freedom."[46] They did not promote a multitude of tongues within their faculties.

The next chapter will look at how commitments particular to theology, and the gifts of grace offered and possessed by those of Christian faith, can and do change the way Christians view intellectual diversity.

---

45. Garvey and Roche, "What Makes a University Catholic?," para. 11.
46. Garvey and Roche, "What Makes a University Catholic?," para. 16.

Part II

Open-Mindedness and Intellectual Diversity after Grace

Therefore, if you have any encouragement from being united with Christ, if any comfort from his love, if any fellowship with the Spirit, if any tenderness and compassion, then make my joy complete by being like-minded, having the same love, being one in spirit and of one mind.

PHIL 2:1–2

7

Intellectual Diversity after Grace

From Nature to Grace

PART I OF THIS book—the first six chapters—concerned the virtue of open-mindedness and the worth of intellectual diversity as viewed through a philosophical, non-theological lens. Part II—encompassing the next three chapters—takes up these same topics but with a new lens, that of grace or the theological virtues of faith, hope, and charity. With the infusion of grace, objects and actions of philosophical study look different, but not entirely so. Between nature and grace—between open-mindedness and intellectual diversity viewed first philosophically and then theologically—exists an organic relationship, a natural trajectory.

In the case of infused open-mindedness (chapter 8), the theological shift entails a view of beliefs as gifts not merely of the created order but of a personal God: awe, wonder, and intellectual gratitude—while remaining formally the same—occur in relationship with a God who enters history. The virtue of faith further restricts the range of propositions that Christians can fully consider or, put differently, enlarges the set of propositions that Christians regard as non-revisable. Theological hope, too, will change, for the better, the will and confidence with which the open-minded person engages in intellectual efforts.

As a reminder, "intellectual diversity" in this project does not mean the presence of a variety of academic disciplines or, say, different genres of literature; rather, it is an experienced state of affairs in which there is disagreement about questions, particularly questions regarded as being of great importance—conflicting beliefs, in other words. Such intellectual diversity takes on a new appearance when viewed through the lens of Christian grace, as I discuss in this chapter. Whereas open-mindedness concerns one's personal mental life and thus beliefs (and, by extension, the possibility of orthodoxy and heresy), the topic of intellectual diversity concerns believers and their traditions (and, by extension, the possibility of heretics).

In Philippians 2:1–2, Paul writes, "Therefore, if you have any encouragement from being united with Christ, if any comfort from his love, if any fellowship with the Spirit, if any tenderness and compassion, then make my joy complete by being like-minded, having the same love, being one in spirit and of one mind." This command from Paul will serve as one of the guiding principles for the next two chapters.

Virtues practiced without grace are liable to fail, hard to sustain, and can, if led too far astray from their ultimate theological context, begin to be malformed. Dietrich Bonhoeffer, for instance, writes about "reason, culture, humanity, and tolerance," and says that Nazism (in his time) led to an alliance between Christian and non-Christian "defenders of these values." He goes on to point out that the concepts of reason, culture, humanity, and tolerance "had [once] served as battle slogans against the Church, against Christianity"—something that is true of the concepts of open-mindedness and the value of intellectual diversity in the contemporary world as well. Nevertheless, in moments of extreme danger, these concepts or virtues, which had become "homeless" in their purely secular form, "now sought refuge in the Christian sphere, in the shadow of the Christian Church."[1] They returned to their origin. "The children of the Church, who had become independent and gone their own ways, now in the hour of danger returned to their mother. During the time of their estrangement, their appearance and their language had altered a great deal, and yet at the crucial moment the mother and the children once again recognized one another."[2] In our modern world, the same can be said of open-mindedness and intellectual diversity. "Reason, justice, culture, humanity, and all the kindred concepts"—such as open-mindedness and intellectual diversity—"sought and found a new purpose and a new power in their origin. This origin is Jesus Christ."[3]

---

1. Bonheoffer, *Ethics*, 58.
2. Bonheoffer, *Ethics*, 58.
3. Bonheoffer, *Ethics*, 58.

The previous chapter ended with Paul Griffiths's remark about the "caress" of an interlocutor who agrees about much while disagreeing about something in particular, or what Griffiths calls the "gift of disagreement," properly done. This is the best that intellectual friendship can be prior to grace. Still, it pales in comparison to intellectual friendship touched by the effects of grace. First, it must be said that grace is possible only because of God's extension of friendship with humans. Aristotle, who understood well the dynamics of true friendship (though without the benefits of knowledge of special revelation), taught that real friendship was only possible among equals. Among virtuous and equal parties, friendship can survive hardship, "but when one party is removed to a great distance, as God is [to us mere mortals], the possibility of friendship ceases."[4] Kings cannot really be friends with their subjects, in other words. It could never have occurred to Aristotle that we humans could be friends with God—that he could be more intimate to us than we are to ourselves, as Augustine said—or that we could close our eyes and fold our hands and speak to the Prime Mover himself. For this, revelation and theological virtues—unknown to Aristotle—were needed. As much as Aristotle knew about the life of virtue, he did not know the good news of John 15:15: "I no longer call you servants, because a servant does not know his master's business. Instead, I have called you friends, because everything I have learned from my father I made known to you." And because of this deficit, Aristotle was unaware of much of what the life of virtue entailed. Put differently, the following prayer (from the service of Evening Prayer in *The Book of Common Prayer*), which assumes a sort of active charity on the part of God towards his human subjects, would have been utterly alien to Aristotle: "Keep watch, dear Lord, with those who work, or watch, or weep this night, and give your angels charge over those who sleep. Tend the sick, Lord Christ; give rest to the weary, bless the dying, soothe the suffering, pity the afflicted, shield the joyous; and all for your love's sake."[5]

Intellectual friendships look different after grace, between fellow Christians, obviously, but also between Christians and non-Christians. Theological charity is now on the scene, causing those who possess it to view their possible union, not just in terms of agreement about truths and acquired virtues, but also to view their possible union in terms of

---

4. Aristotle, *NE* 8.8.
5. Episcopal Church, *Book of Common Prayer*, 71.

union in God and his church. Christians are called to extend charity and friendship even towards those who are not (in the Aristotelian sense) of their same status or of equal virtue, and even to those who are unkind towards them. As Matthew 5:46–47 says, "For if you love those who love you, what reward do you have? Do not even the tax collectors do the same? If you greet only your brothers, what more are you doing than others? Do not even the Gentiles do the same?"

Charity

Practicing the kind of charity called for by Matthew 5:46 means renouncing certain forms of intellectual violence or coercion. The typical language of an interlocutor being "hoisted on his petard" in the course of an argument, or of a particular party not wanting to give "ammunition" to an intellectual opponent, are forms of implied acceptance of the condition of violent intellectual exchange, a state of nature that Christians, granted the gift of charity, are called on to renounce. Instead, we should be willing to turn the other cheek, intellectually speaking, when a conversation partner is unfair to us. So, too, should we engage in acts of "intellectual almsgiving" with our opponents by helping them strengthen their own arguments, even when we disagree with them. In the process, a degree of trust will be established, a trust that, in time, can help achieve the kind of intellectual union in truth that Christians regard as their highest priority (as opposed to "winning" the argument). Almsgiving is a form of sacrifice that keeps the intellectual relationship alive and going, even when it costs the sacrificing party, perhaps in terms of stature, reputation, or energy.

As theologian John Bowlin notes, sacrifices tend to be made for the sake of crossing a divide among persons or groups, "either restoring a broken relationship or generating a new one altogether."[6] Intellectual friendships are no different in this respect. Bowlin offers as a metaphor for Christian sacrifice the act of laying down a bunt in baseball to advance another runner. As in the case of intellectual almsgiving and sacrifice, doing so means one isn't thinking of personal gain. Though he could swing for the fences, "the batter wants neither glory for himself nor honor from others. Rather, he wants to act in obedience to the manager and rescue the stranded runner, and he hopes to be united with each back home.

---

6. Bowlin, "Jesus and Baseball," 2.

For the sake of this end and in light of this hope, a bunt is best."[7] Christians who truly desire to bring their non-Christian (or other Christian) interlocutors "home," where they will finally be reunited with them, can sometimes best accomplish this reunion with acts of intellectual sacrifice, which at times offer the only way to achieve a degree of intellectual atonement among factions.

When considering how intellectual diversity looks different through the eyes of Christian faith, it is helpful to note how secular versions of "intellectual charity" differ from more traditionally theological understandings of the concept. The modern philosopher Donald Davidson, for instance, offered a popular notion of intellectual charity. What Davidson called "radical interpretation," which emerged out of the so-called principals of "logical coherence" and "correspondence," led to a "principal of charity" or interpretative charity towards another person's remarks.[8] Agreement between the parties is maximized by interpreting the other person's words in the manner that gives them the highest degree of reasonability from the standpoint of the interpreter. Charity, however, in its secular form here, makes no mention of communion in truth, as is the natural object of intellectual relationships infused with Christian charity. Intellectual charity for Christians, by contrast, means desiring to be of one mind (intellectually) and one body (sacramentally) with the other person. Without this charity, the agreement that can be accomplished over the meanings of words (as through Davidson's secular principal of charity) is of limited social value and, arguably, of limited epistemic value, too. As 1 Corinthians 13:8 reminds Christians, "Love never fails. But where there are prophecies, they will cease; where there are tongues, they will be stilled; *where there is knowledge, it will pass away."*

Infused with the theological virtue of charity, intellectual diversity looks different to Christians. Augustine, for instance, claims to vary his state of mind and style of speech depending on the class, school of philosophy, and education of the person to whom he is speaking: "Although we owe the same love to all, we should not treat all with the same remedy. And so, for its part, this very love is in pain giving birth to some (Gal 4:19), makes itself weak with others (1 Cor 9:22); devotes itself to edifying some (1 Cor 8:1), greatly fears giving offence to others; bends down to some, raises itself up before others. To some this love is gentle, to others

---

7. Bowlin, "Jesus and Baseball," 4.
8. See Davidson, "Three Varieties of Knowledge."

stern, to no one hostile, to everyone a mother."⁹ Likewise, Paul says in 1 Corinthians 9:9–23,

> For though I am free with respect to all, I have made myself a slave to all, so that I might win more of them. To the Jews I became as a Jew, in order to win Jews. To those under the law I became as one under the law (though I myself am not under the law) so that I might win those under the law. To those outside the law I became as one outside the law (though I am not free from God's law but am under Christ's law) so that I might win those outside the law. To the weak I became weak, so that I might win the weak. I have become all things to all people, that I might by all means save some.

Augustine and Paul were not practicing "strong cognitive empathy," as described in the prior chapter on semblances. They did not assume the truth of the worldview held by each group of people they sought to convert. They simply met the people where they were. Nor did Paul make the mistake of assuming any kind of strong fallibilism: "For God has not given us a spirit of timidity, but of power, love, and self-control. So do not be ashamed of the testimony of our Lord, or of me, His prisoner" (2 Tim 1:7–8). Augustine and Paul made the faith accessible to diverse peoples, granting a freedom to the form of the gospel's message, so that it might be heard. An open-minded evangelist does not presume to know all the varieties of ways the gospel can be spoken and heard. Differences of this kind are acceptable, so long as these differences serve the cause of *sameness* spoken of in Philippians 2:2: "Be of the same mind, having the same love, being in full accord and of one mind. . . . Let the same mind be in you that was in Jesus Christ." Within this "same mind," the differences in question are circumscribed by and seen in the larger context of a more fundamental form of unity through shared beliefs, and, hopefully, shared sacraments.

The infusion of theological charity will also change the substance of friendships between people. Aelred of Rievaulx, an English Cistercian who predated Aquinas, began his text *Spiritual Friendship* by recalling, with approval, Cicero's definition of friendship as being "agreement in things human and divine, with good will and charity."¹⁰ While this form of friendship is available to both Christians and pagans, Christian

---

9. Augustine, *Instructing Beginners in the Faith*, 112–13.

10. Braceland, *Spiritual Friendship*, 67. Special thanks to Ellen Charry for directing me to this text.

friendship and pagan friendship are nonetheless different. To begin with, Aelred is careful not to conflate friendship with charity. For Christians, the law of charity requires that we "welcome into the bosom of love not only our friends but also our enemies."[11] That said, "We call friends only those to whom we have no qualm about entrusting our heart and all its contents."[12] Friendship, on this view, is something made possible by a form or degree of charity that is scarce and made possible by the gift of grace.

How, though, did friendship come to be so scarce, on Aelred's view?[13] The answer is found in the Christian fall narrative. With the creation of Eve, Aelred says, friendship and the kind of charity it requires became part of the very fabric of nature as God intended it.

> So from the very beginning nature impressed on human minds this attachment of charity and friendship.... But after the fall of the first human, with charity growing lukewarm, when cupidity crept in and let private gain supplant the common good, avarice and envy corrupted the splendor of friendship and charity by introducing into the debased morals of mankind contentions, rivalries, hatreds, and suspicions.[14]

After the fall, it was possible to distinguish between charity and friendship (an impossibility before the fall), as true friendship and communion between good people and bad people could no longer exist. "Therefore friendship, which like charity was at first observed among all and by all people, by natural law lingered among the few righteous."[15] This is a loss to creation, to individuals, and to society (as discussed in chapter 1), as "friendship is natural, like virtue and wisdom," things good in and of themselves (i.e., "natural goods"), adding (consistent with the classic definition of virtue) "for all who possess these things make good use of them, and no one entirely abuses them."[16]

---

11. Braceland, *Spiritual Friendship*, 67.
12. Braceland, *Spiritual Friendship*, 67.
13. Augustine at times has a more skeptical view regarding the possibility of true friendship outside the sphere of Christian charity: "[F]riendship is genuine only when you bind fast together people who cleave to you through the charity poured abroad in our hearts by the Holy Spirit who is given to us." *Conf.* 4.4.
14. Braceland, *Spiritual Friendship*, 61.
15. Braceland, *Spiritual Friendship*, 61.
16. Braceland, *Spiritual Friendship*, 61.

Intellectual Diversity within Christian Schools

How should teachers in Christian schools respond to intellectual diversity in the classroom and to what degree should they promote it? Should they make special efforts to incorporate intellectual diversity within their course content, especially regarding ideas they not only disagree with and regard as contrary to Christian teaching but also find potentially harmful to the Christian church? And what, for Christian institutions, are the proper (i.e., faithful) bounds of intellectual diversity within the faculty itself? Should the institution go out of its way, in other words, to hire faculty whose ideas are out of sync with the majority culture of the campus? Should the Christian college or university make a special point of bringing in speakers and productions that push the envelope of intellectual diversity within the school, that even conflict with the stated religious identity of the institution? These are the sorts of questions Christians need to consider in the context of intellectual diversity.

As already argued for in the previous chapter, intellectual diversity, considered in an abstract way, has neither non-instrumental nor instrumental value. It would seem to follow that Christian institutions (as well as their secular counterparts) should not be in the business of intellectual diversity. This, as had been said, is the wrong conclusion for Christian institutions to draw regarding intellectual diversity. It *should* be present in the Christian classroom and, in a qualified sense, deserves a place in the self-understanding of these institutions, but for *missional* and *evangelical*, rather than epistemic, reasons. Intellectual diversity provides the opportunity to bring those who disagree with us back into our intellectual—and thus, hopefully, spiritual—fold, introducing an elevated and perfected form of Aristotelian friendship. The form that this intellectual diversity takes—its boundaries, for instance—will be affected by the infusion of faith, hope, and love, assuming this grace is present. And such a baptized form of intellectual diversity will occur in ways that are unique and beneficial to Christian intellectual engagement with disagreement both internally and externally towards those people who reject the faith on intellectual grounds.

As Calvin College professor Adel Abadeer writes:

> Christian institutions must always be vigilant with regard to their initiation and implementation of diversity, and must separate good from fallen diversity, especially with . . . diversity in ideas. Christian institutions should carefully, based on biblical

teaching and foundations, examine and test them before endorsing or rejecting them (Matthew 7:15).[17]

The line between "good" and "fallen diversity" in the Christian classroom is a tricky one to draw. Classrooms of all kinds were, for instance, both enriched and made more just by their historical inclusion of women and people of color. Such diversity of gender and race (and, more recently, sexual orientation) is often the "diversity" championed in the promotional literature and self-understanding of institutions of higher education. To be clear, these forms of diversity are not the concern of this chapter. Instead, it concerns the value of diversity of ideas or of exposing minds (particularly young, impressionable minds) to many or as many viewpoints as possible. Are Christian environments of learning and teaching made better—made more effective and greater vehicles to the acquisition of faithful "truth"—by the discussion (and serious consideration) of a wide range of views on a particular question?

As discussed in the previous chapter, intellectual diversity within an academic institution (whether secular or Christian) is a natural outgrowth or logical moral consequence of believing in open-mindedness's virtuous nature and the goodness of friendship. Contrary to Mill's optimism about progress in history (as discussed in chapter 5), the Bible and Christian theology give us no apparent reason to believe in such a confident, progressive view of history's arc as regards earthly truths. Our only promise regarding truth predestined to win out concerns a divine truth: that, in the end of time, "every knee shall bow . . . and every tongue confess that Jesus Christ is Lord" (Phil 2:10).

Consider, for instance, the following sentence from the mission statement of Harvard Divinity School: "An exemplary scholarly and teaching community requires respect for and critical engagement with difference and diversity of all kinds."[18] Or the University of Dubuque's—a private university affiliated with the PC (USA) that offers theological seminary programs—description of itself as a place "where a diversity of ideas and experiences are embraced and nurtured."[19] Or Liberty University's (a conservative evangelical institution) commitment to "demonstrate our

---

17. Abadeer, "Seeking Redemptive Diversity," 201.

18. See the Harvard Divinity School's full mission statement at http://hds.harvard.edu/about/history-and-mission.

19. See the University of Dubuque's full mission statement at https://www.dbq.edu/AboutUD/MissionVisionValues.

Christ-like nature by maintaining a culture that . . . promotes achievement of excellence through diversity of ideas and people."[20] Finally, consider remarks on the mission of the University of Notre Dame, made by its current president Father John Jenkins: "Notre Dame takes its commitment to cultivating a diverse intellectual community seriously. In fact, diversity is a moral and intellectual necessity."[21] In all these cases, the general sentiment of the words is reasonably Christian, and yet the bounds of the intellectual diversity to be tolerated and/or celebrated within a specifically Christian tradition and set of commitments is, unfortunately, underspecified or unspecified.

It is understandable, then, that a study performed by professor of education Alyssa Bryant of a small, anonymous, Lutheran liberal arts college in the Midwest found certain confusions and on-the-ground tension among people trying to balance or harmonize their self-understood common Christian identity and commitment to valuing diversity.[22] Bryant polled students, faculty, and staff, asking them questions like "What are the core dimensions of the campus's spiritual climate?" and "How do members of the college community experience the spiritual climate of their institution in light of their diverse identities?" What she discovered in the responses were certain felt strains or even paradoxes with respect to the school's supposed institutional identity or mission and its popular commitments to diversity of all kinds, including its commitment to intellectual diversity. Participants, Bryant summarized, "noted discernable tensions surrounding the college's juxtaposed commitments to its Lutheran denominational heritage and to the ecumenical values implicit in its concern for worldview diversity," making it difficult for them to articulate the school's Lutheran identity.[23] Respondents could not agree, and in many cases could not even figure out for *themselves*, the nature and extent of the institution's Lutheran affiliation, and were unsure how the school was supposed to be "a college of the church, but also one where we embrace diversity." On the other hand, a faculty member at the school was happily surprised upon arriving that, from her perspective, the college approached diversity in such a thoughtful manner:

---

20. Liberty University, "Master of Arts Marriage and Family Therapy," 10.

21. See Notre Dame's Undergraduate Admissions inclusion page at https://admissions.nd.edu/discover/student-life/inclusion/.

22. Bryant and Christy, "Challenge and Promise of Pluralism," 396–422.

23. Bryant and Christy, "Challenge and Promise of Pluralism," 407–8.

> I worried that as an institution of strong faith they wouldn't take diversity and ideas seriously enough . . . and that we wouldn't discuss it as a community or that we'd bury it by ignorance and without faith. We don't do that here I don't think. We talk about the hard issues, we talk about homosexuality, we talk about women in . . . religious roles, we talk about these pieces that I think are . . . currently challenging religious establishments. . . . We don't shy away from those.

No doubt, this faculty member is right to want to resist forms of faith that hide from serious intellectual challenges to some of its beliefs, or that don't handle them in a charitable way when they do. But there remains an important ambiguity in her remarks: when "we" (the pronoun she uses) have discussions about these hard issues, what can "we" share in the way of common commitments that would allow us to address these questions as a Christian (and in this case a specifically Lutheran) institution? Those are the even harder questions right now for institutions such as the one profiled by Bryant.

Though Bryant uses a Lutheran institution for her case study, the same questions and concerns obviously apply to schools affiliated with other Christian denominations. In other words, what makes an institution "Reformed," as in the case, for instance, of Princeton Theological Seminary? Given the amount of confusion on these questions at Christian schools—confusion that is often made worse, not better, by statements from institutional leadership—there is clearly a need to think harder about the proper relationship between intellectual diversity and the Christian faith. To be blunt, when discussions on these Christian campuses regarding what unites their members doctrinally tend to prove divisive (as is often the case), while talk of what makes their members diverse tend to prove agreeable and uniting, it can fairly be asked, with a note of skepticism: can talk of differences (or celebration or embrace thereof) give an institution an identity and sustain it?

Intellectual Diversity within Christian Traditions

How, then, should Christians correctly tolerate intellectual diversity within the bounds of their tradition? Aquinas's commentary on the book of Job offers a nice example of how to benefit from intellectual diversity when the divergent views in question are within the bounds of justice. Aquinas approves of Job's reaction to the friends who offer arguments against him. Though Job is confident in the truth and justice of his opinions, he nevertheless says to his friends, "Despite this, finish what you began to say," so that, as Aquinas glosses, "the truth can come to light from mutual debate."[24]

Likewise, in his *Confessions*, Augustine demonstrates how to tolerate intellectual diversity within an intellectual community—in this case, the kind in which disagreement does not do harm to the truth of something but merely adds possible layers or dimensions to it. The question Augustine addresses concerns how to interpret Moses (whom Augustine thought wrote Genesis) when he speaks of God creating heaven and earth in the beginning, and how the formation of the universe relates to the creation of time, which leads to certain philosophical puzzles. Specifically, Augustine asks whether the words "In the beginning he made" refer to a universe already formed, or only to some unformed matter, merely the physical creation.[25] Augustine sees reason in both interpretations, and, for himself, is unsure which is true. Though there isn't collective agreement on how to interpret this piece of Scripture, Augustine says that a different (and more important) kind of unity can exist in the midst of this (exegetical) disunity: "In this discord of true opinions let Truth itself bring concord, and may our God have mercy on us all, that we may use the law rightly to the end of the commandment which is pure love," he writes.[26] Out of and throughout this intellectual disagreement can still flourish a union in mutual love between the parties. Though we are unable to agree on how to interpret these passages, says Augustine, "Let all of us, whom I acknowledge to see and speak the truth in these words, love one another and also love thee, our God, O Fountain of Truth."[27]

To disagree profitably within a tradition, there must be an already agreed-upon baseline as to what constitutes the essence and boundaries of that tradition. Think of this as the metaphysics of traditions (as opposed to the tradition of metaphysics) or the metaphysics of ideas. This chapter assumes that Aristotle's insights about change and substances/accidents of things in the world are equally applicable to the metaphysics of ideas and traditions of thought. That is, certain things must persist for a tradition to remain itself. Put in Aristotle's metaphysical terminology,

---

24. Aquinas, *Literal Exposition on Job*, chapter 6, lesson 2.
25. Augustine, *Conf.* 12.29–30.
26. Augustine, *Conf.* 12.30.
27. Augustine, *Conf.* 12.30.

there must be an enduring or "primary substrate" within an intellectual tradition. This is the quality (or set of propositions or assumptions) it cannot afford to lose, lest it cease to remain itself.[28] Like organisms, traditions swap matter over time, but they also come into and go out of existence.

It is important to stress that believing that Christianity generally, and Christian denominations specifically, have certain essences is not the same as naively insisting that traditions never change. When Martin Luther protested, "Here I stand" (forget whether or not he actually said it), his "here" was not identical with the "here" of the modern-day Lutheran. Recall Heraclitus's observation that no man steps in the same river twice. But conceding this much doesn't require us to conclude that Luther therefore stands alone (just like the rest of us)—that his *hereness* does not stand in some real relation (via a persisting form) to the *thereness* of the church that still bears his name.

It could be objected at this point that Heraclitus's river metaphor is the wrong one, and that a better aquatic metaphor is needed. In *On Certainty*, Wittgenstein speaks of traditions of certain world-pictures as like riverbeds. "The mythology," he says, referring to any intellectual tradition, "may change back into a state of flux, the river-bed of thoughts may shift. But I distinguish between the movement of the waters on the river-bed and the shift of the bed itself; though there is not a sharp division of the one from the other."[29] It is this last contention (the denial of a "division") that places Wittgenstein in tension with the version of essentialism defended in this chapter.

Wittgenstein continues the metaphor: "And the bank of that river consists partly of hard rock, subject to no alteration or only to an imperceptible one, partly of sand, which now in one place now in another gets

---

28. "The matter comes to be and ceases to be in one sense, while in another it does not. As that which contains the privation, it ceases to be in its own nature, for what ceases to be—the privation—is contained within it. But as potentiality it does not cease to be in its own nature, but is necessarily outside the sphere of becoming and ceasing to be. For if it came to be, something must have existed as a primary substratum from which it should come and which should persist in it; but this is its own special nature, so that it will be before coming to be. (*For my definition of matter is just this—the primary substratum of each thing, from which it comes to be without qualification, and which persists in the result*). And if it ceases to be it will pass into that at the last, so it will have ceased to be before ceasing to be." Aristotle, *Phys.* 192a, emphasis added.

29. Wittgenstein, *On Certainty*, §97.

washed away, or deposited."[30] The reference to "rock" here is intriguing for it may or may not function like an essential form to the tradition in question. The course of the Colorado River, for instance, has greatly changed over time but it remains the Colorado River because, among other things, its origin and eventual destination remain the same. Whatever is the case regarding the hardness of Wittgenstein's rock, and whether or not Wittgenstein's imagined river has locks, it certainly (from the essentialist standpoint, and as concerns the Christian tradition) has "hinges" (as admitted by Wittgenstein in chapter 4) at every step along the way.

When our Lord stepped into the water of the River Jordan for baptism, he immersed himself in a river physically somewhat different from the one in which John had already baptized others. And yet, that river was nonetheless the same river, intellectually and spiritually speaking. Our Lord's river was not Heraclitus's but neither, it seems, was it Wittgenstein's river. The far bank of the Jordan may change with time in its natural elements, but its spiritual and intellectual significance and meaning remain the same: it was, is, and always will be the boundary of the promised land, into which the Israelites crossed, and across which Christians believe death or a certain release from the trials of life (as expressed in multiple slave spirituals) will finally take us, where we will finally be reconciled with God and finally come home as a people of God, Jews and Christians alike.

The idea that intellectual traditions, Christianity included, can survive having every aspect of their constitution replaced (recall Theseus's famous ship here) and still remain themselves is an illusion. Richard John Neuhaus observed that this point has failed to occur to many cradle Roman Catholics in America, it perhaps being more obvious from the "outsider's" perspective of Neuhaus, a Lutheran-turned-Catholic. He calls this confidence a version of "ecclesiastical fundamentalism" that "seems to believe that—after every form of doctrine, discipline, authority, and communal identity has been abandoned—the Roman Catholic Church will endure so long as there is something to call 'Catholic.'"[31] But

---

30. Wittgenstein, *On Certainty*, §99.

31. Neuhaus, *Catholic Moment*, as quoted in Douthat, "Why I Am a Catholic," paras. 11–12. It should be pointed out that Neuhaus's remarks apply to a great many other things as well—baseball, democracy, marriage, etc.—in which fundamental changes can lead to different substantial forms. Understandably, though, we care a great deal more about some possibilities than others. Whether "baseball" played with

why think this, as Neuhaus rightly asks? Neuhaus recounts a conversation with a priest who imagined, in a longing way, a "renewed" Catholic Church that would in just about every way—from democratically elected pastors, to open conventions that would decide church positions—look like most mainline Protestant denominations. To which Neuhaus wondered how it can be that this "dismantling of the house piece by piece" could occur while

> confidently asserting that the house is indestructible. Curiously, this particular priest harshly criticized [Pope John Paul II] because "he talks about the church as though it were an abstraction." Yet the church this priest describes—decontextualized, dehistoricized, and deprived of all its thus and so-ness—will, he believes, forever remain the Roman Catholic Church in which he made his first Communion and his ordination vows.[32]

For Paul Griffiths, the Roman Catholic theological tradition in which he sees himself as operating must entail doctrinal discovery of certain kinds and cannot be (on pain of incoherence or self-destruction) completely open and nonrestrictive in its understanding of Catholic theology. The sad consequence of a lack of agreement on this basic matter can lead two scholars, both of whom think they are doing Catholic theology, to be unable to recognize what the other is doing *as* Catholic theology. "There that dispute must remain," Griffiths concludes. But all hope is not lost. "What each of us can do in such a case," he advises, "is do what we do, hope to make beautiful the [intellectual] artifacts we produce, and show them, in humility and love, to those engaged in other enterprises.... The beauty and the passion of Catholic theology is in large part given to it... by its intrinsic responsiveness to authority. That not all Catholics see it this way is a matter for lament."[33]

Responses to Griffiths's remarks have only underscored the point he rightly makes. Cathleen Kaveny, for instance, replied by reiterating her belief that the Catholic Theological Society of America (CTSA)—the professional guild for Catholic theologians whose activity prompted Griffiths's statements—should "accommodate as wide as possible a range

---

a designated hitter has evolved into a new substantial form is of less interest (or should be) to modern-day Christians than whether we stand in the same tradition as the early church.

32. Neuhaus, *Catholic Moment*.
33. Griffiths, "Theological Disagreement," 34.

of theological opinion."³⁴ But how "wide" is too wide? More, Kaveny's distinction between the Christian community and the academic sphere is revealing. She writes,

> I do not think it is a breach of ecclesial communion if one group [within the CSTA] decides it can do better work within a more narrowly defined theological context. Leaving the CTSA isn't leaving the church. An academic conference is not the Body of Christ, after all. And within the church, there has always been ample room for different groups to pursue their calling in parallel, inconsistent, and sometimes contesting ways. Jesuits aren't Franciscans, who in turn definitely aren't Benedictines.³⁵

While this might be true, Kaveny's remarks do not address Griffiths's central point and concern: that commitments to certain kinds of scholarship within certain boundaries governed by certain shared assumptions reflect certain shared ecclesiastical communions—the orders she lists being all members of the same church. After all, where else would such boundaries come from? And what does it say about the kind of scholarship being done if it doesn't derive from ecclesial boundaries?

Consider, also, this response from Michele Saracino: "Why does Griffiths want this model of theology? . . . Is it that he needs certainty? What is the problem with saying [that] theologizing is more of a negotiation? . . . Think of all the life that is symbolically saved by an understanding of . . . Christian teaching not as proclamation—but as dissent and dialogue."³⁶ Saracino's rhetorical questions are, in fact, nicely representative of the wider confusion regarding the proper Christian views of open-mindedness and the value of intellectual diversity that this project, taken as a whole, seeks to address. As argued in chapter 3, the "need for certainty" is a misleading phrase, as Catholic theology—just like marine biology, or Malaysian history, or any intellectual endeavor—must begin with certain shared assumptions and boundaries about which one is functionally confident. More, certain propositions are not, cannot morally *be*, live propositions for these endeavors to function, just as for Christians, additionally, certain items in the deposit of faith are not open to dissent and dialogue; indeed, they must, contrary to Saracino's words,

---

34. Kaveny, "No Academic Question."
35. Kaveny, "No Academic Question."
36. Saracino, "Response to Paul Griffiths' 'Theological Disagreement,'" 38.

be proclaimed, as in response to Jesus' question in Matthew 16:15, "Who do you say that I am?"

Theologian Ellen Charry, in keeping with the trajectory of Griffiths's remarks, observes how certain tenets of the faith impose limits upon the acceptable range of intellectual diversity within the church. Concerning this necessary baseline of beliefs, "Neither modern science, high-minded values, nor personal experience can authorize changes in Christian doctrine and practice apart from historically agreed upon creedal categories," writes Charry. Christian belief and practice, she says, "are not like a Kandinsky painting that can be thought of as right side up no matter which direction one views it from."[37] The hard part, as Charry points out, is figuring out when disagreements on issues warrant church division. When is intellectual diversity intolerable within a church body, in other words? Charry rightly sees the real possibility that there is no neutrality on these matters, since (in the Anglican tradition to which she is referring) priests must follow their bishops, so "a move to include the disenfranchised effectively disenfranchises others. What looks to some like 'leaving the church' is to others being left by the church."[38]

Theologian Kevin Hector, looking for another way, has advocated for replacing the traditional stabilizing forces of Scripture and ecclesial decisions with actions of the Holy Spirit. Consistency would no longer come from the top-down but from the bottom-up, as "the Spirit is publicly mediated, yet cannot be identified in advance with the authority of any person or the configuration of any prevailing order; rather, the Spirit is continually reconfiguring that order from within."[39] Hector's failure, however, to specify the extent to which this Spirit can be "public" (all those baptized? all who self-identify as "Christian"?) without ceasing to be Christian is problematic and finally leaves his proposal unhelpful.

The Value of Heresy

"Bar the way of heresy and what's left is orthodoxy" is a way of thinking that was once popular in forms of Western Christianity. It has, by and large, fallen out of favor today among Western Christians, particularly among mainline Protestants. The mainline churches for the most part

---

37. Charry, "Same-Sex Relationships," xv.
38. Charry, "Same-Sex Relationships," xvii.
39. Hector, *Theology without Metaphysics*, 286.

no longer find doctrinal heresy to be a useful concept for defining the content of their faith. The history that led to this transformation concerning the sources of self-identity is a story unto itself. For the purposes of this chapter, it is sufficient to note that it was not always so, and that there remain good theological reasons for thinking that heresy (and its inverse concept, "orthodoxy") is a useful, perhaps even indispensable, concept for understanding the essence of Christianity and of particular denominational identities—that the delineations of heresies are a gift from earlier Christians who, like guides, traveled intellectual paths before us, leaving behind a kind of map that we call the deposit of faith.[40] Heresy, it will be further argued, is thus an important subject for Christians trying to figure out how to view intellectual diversity through the eyes of grace. More, the concept of heresy is essential to Christianity because Christianity is a tradition that, by its own self-understanding, is not defined by class, race, gender, etc., but rather partially by what its adherents believe. As theologian Ben Quash reminds us:

> To our modern liberal ears an interest in the right and wrongs of doctrine may sound a bit of a pedantic interest to have—and even a recipe for intolerance and persecution. . . . But there is a very good and positive reason why Christianity has been so concerned about orthodoxy, or right belief. From its very beginnings, Christianity said that neither your race, nor your sex, nor your social class, nor your age could ever be a bar to full membership of Christ's body, the Church. Anyone could be a Christian. . . . This was radical stuff. What, though, was left to mark a Christian out from a non-Christian? The answer was: your faith—what you believed in, as embodied in your practices and confessed with your lips. The Church's identity and integrity were expressed in orthodoxy: the confession (and enactment) of a collective belief. Christianity was open to anybody, but had definite convictions. That's why heresy was a matter to be taken seriously, because it called those convictions into question. It threatened a crucial thing that bound the Church together and made Christians Christians.[41]

---

40. That a "heresy" is only so after the fact of an authoritative church council having weighed in does not change the truth of these statements. As the adage goes, "Origen was not a heretic but Origenism *is*."

41. Quash, "Prologue," 1–2. Roman Catholic readers of Quash would likely add that, in addition to adherence to a set of defined beliefs, certain sacramental communion with the living church is required for full Christian identity.

From the standpoint of Christianity, intellectual diversity can only be tolerated internally within a restricted range of beliefs. Thus, what Aquinas calls "fraternal correction" is a necessary, even morally obligatory, aspect of the Christian life. In a section in his *Summa* on the topic of tolerating heresy, Aquinas tellingly says nothing about the *value* of dissenting opinion within the church on matters pertaining to the faith. Quite the contrary, he quotes approvingly Jerome's commentary on Galatians 5:9: "Cut off the decayed flesh, expel the mangy sheep from the fold, lest the whole house, the whole paste, the whole body, the whole flock, burn, perish, rot, die."[42] What starts small can smolder and grow if it is not properly, sometimes coercively, dealt with. "Arius," as Jerome goes on to say, "was but one spark in Alexandria, but as that spark was not at once put out, the whole earth was laid waste by its flame."[43]

Before Aquinas, Augustine wrote an entire handbook cataloging the known heresies of his time (he described eighty-eight in total). He demonstrates a kind of intellectual humility in acknowledging that there are, no doubt, many heresies he is unable to know about and, moreover, that even those he does detail are not "as well understood by a stranger as by its own believers."[44] He is quick to add, though, that it is nevertheless "of great value to be able to avoid those errors which I have included in this work, once they have been read and understood."[45] That many believers do not know the ins and outs of these heresies or how to argue against them is beside the point. "It is of great advantage," Augustine writes, "to the faithful soul to know what he must not believe, even if he cannot refute [these heresies] by skill in argumentation."[46] Aquinas thought similarly.[47] Interestingly, Augustine finished his text on known heresies

---

42. *ST* II-II.11.3.

43. *ST* II-II.11.3.

44. See "To Quodvultdeus on Heresies" in Augustine, *Letters of Saint Augustine*, 128–29.

45. See "To Quodvultdeus on Heresies" in Augustine, *Letters of Saint Augustine*, 129.

46. See "To Quodvultdeus on Heresies" in Augustine, *Letters of Saint Augustine*, 129.

47. Aquinas: "A twofold knowledge may be had about matters of belief. One is the knowledge of what one ought to believe by discerning things to be believed from things not to be believed: in this way knowledge is a gift and is common to all holy persons. The other is a knowledge about matters of belief, whereby one knows not only what one ought to believe, but also how to make the faith known, how to induce others to believe, and confute those who deny the faith. This knowledge is numbered among the gratuitous graces, which are not given to all, but to some." *ST* II-II.9.

by promising to take up the question of what makes a heretic in his next volume. Unfortunately, he never got around to composing this work.

The difference between the term "heresy" and the term "schism" is important to discussions about the limits of tolerating intellectual diversity within the Christian tradition. Schism, in the classic understanding, is a form of disagreement that has yet to result in a full ecclesial separation—a division of opinions prior to a formal split. Heresy, on the other hand, entails continuing to choose for oneself (the etymology of the word) after a person has been corrected by church authorities, thereby cutting oneself off from the church body. This is why, as mentioned earlier, Origenism can be regarded today as a heresy while Origen, during his own life, was not a heretic. Augustine puts the distinction this way: "Heretics by holding false notions of God violate the Faith itself," whereas "schismatics by unrighteous rendings asunder, break away from brotherly love, although they believe the same things as ourselves."[48] Augustine probably had the Donatists in mind when drawing this distinction, since in many ways Donatism resembled the Catholic Church in its recognition of the same books of Scripture and use of the same sacraments; what it lacked, in Augustine's view, was the charity or brotherly love that would unite (or re-unite, as was the case) Donatists to the principal church body, thereby making their actions tantamount to heresy, which Augustine elsewhere speaks of as "a schism grown old."[49]

From the Christian perspective, a certain degree of schism, therefore, is tolerable so long as it doesn't violate the (admittedly contestable) nonnegotiable items found in the deposit of faith, and so long as it is carried out in a spirit of charity, and so long as the adherents of the heterodox beliefs don't persist in those beliefs after a formal church body (whose identity and authority is admittedly contestable as well) has decided against them. Thus, it could be argued that, with the reception of the new supernatural virtues of faith and charity, a new *vice* (one without an acquired form) is made possible as well: the heretical will, or, more explicitly, the habit of mind that makes a person content with segregation

---

48. Augustine, *De Fide et Symbolo*, 21.

49. Aquinas, it should be said, used the labels differently but maintained the same general distinctions between the concepts, writing, "Heresy and schism are distinguished in respect of those things to which each is opposed essentially and directly. For heresy is essentially opposed to faith, while schism is essentially opposed to the unity of ecclesiastical charity. Wherefore just as faith and charity are different virtues, although whoever lacks faith lacks charity, so too schism and heresy are different vices, although whoever is a heretic is also a schismatic, but not conversely." *ST*, II-II.39.

and polarization within the body of Christ, a product of lacking the full charity and humility that would avoid such outcomes.

Charity in the Face of Intellectual Diversity

Augustine's homilies on 1 John offer a helpful example of the role of Christian charity in the face of intellectual diversity. The homilies are anti-Donatist texts in which he uses the trope of love to invite the Donatists back into the Catholic faith while condemning them at the same time. Skeptics might discount the style and strategy as merely a bit of rhetoric (in the worst sense of the word) or, worse, a power play on the part of a bishop disguised as an invitation born of charity. But these skeptics would be wrong and their mis-assessment would be typical of misunderstandings of how Christian charity functions in the face of intellectual diversity. The first thing to note in the homilies is that Augustine, as with Aquinas, evinces no signs (in response to the intellectual diversity he sees around himself) of the kind of strong fallibilism discussed in chapter 4; nor does he display any signs of the kind of conformism discussed in chapter 5. Augustine writes, "He that loves his brother, bears all things for unity's sake."[50] Imagine, he says, that someone offends you. He may be a bad man, or you may just think he is a bad man, or you might be unsure. The point is, do you abandon all such men? If so, you abandon many, many people, says Augustine. This, Augustine implies, is what the Donatists have done. "What sort of brotherly love," he asks, "is that which has appeared in these persons? While they accuse the Africans, they have deserted the whole world!"[51]

Similarly, in reflecting on 1 John 2:10 ("He that loves his brother abides in the light, and there is no occasion of stumbling in him"), Augustine asks rhetorically (again, with obvious reference to the Donatists), "If we be in unity, what means it that there are two altars in this city? What, that there are divided houses, divided marriages? That there is a common bed, and a divided Christ?"[52] Note how different these notions of charity are from the more secular versions of intellectual charity described earlier.

---

50. Augustine, *Homilies on the Gospel*, 1107.
51. Augustine, *Homilies on the Gospel*, 1107.
52. Augustine, *Homilies on the Gospel*, 1107.

In response to the possible objection that Augustine's supposed charity is actually a form of *un*charitable coercion, Augustine points out how a true friend, how true charity (as in the case of fraternal correction mentioned in Aquinas), must be willing to correct (to "call out" in modern parlance) those who are doing harm to the deposit of faith or the church body by continuing to espouse opinions contrary to fundamental church teachings after having been told to stop. As Augustine says, a person who actually hates another will feign friendship with him, and praise him for doing something that is vicious and dangerous to him, because he secretly wishes him ill. On the contrary, a true friend, possessing true charity, "sees his friend doing something of the same sort [and] he calls him back; if he will not hear, he uses words even of castigation, he scolds, he quarrels." Augustine, aware that his readers may be surprised that he is approving of "quarrelling," because such behavior would seem to be at odds with the spirit of Christian peace, hastens to add that quarreling is sometimes appropriate. "Behold, hatred shows itself winningly gentle, and charity quarrels! Stay not your regard upon the words of seeming kindness," which could actually be born of hatred, "or the seeming cruelty of the rebuke," which could actually be born of real charity. "Look," says Augustine, "into the vein they come from; seek the root whence they proceed. The one is gentle and bland that he may deceive, the other quarrels that he may correct."[53]

Importantly, in these cases of sacrifice, the object in sight is God, and the medium is love of God, even if in the foreground are one's neighbor and one's love of neighbor. Think of this as a form of intellectual hospitality. Aquinas, for instance, speaks of the types of religious life in his *Summa*, noting that although different kinds are called for, all are directed ultimately to God. All forms of the religious life, he says, are "directed to the perfection of charity, which extends to the love of God and of our neighbor. Now the contemplative life, which seeks to devote itself to God alone, belongs directly to the love of God, while the active life, which ministers to our neighbor's needs, belongs directly to the love of one's neighbor."[54] This love of neighbor redounds to God, as Matthew 25:40 reminds us ("What you have done to the least of my brethren, you did to me"). In referring such services to God, they are made into sacrifices. Thus, there is, arguably, a charism-based metaphor to be found

---

53. Augustine, *Homilies on the Gospel*, 1107.
54. *ST* II-II.188.

here, as concerns the dimensions of the Christian intellectual life in the face of intellectual diversity: sometimes correction is called for, sometimes it is right to simply attend to internal issues, and sometimes it is proper to court, to woo with love, those who disagree. To complete the analogy, note how Abbot Nesteros distinguishes the various aims of religious orders: "Some direct their intention exclusively to the hidden life of the desert and purity of heart; some are occupied with the instruction of the brethren and the care of the monasteries; while others delight in the service of the guesthouse," i.e., hospitality.[55]

The Sadness of Intellectual Diversity

In the preface to his *Retractions* Augustine remarks, "[M]any teachers arise when there are different and mutually opposed opinions. But when all utter the same words and speak the same truth, they do not depart from the teaching of the one true Teacher."[56] It's an interesting statement and little commented upon, as secondary scholarship has been concerned by and large with his preceding comment that, as bishop, he was seldom allowed to remain silent on matters, an indication of the burdens he felt as a leader. The quoted sentence would seem to suggest that teachers are an unfortunate necessity after the fall (a fall into intellectual discord and disagreement) and emerge, because they must, to try to bring some (imperfect) order back to things. True, perfect agreement is only possible for God and in God, and will not exist until the end of time. Disagreement, to carry out this line of thought, is a result of sin, the consequence of no longer being of one mind, having first come about in history when Eve (and not yet Adam) believed in the goodness of eating the apple. Disagreement, as consequence of sin, actually predates suffering and death. Atonement, then, has an intellectual dimension: that of being, again, of one mind in Christ.

Augustine, in this connection, seems to suggest in his *City of God* that disagreement within a school of thought casts serious doubt on the truth of its general views. The incarnation, he implies at times, so democratized truth that any school of thought or spirituality that cannot agree within itself, or that is achievable or understandable to only a select few, such as Platonism, must not be the true philosophy, must not be the

55. *ST* II-II.188.
56. Augustine, *Retractions*, 4.

correct way to God. Returning, though, to the relevant portion of the *City of God*, Augustine speaks about the "discord of philosophical opinion." Many of these philosophers, Augustine admits, were intelligent and had the right intentions: "They seem to have labored in their studies for no other end than to find out how to live in a way proper for laying hold of blessedness."[57] Given this, he asks, "Why, then, have the disciples dissented from their masters, and the fellow-disciples from one another?" They have pursued these things of "human sense and human reasonings."[58] And this is not enough when it comes to the most fundamental questions about existence. As Augustine says, "But what can human misery do, or how or where can it reach forth, so as to attain blessedness, if divine authority does not lead it?"[59] Discord among the secular philosophers is inevitable, as human sense and reasoning lead us this way and that way.

After listing multiple examples of philosophical schools that have disagreed over issues like the immortality of the soul, or whether nature is governed by chance or by laws, Augustine associates these schools and the gymnasium with the City of Man. He asks, "Has it not held in its bosom at random, without any judgment, and confusedly, so many controversies of men at variance, . . . about those things which make life either miserable or happy?"[60] He then reminds his readers that Babylon means confusion. The Israelites, by contrast, were a city, a people, who were blessed to receive the commands of God, about which there could be no confusion or questioning of authority. If God says, "Honor your father and mother," then this is commanded and there is no room for disagreement about it, says Augustine. As to the question of how it can be, then, that some pagan philosophers came, in certain places, to similar ethical conclusions as the Decalogue or similar general knowledge of God but did so without the gift of revelation, Augustine insists that these truths were still sent down from on high, and issued from God.

> Whatever truth certain philosophers, amid their false opinions, were able to see, and strove by laborious discussions to persuade men of—such as that God had made this world, and Himself most providently governs it, or of the nobility of the virtues, of the love of country, of fidelity in friendship, of good works and everything pertaining to virtuous manners, although they

---

57. Augustine, *City of God*, Book 18, Chapter 41.
58. Augustine, *City of God*, Book 18, Chapter 41.
59. Augustine, *City of God*, Book 18, Chapter 41.
60. Augustine, *City of God*, Book 18, Chapter 41.

knew not to what end and what rule all these things were to be referred—all these, by words prophetic, that is, divine, although spoken by men, were commended to the people in that city, and not inculcated by contention in arguments, so that he who should know them might be afraid of condemning, not the wit of men, but the oracle of God.[61]

For the purposes of this chapter, it is worth highlighting that Augustine discounts the value of collective disputation as a means of arriving at truth; indeed, he seems to imply the opposite: that, without instruction from the one true Teacher, disagreement and confusion are bound to result.

This does not mean, of course, that Christians cannot learn much from non-Christians. In speaking of the liberal arts, for instance, John Calvin wrote:

> Men are endued with a general apprehension of reason and understanding. Yet it is such a universal blessing, that every one ought to acknowledge it as a peculiar favor of God. To this gratitude the Author of nature himself abundantly excites us, by his creation of idiots, in whom he represents the state of the human soul without his illumination. . . . Whenever therefore we meet with heathen writers, let us learn from that light of truth which is admirably displayed in their works, that the human mind, fallen as it is, . . . is yet invested and adorned by God with excellent talents. If we believe that the Spirit of God is the only fountain of truth, we shall neither reject or despise the truth itself, wherever it appear, unless we wish to insult the Spirit of God. . . . Now, shall we deny the light of truth to the ancient lawyers who have delivered such just principles of civil order and probity? Shall we say that the philosophers were blind in the exquisite contemplation and in their scientific description of nature? Shall we say that those who by the art of logic have taught us to speak in a manner consistent with reason, were destitute of understanding themselves?[62]

This is the proper Christian way of dealing with intellectual diversity. Consider, also, as a more specific example, Calvin's use of Arabic numerals in his personal correspondence (those letters dated 1551 and 1562).[63]

---

61. Augustine, *City of God*, Book 18, Chapter 41.
62. Calvin, *Institutes of the Christian Religion*, 287–88.
63. Special thanks to Elsie McKee for highlighting this fact for me.

Arabic numerals were a cultural import through the Iberian Peninsula around Calvin's time, brought by Muslims in the thirteenth and fourteenth century. Interestingly, unlike his personal correspondence, Calvin's first book in 1532 used Roman numerals (the text of the book we have today is a print, but most likely a faithful translation). Though Calvin is open-minded and Christian in his relationship with intellectual diversity in the above example, he was, no doubt, an imperfect man, as was shown by his deadly intolerance towards Servetus, his intellectual foe.

How Christians Should Disagree

The reception of the work of theologian Robert Jenson serves as a revealing case study for the value of intellectual diversity within theology. Consider George Hunsinger's otherwise critical review of Jenson's *Systematic Theology* in which Hunsinger pays passing respect to the daringness of Jenson's project.[64] He writes, "The single-minded rigor with which Jenson thinks through the utter novelty of his proposals can only be admired," and "It is not nothing . . . to spit in the eye of the Zeitgeist, come what may."[65] Hunsinger sees Jenson's work as the culmination of a radical thought experiment that, thanks to Jenson, can finally be confirmed as a failure. Unmentioned by Hunsinger, however, is any note of gratitude for what Jenson has done for theology, for the intellectual diversity and refinement he has brought to the discipline. Arguably, owing to Jenson's intellectual creativity and stubbornness, all theologians (Hunsinger included) stand in a better position to understand God's identity. Dead ends can prove instructive. That said, a critic in Hunsinger's position may be excused from feeling or expressing gratitude towards Jenson, if, on the critic's view, the resulting diversity is more harmful than beneficial to the cause of Truth; i.e., despite its other undeniable merits, Jenson's project does *not* profit theology insofar as it leads people astray from the truth about God. But, even if this were the case (it is unclear if Hunsinger thinks so), Augustine's example of how to court the Donatists is still to be followed: those who are in need of correction, perhaps even for opinions contrary to the deposit of faith, must be argued with in the spirit of *charity*.

---

64. Hunsinger, "Robert Jenson's *Systematic Theology*," 161–200.
65. Hunsinger, "Robert Jenson's *Systematic Theology*," 161–200.

Maintaining such a spirit of charity is not always easy. Theology, among the disciplines, is an especially high-stakes game. Topics like God's true identity and how God expects us to live are believed to have consequences for the fates of souls—what, then, could be more important? Given this, we should expect theological disputes to be especially devoid of the spirit of charity and to be among the most combative in the academy; we should expect, too, theologians to be the most closed-minded and disinterested in intellectual diversity—a sobering thought, were it not for the fact that Christians and their theology are also unique in another, far more positive, respect. Christians can assume that their intellectual relationships are, as mentioned earlier, graced by the theological virtues of faith, hope, and love—enabling them to take up, heal, and transform the intellectual Machiavellianism that characterizes an academic state of nature into something else, something better. That Christian scholars are often no better than their pagan counterparts in this respect does not disprove the reality of these intellectual graces. It merely lays bare a sad neglect for the infused intellectual virtues among Christian scholars, who have yet to become what they are called to be: members of a beloved community of learning. As theologian Bruce McCormack remarks, "Polemics certainly have their place." But they should "always be respectful, never obsessive," and must never "be allowed to subvert that awe before the subject matter which turns even the most learned theologian into a person filled with childlike wonder and the joy of discovery," just as, this chapter wishes to stress, polemics should never be allowed to subvert or pollute the *charity* that Christians should feel and show towards people with whom they disagree.[66]

Is it possible that we, a circle of believing scholars, can preach the gospel in the way that we approach disagreement, in the way we listen, learn, and teach? If we do, if we model the virtues of the mind, both our faith and scholarship will benefit, and, as is the case whenever virtue is practiced, those outside our circle will be drawn to our way of life and, with it, our message.

The next chapter will take up the question of how the virtue of open-mindedness is changed by the infusion of Christian grace.

---

66. McCormack, "Let's Speak Plainly," 65.

8

Infused Open-Mindedness

General Changes

How is the natural virtue of open-mindedness elevated by supernatural grace, particularly the gift of faith? When infusion occurs, the object of open-mindedness shifts from goodness to God, and its exemplar becomes the person of Jesus Christ, giving open-mindedness a new appearance while retaining its general form. Though Aquinas reserves the concept of divine "infusion" for the reception of the theological virtue of charity alone, this chapter will, additionally, speak of the "infusion of faith" and "infusion of hope." Each phrase should be interpreted as referring to the reception and consequences of these particular graces (faith and hope) that are, admittedly, only made possible by the initial reception of divine charity (God's extension of friendship to us).

The reception of the Christian faith by the open-minded person changes how he or she views intellectual humility. Call this new reality epistemic grace. Theologian Steven Pardue's recent book *The Mind of Christ: Humility and the Intellect in Early Christian Theology* discusses this change, drawing heavily on the work of Gregory of Nyssa (an important voice in chapter 9).[1]

Pardue points out a strong relationship (noted in chapter 4 of this book) between a person's metaphysical commitments and the way in which he or she values epistemological virtues such as humility. In other words, if one begins with Kant's assumptions about the distinction between the noumenal and the phenomenal worlds, what constitutes

---

1. Pardue, *Mind of Christ*.

open-mindedness (and thus proper intellectual humility) is going to follow from these assumptions. By comparison, Thomas Aquinas considered it a vice to spend too much time thinking about worldly things and lose sight of the more important matters: things invisible and in the life of the world to come. While acknowledging that a great many modern Protestant theologians like himself simply take the previous Kantian metaphysical assumption for granted, Pardue instead laments that "Christians have mistakenly attached their understandings of epistemic humility to an insufficiently Christian view of the world," often without knowing it.[2] What makes this notion of intellectual humility un-Christian is its failure to take into account the history-changing event of the incarnation, according to Pardue. Note, though, how Pardue's reason for rejecting modern notions of intellectual humility is different than Aquinas's, discussed in chapter 4. Aquinas's notion of intellectual humility was centered on the metaphysical hierarchy found in the great chain of being, discernable prior to and apart from knowledge of the incarnation, whereas Pardue appears to assume that Kant's distinction would hold true had it not been for the incarnation. As Pardue writes, "It is precisely the metaphysical significance of the incarnation of God the Son that explodes the late modern vision of intellectual humility," as evident in Kant's apophaticism, which offers an overly constricted version of intellectual humility.[3] When Christ entered time, the infinite became finite, the transcendent became immanent, the word became flesh, and heaven came to earth. The new activity of divine grace made possible by this event expands human limits.

That grace changes what counts as intellectual humility, and thus the content of virtuous open-mindedness seems certain, at least from a virtue ethics standpoint. But there is no consensus on how and where the embrace of faith redraws the acceptable boundaries of humility. These boundaries depend on which theologians you happen to be reading. For some, the lingering doubt in the statement "I might be wrong about *that*" seems to no longer apply to select articles of the faith. Just what these articles are is itself an assortment, but one can nevertheless identify such elements in the thought of many figures, while other voices in the Christian tradition have continued to reason as if faith and doubt are fully compatible, as if all beliefs are still up for discussion.

---

2. Pardue, *Mind of Christ*, 172.
3. Pardue, *Mind of Christ*, 182.

And it is here that the Christian faith will come into greatest tension with the modern pluralist society in the eyes of some, since, after faith, there will be a set of propositions (fundamental tenets of the faith) that cannot be called into question, because they are products of early, authoritative, and ecumenical church councils such as Nicaea and Chalcedon, prior to later ecclesial divisions within Christianity. Among these beliefs would be, for instance, the divinity of Jesus, that Jesus was fully human, that God is one yet three persons, other tenets found in the Apostle's Creed, etc. For Christians, there is no going "behind" Chalcedon, so to speak, as its formulations are normative and inseparable from Christianity in its wake; theological reimaginings must assume as much and thus remain of the near side (theologically) of the ecumenically universal councils, where they are free to propose and speculate without risking the charge of heresy.[4] Again, this is disputed within the theological tradition. On one side are Christian thinkers (usually though not always modern) like the philosopher Charles Taylor, who view their faith in epistemic terms that a modern critic of religion will find more amenable to modern cultural pluralism.

According to Taylor, whether we see God as a threat or distraction from human happiness or instead as the natural goal of human flourishing is not a question that every person has honestly grappled with in any honest way. Many, as Taylor puts it, have not "stood in that open space where you can feel the winds pulling you, now to belief, now to unbelief."[5] Instead, many will themselves to believe or *not* believe, even

---

4. To return to a topic mentioned in the previous chapter, if one believes that there are such fixed, foundational elements in Christianity, it naturally follows that such beliefs, interestingly, should be exempted from any kind of prayer for (as-needed) fraternal correction. Believing that the doctrinal formulations and ecclesial decisions of the early Christian church are binding for future Christians means taking a different view of the supposed benefits of any intellectual creativity in such matters. In response to the arguments by "disruption" enthusiasts like Clayton Christensen and Peter Thiel (discussed in chapter 6), any lost innovations due to docility towards and willed conformity with these formulations are not, in the final estimate, true losses in the eyes of the church. The inevitable preclusion of some theological creativity and possible theological innovations as a consequence of the attitude of docility (or intentional *un*originality) toward conciliar formulations of the faith can only be seen as beneficial losses from the perspective of the church, while, by contrast, they can only be seen as true losses when working with a purely techno-economic model of human agency and goals. Likewise, the intellectual DNA of the Christian faith, in its formation and development, cannot be a form of open-source software but is, rather, very much a proprietary system, a fact, that, from the Christian perspective, is a blessing.

5. Taylor, *Secular Age*, 549.

as they consciously tell themselves that their decision is the product of objective reason.

Taylor says the condition of the modern believer is one in which

> we cannot help but be aware that there are a number of different construals, views which intelligent, reasonably undeluded people, of good will, can and do disagree on. We cannot help looking over our shoulder from time to time, looking sideways, living our faith also in a condition of doubt and uncertainty.[6]

According to Taylor, the modern believer cannot, like Augustine or Aquinas, believe with uncertainty, without looking over his shoulder and asking himself, "Do I have this wrong?" Something has changed. Various explanations could be given for what has changed and why. Taylor has his own but, for the purposes of this paper, it need only be noted that this form of modern faith is at odds with what has been previously said about the nature of virtuous open-mindedness and the semblance of strong fallibilism.[7] It must also be said that there is, on this point, an unsettling natural conclusion to be drawn about the character of much of modern religious faith in the West according to the logic of this book. To the extent that Taylor is here speaking about the deposit of faith, and assuming Augustine and Aquinas are correct about these matters even in our pluralist times, then Taylor and so many of us fellow believers who at times feel the winds of which he speaks are not simply living a new kind of modern Christian faith that is befitting of our times, but rather we are people of *weak* faith—an unsettling realization.

If interpreted as speaking about the basic articles of faith rather than (as some readers claim) the internal development of doctrine while entertaining no doubts about the basic articles,[8] then Cardinal Joseph Ratzinger could be placed alongside Taylor, writing,

---

6. Taylor, *Secular Age*, 110.

7. Elsewhere, Taylor seems to espouse what this project has characterized as a virtuous open-mindedness or intellectual humility born not of doubt but merely a sense of human limitations. As Taylor says, "None of us could ever grasp alone everything that is involved in our alienation from God and His action to bring us back. But there are many of us, scattered through history, who have had some powerful sense of some facet of this drama. Together we can live it more fully than any of us could alone. . . . Our faith is not the acme of Christianity, but nor is it a degenerate version; it should rather be open to a conversation that ranges over the whole of the last 20 centuries (and even in some ways before)." Taylor, *Secular Age*, 754.

8. To quote Pope John XXIII: "The substance of the ancient doctrine, contained in the 'deposit of faith,' is one thing; its formulation is quite another."

> No one can lay God and his Kingdom on the table before another man; even the believer cannot do it for himself. But however strongly unbelief may feel justified thereby, it cannot forget the eerie feeling induced by the words "Yet perhaps it is true." That "perhaps" is the unavoidable temptation it cannot elude, the temptation in which it, too, in the very act of rejection, has to experience the unrejectability of belief. In other words, both the believer and the unbeliever share, each in his own way, doubt and belief, if they do not hide from themselves and from the truth of their being. Neither can quite escape either doubt or belief. . . . Perhaps in precisely this way doubt . . . prevents both from enjoying complete self-satisfaction; it opens up the believer to the doubter and the doubter to the believer.[9]

Taylor and (perhaps) Ratzinger regard their faith in a way that other Christian thinkers would advise against. This project has also maintained, contra Ratzinger's remarks, that a virtuous form of open-mindedness can save different sides of an argument from being "shut up in their own worlds," without requiring any side to have doubts about its beliefs.

Augustine, for instance, in answering the "skeptics" of his own day, took the position that true faith admits of no doubts (even if its self-understood knowledge is limited). Of course, Augustine lived 1600 years before Taylor and Ratzinger and before the advent of modern pluralism. Even so it would be misleading to think that Augustine was unfamiliar with intellectual pluralism, for his time and place certainly had its share. Augustine lent support to the conviction that true faith admits of no doubts. In a section in *City of God* entitled "How Different the Uncertainty of the New Academy is from the Certainty of the Christian Faith," he writes, "As regards the uncertainty about everything which Varro alleges to be the differentiating characteristic of the New Academy, the city of God thoroughly detests such doubt as madness. Regarding matters which it apprehends by the mind and reason it has most absolute certainty," though Augustine admits that such "knowledge is limited because of the corruptible body pressing down the mind."[10] As the Apostle Paul says, we now know "through a glass darkly." All the same, if one who trusts his senses is sometimes deceived, "he is more wretchedly deceived who fancies he should never trust them."[11] Most importantly,

---

9. Ratzinger, *Introduction to Christianity*, 46–47.
10. Augustine, *City of God*, Book 19, Chapter 18.
11. Augustine, *City of God*, Book 19, Chapter 18.

Christians must, says Augustine, believe in "the Holy Scriptures . . . by which we walk *without doubting* whilst we are absent from the Lord." Provided such faith "remains inviolate and firm, we may without blame entertain doubts regarding some things," but only those things "which we have neither perceived by sense nor by reason, and which have not been revealed to us by the canonical Scriptures, nor come to our knowledge through witnesses whom it is absurd to disbelieve," such as those present in the Gospels.[12]

Doubt and the Infusion of Faith

Is there something about the very nature of faith that permits no uncertainty? Literary theorist George Steiner, a non-Christian looking from the outside in, appears to think so. "To achieve finalities of meaning," he writes, "one must punctuate. One must arrest the cancerous throng of interpretations and re-interpretations. The explicative and legislative decrees promulgated by Rome and by the custodians of orthodoxy in medieval Paris, the doctrinal-metaphysical enclosedness of Aquinas' *Summa*, can be understood as a series of attempts at hermeneutic 'end-stopping.' In essence, they proclaim that the primary text can mean *this* and *this*, but not *that*." By this logic, heaven is the exact opposite of eternal reinterpretation and commentary.[13] Hell, it turns out, truly is the committee meeting that never ends. Steiner defines heresy as "un-ending re-reading and evaluation," which "refuses exegetic finality. The heretic is the discourser without end"—a description consistent with the arguments about heresy made in chapter 7. The heretic's fresh translations, says Steiner, "even where they profess, strategically, a return to the authentic source, even where they allege that the understanding of the primary text will be made plainer and more relevant to the needs of an unstable world," create a harmful "open-ended, disseminative hermeneutic."[14]

Theologian John Henry Newman speaks of religious faith in a similar manner. He asks, rhetorically, "Would any one ever call him certain that the Apostles came from God, if after professing his certainty, he added, that perhaps he might have reason to doubt one day about their

---

12. Augustine, *City of God*, Book 19, Chapter 18, emphasis added.
13. Steiner, *Real Presences*, 44.
14. Steiner, *Real Presences*, 45.

mission?"¹⁵ Any such "perhaps" signals an unfortunate and "real, though latent, doubt, betraying that he was not certain of it at present," writes Newman.¹⁶ Indeed, chapter 5 made this same argument regarding all beliefs, not just religious belief, and the truth of Newman's observation undermines the notion that strong fallibilism can provide the basis for any belief. Newman points out that "to make provision for future doubt, is to doubt at present." We can "love by halves, [or] obey by halves," but we cannot "believe by halves."¹⁷

If Steiner and Newman are correct about the true nature of religious beliefs, then it would seem that some modern critics of religion might be warranted in fearing the influence of religious beliefs in modern civil discourse within a pluralist society. If such systems of belief are built on dogmas that, at minimum, are non-conducive to discourse within a pluralist cultural setting and, at worst, give excuse or motivation for violence, then the critic would appear to have a point. It looks like a bait-and-switch maneuver on the part of Christian virtue ethicists recommending open-mindedness to others while availing themselves of certain exceptions for particularly cherished beliefs of their own. This is an understandable reaction. But arriving at this conclusion without further investigation would be to ignore the gifts of hope and charity.

By way of illuminating the contrast, there exists a Christian variant of Hegelianism that would seem to deny the possibility of such closure of truths. Hegel leaves us with a version of history that is never fully resolved, never fully confident that it has reconciled itself with God's law. As James Wetzel observes, "There is no closure in Hegel's absolutism, no end to the intersubjective negotiation of norms, to ventures of mutual recognition, to the unanticipated ingenuity of a heterogeneously social dialectic; . . . If there is anything absolute about Hegel, it is his disdain for absolutist thinking."¹⁸ Such a sentiment, the very target of Steiner's, is at odds with the version of faith-infused open-mindedness being defended in this chapter.

The notion that there are "right answers" or premises which have been arrived at and are now binding and non-negotiable for anyone who wants to call herself a "Christian" will upset some believers. But many

---

15. See "Faith and Doubt" in Newman, *Discourses*, 215.
16. Newman, *Discourses*, 216.
17. Newman, *Discourses*, 216.
18. Wetzel, "Absolute Augustine," 8.

Christians make such assumptions, and this chapter will argue that these assumptions are the result of the infusion of faith into the virtue of open-mindedness. A month after the close of Vatican II, Pope Paul VI responded to some of the more original interpretations of the council, saying that while

> the council opens many new horizons to biblical, theological, and humanistic studies, . . . it does not allow that arbitrariness, servility, uncertainty and desolation which characterize so many forms of modern religious thinking, when it is deprived of the assistance of ecclesiastical *magisterium*, to enter into the philosophical, theological, and scriptural schools of the Church.[19]

A year later, the Holy Father restressed the functional importance of the magisterium, cautioning listeners "to avoid the danger of certain broad opinions which insinuate an arbitrary evaluation of the council almost as if this great ecclesiastical event could justify a concept of Catholicism different from that already well defined," while also "authoriz[ing] free suppositions of different and discordant religious ideologies," even if they still contain "a sense and love of the Catholic religion."[20]

Although Protestantism does not officially have a magisterium, it often operates with its own versions of such authority. For Karl Barth, it was the word of God, about the truth of which he entertained no doubts. In fact, Barth dismissed as un-Christian any concept of "tolerance" that did not begin and end with Christ's mercy: "A truly theological treatment of religion and religions . . . will need to be distinguished from all other forms of treatment by the exercise of a very marked tolerance towards its object"—as is the case for open-mindedness as well.[21] This tolerance, says Barth, "must not be confused with the moderation of those who actually have their own religion or religiosity, and are secretly zealous for it, but who can exercise self-control, because they have told themselves or have been told that theirs is not the only faith, that fanaticism is a bad thing, that love must always have the first and the last word."[22] Note, again, the strong parallels between Barth's remarks here and the general arguments made about the properly non-fallibilist-based notions of virtuous open-mindedness made in this project.

19. As quoted in Grisez, "Academic Freedom and Catholic Faith," 20.
20. Grisez, "Academic Freedom and Catholic Faith," 20.
21. Barth, *Church Dogmatics*, I/2, 102; hereafter *CD* in footnotes.
22. Barth, *CD*, I/2, 102.

Barth insists that tolerance toward other religions must be "informed by *the forbearance of Christ*, which derives therefore from the knowledge that by grace God has reconciled to Himself godless man and his religion. It will see man carried, like an obstinate child in the arms of its mother"—the same metaphor used by Bonhoeffer in the previous chapter—"by what God has determined and done for his salvation in spite of his own opposition. . . . [I]t will neither praise nor reproach him." Rather, it will see his situation for what it is, even if the godless man and his religion cannot see it for themselves, able to understand it "*not because it can see any meaning in the situation as such, but because it acquires a meaning from outside, from Jesus Christ.*"[23] Needless to say, Barth's attitude changes the character of his open-mindedness in certain respects. Elsewhere, when commenting on the effort towards the union of the churches beginning in the eighteenth century, Barth criticizes it to the extent that it originated out of an idea of shared tolerance and civility:

> The serious criticism to which this mode of union is open cannot be ignored. *The concept of toleration* (of the variety whose basis lies in realization of religious pluralism, or that fanaticism is a bad thing, etc.) *originates in political and philosophical principles which are not only alien but even opposed to the Gospel.* Their triumph within the various churches was a symptom of inward weakness and not of strength.[24]

As if that weren't enough, Barth continues, "Nor can we think and speak dogmatically on the assumption that in another place we could do the same thing just as well and legitimately in another way. Properly speaking, there is no such thing as dogmatic tolerance."[25] That is a remarkable statement. While Barth never actually parts ways with the formulations of the early creeds and councils, he refrains from locating in them a source of "absolute" authority, opting instead for a merely "relative" one. The church, he says, has authority "by not trying to speak out as though it were infallible and final, but by subordinating itself to Jesus Christ and the Holy Spirit in the form in which Jesus Christ and the Holy Spirit is actually present and gracious to it."[26] The authority of the church's confessions are agreements that may someday be questioned,

---

23. Barth, *CD*, I/2, 102, emphasis added.
24. Barth, *CD*, I/2, 102, emphasis added.
25. Barth, *CD*, I/2, 102, 80.
26. Barth, *CD*, I/2, 102, 135.

transcended, and corrected, but the *word of God* can never be, at least for Barth. All truths and all knowledge—Christian or non-Christian—must finally answer to this word and be measured by it.[27] And to what does this word answer? Only itself. It is self-authenticating and nonnegotiable, meaning that, for Barth (and for this project as well), any virtuous form of open-mindedness must, for Christians, be changed by the infusion of faith in the truth of Jesus Christ. As Barth writes, "[T]he declaration of the prophecy of the life of Jesus Christ is valid as and because it is a declaration concerning the life of Jesus Christ. But is not this begging the question?" The argument is circular, and Barth knows this, celebrates it even, in light of the truth of Christ, it "is legitimate and obligatory."[28]

Open-Mindedness in the Bible

To begin with, what does the Bible say about faith and doubt? On asking God for increased wisdom, James 1:6–8 instructs us, "But let him ask in faith, with no doubting, for the one who doubts is like a wave of the sea that is driven and tossed by the wind. For that person must not suppose that he will receive anything from the Lord; he is a double-minded man, unstable in all his ways."

When combined with faith, open-mindedness entails openness to God's will (whatever it may be) without presuming to know what it is. Concerning future signs of Christ's return, Matthew 24:36 assures us: "But about that day or hour no one knows, not even the angels in heaven, nor the Son, but only the Father." Mary's instruction to the Canaanite wedding servers, "Do whatever he tells you" (John 2:5), is an act of open-mindedness. The same is true of James 4:13–15: "Come now, you who say, 'Today or tomorrow we will go into such and such a town and spend a year there and trade and make a profit'—yet you do not know what tomorrow will bring. What is your life? For you are a mist that appears for a little time and then vanishes. Instead you ought to say, 'If the Lord wills, we will live and do this or that.'"

Was Jesus open-minded? This is not an easy question to answer. If one regards his divine attribute of omniscience as present from the beginning of his life, then it is hard to see how there could have been any room

---

27. See, for instance, Barth's discussion of the relation of the "phenomenal" man to the "real" man in *CD* III/2.

28. Barth, *CD* IV/3, 82.

for the virtue of open-mindedness (as it has been defined in this book) to operate. Perhaps, though, his prayer at the Mount of Olives could be interpreted as a kind of faithful open-mindedness in which he did not fully know but was already open to learning and ready to be obedient towards the will of the Father: "Father, if you are willing, remove this cup from me; yet, not my will but thine be done" (Luke 22:42).

Christians are called to face the uncertainty of the future and unknown knowledge from non-Christians with the certainty of faith. As Psalm 27 tells us: "The Lord is my light and my salvation—whom shall I fear? The Lord is the stronghold of my life—of whom shall I be afraid?" We have reason to fearlessly engage any and all, to be open to God wherever we should find him and whatever his will might be.

That said, the gift of faith also *constricts* open-mindedness. Christians cannot be "open" to predictions about the end of history that do not accord with their belief that every knee shall bow and every tongue confess that Jesus is Lord. In addressing the Athenians, the Apostle Paul mentions their town altar "To the Unknown God."[29] This, he explains, is the God of whom he preaches. We're told that some of the Athenians converted upon hearing Paul's words: "Among them was Dionysius, a member of the Areopagus, also a woman named Damaris, and a number of others" (Acts 17:22–34). Though it goes unsaid, the acquired open-mindedness symbolized by the altar to the unknown God is transformed for Dionysius and Damaris upon their conversion. The altar "To the Unknown God" was, for them, no longer. *That* God was now known, and beside him there are no others.

Christian Mission as Case Study

An old bronze plaque outside the campus center at Princeton Theological Seminary reads:

> OF THESE THE WORLD WAS NOT WORTHY
> *Walter Macon Lowrie* class of 1840
> Thrown overboard by pirates in the China Sea in 1847
> *John Edgar Freeman* class of 1838
> *Robert McMullin* class of 1853
> Who with their wives were shot by order of Nana Sahib in 1857 at Cawnpore, India

---

29. Acts 17:23.

Levi Janvier class of 1840
Stabbed by a Sikh fanatic at Ludhiana, India 1864

Isidor Loewenthal class of 1854
Shot accidentally or by design at Peshawar, India

John Rogers Peale class of 1905
Killed with his wife by a mob at Lien Chou, China 1905

Passing by the plaque on a regular basis, I continually marvel at the courage and faithfulness of these Christian missionaries, at what they did, and how they died. But there is another dimension to their lives worth commenting on as concerns this project. Their choices in life, and whatever journals and letters they left us, suggest something about what their views of open-mindedness and intellectual diversity might have been. Given the greatness, and in some cases apparent saintliness, of their witness, their voices deserve a hearing and should be received with a degree of authority and reverence, particularly by modern Presbyterians, their ecclesial descendants.

Walter Lowrie, listed first on the plaque, was a nineteenth-century Presbyterian missionary to China. Lowrie's memoirs, collected after his death by his brother, describe his experiences. Reading them, one is struck by the fear Lowrie initially felt at the thought of being a missionary, knowing that it meant leaving everything behind for good, and undertaking severe duties and deprivations.[30] And he didn't let this fear stop him. He was motivated by his desire to bring the Christian faith to those who did not yet have it. In a letter to his father, dated March 1837, Lowrie wonders aloud, "Who," given all the challenges faced by a missionary, "is sufficient for these things? Yet if I know my own heart, I am willing to live or die for the heathen."[31]

A few months later, in a letter to an old seminary friend John Lloyd, whom Lowrie persistently tried to recruit as a missionary to the Far East, Lowrie asks Lloyd,

> Do you yet hear the voice, "Come over and help us," and the wailing cry, "And what then?" as it rises from the death-bed of the Hindoo, and, borne across the waste of waters, reaches our ears both from the east and the west, swelled as it is, and heightened and prolonged by the addition of innumerable others? Or

---

30. Lowrie, *Memoirs of the Rev. Walter M. Lowrie.*
31. Lowrie, *Memoirs of the Rev. Walter M. Lowrie*, 15.

does it die away among the crumbling ruins of heathen temples, unheard and unheeded, save by the infidel and the deist?[32]

Lowrie's letters contain no hint of strong fallibilism or conformism in the face of pluralism. His words and actions, at every step along the way, reflect his belief that it would be better if the people of the Far East (Hindus, Confucians, etc.) were baptized as soon as possible. Lowrie clearly believes Christianity's claim to absolute truth.

In May of 1842, upon departing for China, Lowrie found himself already mourning his home and friends. Nevertheless, he persisted, feeling that God was sustaining him. As an interesting point of historical comparison, Lowrie's entries at sea during this period occur at the same time that Melville (discussed in chapter 5) was a common sailor on a whaling expedition in the South Pacific; Melville was not far from Lowrie's approximate location at that time. Melville's experience, of course, would go on to provide him with the material for *Moby Dick*. As mentioned in chapter 4, *Moby Dick* is, according to interpretations like Dreyfus's, *the great tract against Western monotheism and the quest for absolute, transcendent truth*. The idea of Lowrie's *Ship Huntress* and Melville's *Acushnet* passing each other, two ships at night, is not only a strange possibility of history but also an apt symbol of passing currents in intellectual history, with Melville's on the ascent, and Lowrie's on the decline and defense. Melville, while privately ruminating about the truly "wicked book" (as he described it to Nathaniel Hawthorne) whose content was taking shape inside his head, could have looked out on the same waters as Lowrie.

Lowrie's journal entries continue after he reaches China and begins his missionary work. Faced with intellectual diversity (to use the language of this project) concerning certain cultural practices in the Amoy area where he spent most of his time, Lowrie does not flinch in his beliefs about right and wrong in the eyes of God. He notes at one point that infanticide "is very common" in the province. According to the estimates of missionaries who had preceded him, nearly one-fifth of the children were perishing by the hands of their own parents. Lowrie recounts in his journal an episode in which a poor man said to his missionary colleague, "Teacher, before you came, I killed five of my children; I would not do it

---

32. Lowrie, *Memoirs of the Rev. Walter M. Lowrie*, 19.

now, for you have showed me that it is wrong, but before you came I did not know that. Who was there to tell me?"[33]

Later that same year, in a letter to "The Society of Inquiry in the Western Theological Seminary," Lowrie gives advice to missionaries-in-training, telling them to come with a spirit of Christian charity. At this point in his work in China, Lowrie had already learned Chinese and had become familiar with the local cultural and spiritual practices of the Chinese people in his region. He came to respect the people greatly. Without condescending to them, he believed he was bringing them absolute truth in the form of the Christian faith. He writes to the seminarians,

> I trust you have none of those romantic notions that will induce you to think a missionary a superior being.... We come from different parts of the world with different views, from the influences of very different states of public feeling.... In such circumstances, it is natural to expect great diversity of views, and nothing but the spirit of meekness, and forbearance, and love will enable you to live happily with your fellow-laborers.[34]

It is Christian charity that makes possible a nonhostile presentation of the gospel as universally true within an environment of intellectual diversity, just as it did for Augustine in his dealings with the Donatists (as described in the previous chapter). Lowrie never wavered in his faith. Later in his career, Lowrie recounts telling a Chinese villager that his "belief in the doctrine of election was as firm as my belief in my own existence."[35] Such confidence was born of the infusion of the theological virtue of faith.

This gift of grace did not, however, make Lowrie *less* open-minded. Demonstrating what infused open-mindedness looks like, Lowrie wrote to his brother John Lowrie in 1847, insisting that "the Chinese are no fools, and they have said and done things worthy of great renown. I begin to have a real veneration for Confucius, and to doubt whether any heathen philosopher ever saw so much truth as he did." That said, Lowrie then adds, one must not "neglect of the far more important duties of one whose chief business it should be to know nothing but Christ, and him crucified."[36] In the end, it is the story of Christ's life and death that defines

---

33. Lowrie, *Memoirs of the Rev. Walter M. Lowrie*, 178.
34. Lowrie, *Memoirs of the Rev. Walter M. Lowrie*, 202.
35. Lowrie, *Memoirs of the Rev. Walter M. Lowrie*, 231.
36. Lowrie, *Memoirs of the Rev. Walter M. Lowrie*, 358.

true wisdom to the open mind infused by charity and faith. Convincing the Chinese of the truth of the gospel proved an uphill battle for Lowrie and he occasionally wonders if he has accomplished anything in his mission. In a journal entry in Ningpo in 1847, Lowrie explains one source of frustration:

> After repeating over and over again, the statements about God as eternal, true, and holy, they are sure to confound all you say with their own gods. This is not because they do not understand what I say, for I find that I am pretty well understood; but because, first, they cannot conceive how it is that their own gods are false gods.[37]

Later that same year, as Lowrie traveled by sea to another Chinese city, his boat was intercepted by a pirate ship. The crew was robbed and thrown overboard (as the plaque at Princeton Seminary records). According to a survivor's account, in one last act of faith, just before being pushed overboard, Lowrie threw his Bible on the deck of the ship, in the hope, presumably, that someone else might pick it up, read it, and come to believe in Jesus Christ.[38]

Infusion of the Theological Virtue of Hope

Intellectual hope is the belief that reality won't let us down, that our intellectual prayers won't go unanswered. Theologian Josef Pieper, for instance, mischaracterizes Aquinas's attitude on this matter, while

---

37. Lowrie, *Memoirs of the Rev. Walter M. Lowrie*, 366.

38. Many Chinese did, of course, come to believe in Christ, but not until long after Lowrie's death. For the first 150 years of Protestant missions, Christianity experienced relatively little growth in China. When missionaries were expelled from the country in the 1950s, Christians were still few in number. Indeed, it would take two centuries after Lowrie's death for the full fruits of efforts like Lowrie's to be realized. But with the reforms in religious liberties beginning in recent decades, Christianity has finally flowered in China in the way Lowrie hoped for. By some estimates, there are as many as 130 million Christians in China (comprising 10 percent of the population), a hundredfold increase during the last sixty years. Fenggang Yang, a professor of sociology at Purdue University and respected scholar on Christianity in China, has written, "By my calculations China is destined to become the largest Christian country in the world very soon. It is going to be less than a generation. Not many people are prepared for this dramatic change." If Yang's predictions are correct, by 2030 China will have a Christian population of over 247 million, exceeding individually that of Mexico, Brazil, and the United States. Walter Lowrie would be pleased. Fenggang Yang as quoted in Blumberg, "China on Track," para. 3.

simultaneously misstating the Christian case for intellectual hope. Commenting on Aquinas's notion of the "pilgrim man," Pieper states, "It is wholly impossible for 'pilgrim man'—and hence cannot constitute a valid goal for him—to escape from uncertainty into absolute certainty. Absolute certainty is unattainable, even in principle, for *homo viator*."[39] Instead, we should take refuges in God's decrees.[40] The vice of presumption, according to this logic, is a denial of our condition in the *status viatoris* or as pilgrims. Pieper stresses that presumption of this kind, which believes it has achieved finality in truth, makes hope unnecessary. Yet, Aquinas's description of the pilgrim man contains none of the unnamed fallibilism in Pieper's exegesis of the concept; instead, Aquinas speaks only of the importance of man to never forget that he is higher than animals (who are not "on their way" anywhere) and lower than the angels (who have already arrived, so to speak).

The infusion of Christian faith into open-mindedness comes with another benefit: it gives Christians confidence in the face of biographical contingencies that factor in to all our conclusions and beliefs. Trusting that divine providence is guiding human history entails, by extension, trusting that divine providence is guiding our personal thoughts and conclusions. John Calvin was well aware of the physical hazards of life, but his logic, and his theological response to these hazards, applies equally well to the intellectual pitfalls and harmful influences that seemingly lie everywhere, potentially leading us away from the truth, towards mistaken beliefs. As Calvin writes,

> Innumerable are the evils that beset human life. . . . Embark upon a ship, you are one step away from death. Mount a horse, if one foot slips, your life is imperiled. Go through the city streets, you are subject to as many dangers as there are tiles on the roofs. If there is a weapon in your hand or a friend's, harm awaits. All the fierce animals you see are armed for your destruction.[41]

Calvin can come across as overly paranoid until one recalls that, during his lifetime, life was much more dangerous than in modern times—it was, statistically, more fragile. And, yet, translated into the intellectual medium of this project, what Calvin observes hasn't changed at all: there are so many ways and opportunities to be misled in one's beliefs, and sober reflection on this fact can prove dispiriting, almost paralyzing. Upon

39. Pieper, *Faith, Hope, and Love*.
40. Pieper, *Faith, Hope, and Love*, 128–29.
41. Calvin, *Institutes of the Christian Religion*, I.XVII.10.

such reflection, a degree of intellectual hypochondria is understandable. What, then, is the appropriate solution? For Calvin, as regards the physical dangers of life, the option of self-cloistering was not a helpful remedy. "But if you try to shut yourself up in a walled garden," he says, "seemingly delightful, there a serpent sometimes lies hidden. Your house, continually in danger of fire, threatens in the daytime to impoverish you, at night even to collapse upon you."[42] Intellectual self-segregation, by which an individual might intentionally avoid any encounters with ideas or arguments other than his own, never venturing intellectually beyond the personally built walled gardens of his own mind, will not get rid of the intellectual pitfalls that come with being a finite creature. The serpent still lurks in the privacy of our own minds.

No matter what a man does, it seems that he is resigned to this miserable condition, "as if he had a sword perpetually hanging over his neck." That same sword hangs over our necks intellectually. And, yet, for Christians, the same comfort enjoyed by Calvin in response to this threat can be enjoyed in the face of the contingencies and hazards in our intellectual lives. To end the story with the situation Calvin describes above would be to give sin, fallen-ness, and finitude the last word. "Yet," says Calvin, "when the light of providence has once shown upon a godly man, he is then relieved and set free not only from the extreme anxiety and fear that were pressing before him, but from every care."[43] In the words of *The Heidelberg Catechism*, "not a hair can fall from my head without the will of my Father in heaven; in fact, all things must work together for my salvation." I cannot commit a single, even trivial, intellectual misstep (many of which, no doubt, I will commit in my life) without the will of the Father in heaven. When I possess theological faith, hope, and love, then all things—all ideas met with an open mind and all intellectual diversity—work together for my salvation and for the providential ordering of the world.

The infusion of the theological virtue of hope elevates and perfects the acquired virtue of open-mindedness by strengthening its confidence in arriving at absolute truth, despite the many and real obstacles faced by finite minds in this effort. Philosopher of science Michael Polanyi understood this challenge. The conceptual tools at our disposal, he says, are the products of local cultures and particular times, and, of course, are always

---

42. Calvin, *Institutes of the Christian Religion*, I.XVII.10.
43. Calvin, *Institutes of the Christian Religion*, I.XVII.11.

to some extent polluted by desire for power and privilege. Despite all this, says Polanyi, we are called, as scientists and as creatures of God, to strive for, claim, and take responsibility for judgment with what he calls "universal intent." As he says, "I accept these accidents of personal existence as the concrete opportunities for exercising our personal responsibility. *This acceptance is the sense of my calling.*"[44] Despite the realization that our intellectual standards for truth are self-set and circular, the responsible mental agent "does not do as he pleases, but compels himself forcibly to act as he believes he must."[45] If we do not, we remove ourselves from contact with reality.

Indeed, Polanyi goes so far as to apply the Pauline scheme of redemption to his professional work. About the aspirations of the human desire to know and to know fully and truly, Polanyi writes,

> Our subjective condition may be taken to include the historical setting in which we have grown up. We accept these as the assignment of our particular problem. . . . The stage on which we thus resume our full intellectual powers is borrowed from the Christian scheme of Fall and Redemption. Fallen Man is equated to the historically given and subjective condition of our mind, from which we may be saved by the grace of the spirit. . . . We undertake the task of attaining the universal in spite of our admitted infirmity, which should render the task hopeless, because we hope to be visited by powers for which we cannot account in terms of our specific capabilities. This hope is a clue to God.[46]

The theological twist in Polanyi's final sentence is suggestive, as it hints at the direction taken in this chapter: that such a hope is not just a clue *to* God but rather a gift of believing *in* God.

How does the virtue of hope change open-mindedness in the act of prayer? It gives us confidence in the reality and goodness of the unknowable and as yet unimaginable. In a letter to a widow named Proba, Augustine says that we should ask for only one thing in prayer: the "blessed life." And yet, he adds, we don't actually know what this "life" consists of, only that it is what we

---

44. Calvin, *Institutes of the Christian Religion*, I.XVII.11.
45. Calvin, *Institutes of the Christian Religion*, I.XVII.11.
46. Polanyi, *Personal Knowledge*, 342.

thirst for in prayer so long as we live in hope, not yet seeing that which we hope for, trusting under the shadow of His wings before whom are all our desires, that we may be abundantly satisfied with the fatness of His house.... At the same time, because this blessing is nothing else than the "peace which passeth all understanding," even when we are asking it in our prayers, we know not what to pray for as we ought.[47]

Infused Open-Mindedness in the Modern World

Practicing open-mindedness as I have defined it does not mean doubting one's own currently held beliefs. It does not require the atheist, the Cartesian, or the monarchist to stop believing as he currently does or to believe those defining principles any less when engaging in civil discourse. The fear on the part of many, particularly religious people, that this *is* what is required by discourse within a pluralistic society, can lead to a retreat into cultural localism (a bunker mentality) that can only be adversarial toward pluralism. This is unfortunate because, if what has been argued (in chapter 4) about the false consciousness of strong fallibilism is correct, then being open-minded and civil conversation partners requires no such thing. What open-mindedness *does* require is openness, willingness, even a desire to learn from those with whom we disagree, to engage other subcultures, to work toward greater collective knowledge, toward wider agreement on important issues—confident that this is possible because we believe that God is Truth and God is one, and thus that Truth is one.

The theological gift of faith alters the virtue of open-mindedness by giving it an expanded horizon. The world opens up. Christ, the hermeneutical key to the universe, unlocks doors to truths and experiences

---

47. Augustine, *Letters of Saint Augustine*, 163; As regards the difference that Christian hope makes to open-mindedness, it should be pointed out that, to the extent that an individual does not assume (as many modern intellectuals do not) the unity of the Platonic transcendentals of the True, the Beautiful, and the Good, then the new reception of Christian faith and hope will, for this individual, also entail a new belief in the unity of these transcendentals, something the Christian tradition has always insisted on. An open mind that aims for the Good will now believe itself to be simultaneously seeking the True. Reality can't let Christians down, because Truth, Beauty, and Goodness all lead to and come from the same thing: God. For an interesting comparison with this perspective, and evidence of the epistemic anxieties and uncertainties resulting from the modern severing of these transcendentals from one another, see Nehamas, *Only A Promise of Happiness*.

previously unattainable (even to those with acquired open-mindedness). So, too, is the "old" world made new, as secular knowledge takes on added dimensions.

The open-minded Christian is willing to learn from brothers and sisters in the faith who think differently, including the community of the dead. Christian theologians should offer their theories with humility and open-mindedness toward both God *and* their fellow believers. We must, though, be open to being persuaded by each other. We must be open to the possibility that we are not only wrong about some things but wrong about a great many things. Those who are happy to dismiss strong fallibilism but are frightened of possible future conversions from practicing open-mindedness and thus suspicious about the price of admission to this kind of public discourse should be reminded of what pragmatists like Bilgrami (in chapter 4) have taught us. If we have such worries now, they are not actually the result of the fact of pluralism or the potential consequences of cultivating natural or infused open-mindedness (even if self-consciously one may think they are). Rather, they are the product of already-existing doubts about our current beliefs, unrelated to the circumstances of pluralism, generated by (in the case of infused open-mindedness) beliefs that are at odds with a more orthodox set of convictions. Admitting this may be upsetting. But those of real faith have no reason to be afraid of pluralism. As Scripture reminds us, "God has not given us a spirit of fear, but of power and of love and of a sound mind" (2 Tim 1:7).

9

Open-Mindedness and Intellectual Diversity after Death

Transition to the Afterlife

THE PRECEDING CHAPTERS HAVE confined themselves to the nature of open-mindedness and intellectual diversity in the immanent world during our mortal lives, and, to a lesser extent, in the pre-fallen world spoken of in Scripture. This chapter, by contrast, speculates about the postmortem fate of open-mindedness and intellectual diversity. True to the spirit of Aquinas in which final causes are indicative of natures—where a creature's teleological end is more illuminating than its (temporal) beginning and efficient causes—the arguments offered in this chapter attempt to do more than merely add an epilogue to the rest of the project; rather, they aim to form a frame around the entire book, a closing preface of sorts. It would be more accurate to say, in hindsight, that chapters 1–8 have been, all along, *pulled* by the beatific destinies to be discussed in this chapter than to say that the non-final causes described in chapters 1–8 have *pushed* for any produced verdicts regarding open-mindedness and intellectual diversity in the afterlife. Indeed, what remains for and awaits human creatures after death, especially souls in heaven, can often tell us more about what it means (or what it meant) to live a mortal life than the lives themselves, when studied in their earthly phase.

Summary of Arguments

In heaven there is no learning. Christian paradise provides a never-ending intellectual Sabbath or mental repose, a ceasing of our intellectual labors (now no longer necessary), after which we will, as God does in Genesis, conclude that all is good, that everything makes sense.[1] We will drink from a well of wisdom and never thirst again (John 4:14). In heaven, minds are blissfully *closed*. There is no more need for studiousness, as the *visio dei* replaces the desire to know because this desire has been fulfilled by perfect knowledge. Intellectual hope (that reality won't let us down), intellectual imagination, and intellectual fortitude cease to be necessary, for we will finally see face-to-face, as Paul says.

There are no more moderates in heaven. Docility, whereas before a virtue that was authority-relative, becomes an unconditional virtue in heaven, where there is only one authority. In heaven we are relieved of any intellectual irony, skepticism, or intellectual fallibilism. Strong cognitive empathy, liable to viciousness in our earthly lives, becomes our new shared reality, as we all know each other's minds with perfect intimacy, though the result is never harmful and always adds to God's glory.

In heaven there is no disagreement. No disagreement about the facts of existence, the meaning of life, about what was morally "right" or "wrong" in a given circumstance, or (above all) about God's true nature and purposes. We are no longer Baptists and Methodists but merely Christians reunited with God. We are no longer Barthians or superlapsarians or anything of the like because we will all simply be knowers of the sole indisputable truth (whatever it turns out to be), seen, for the first time, face-to-face. There are no more schools of thought or –isms to speak of at all. Presumably, the subordinationists (provided they are in the company of the blessed, too) will realize the error of their thinking and join the creedal consensus, joyfully, on Christ's coequality with the Father. Some intellectual factions will be proven right, once and for all, others wrong, but, importantly, this will not be cause for embarrassment or sadness on the part of those whose beliefs are corrected. Quite the contrary, insofar as the absence of final closure (and the presence of intellectual diversity)

---

1. It is reasonable to think that there is no learning in hell either (consider James 2:19: "You believe that there is one God. Good! Even the demons believe that—and shudder")—the difference being, of course, that the Truth made known is cause for peaceful bliss for those in heaven while the same Truth is cause for peace-less shudders among those in hell.

was a lamentable condition to begin with, we will all be overjoyed to finally possess such enlightenment and to bid farewell to collective disagreement. Indeed, the heavenly pleasure of finally knowing the Truth, even if proven wrong by it, will far exceed the joy of discovery that lacks total consensus occurring in one's mortal life. It could even be argued that to desire the first more than the second, in this life, sets one on the path to intellectual virtue.

Because learning ceases in heaven, so too will open-mindedness. Both become unnecessary and superfluous. The deficiency or absence (of complete knowledge) to which open-mindedness was the proper response (intellectual unrest) will no longer exist. That open-mindedness's going away will be a good thing need not suggest that its existence in this life was a bad thing or that it wasn't a virtue all along. Many things that are virtuous in this mortal life (courage, temperance, prudence, etc.) will become wonderfully obsolete in the grander existence that awaits us after death. The existence of intellectual diversity, on the other hand, was always lamentable, even in the created world, though it was an inevitable result of the intellectual faction-ism that characterizes the fallen human state. Open-mindedness and intellectual diversity were not part of Adam and Eve's paradisiacal condition and neither, it is the natural conclusion of this book, should we expect them to be part of the afterlife.

Augustine

For Augustine, heaven is a long-awaited peace (*quies*) for restless souls.[2] We find rest by desiring the right thing for the right reason, and getting it. Thus, in the life to come, we must have a complete knowledge and experience of God, whom we desire by nature to know and love. Short of this, our souls continue to desire something they lack. In heaven, says Augustine, faith and hope are no longer necessary, but love waxes all the more: "But sight shall displace faith; and hope shall be swallowed up in that perfect bliss to which we shall come: love, on the other hand, shall wax greater when these others fail."[3] In a similar fashion, what this project has called intellectual hope, intellectual charity, and open-mindedness all pass away, but goodness and truth wax greater.

---

2. Augustine, *City of God*, Book 19, Chapter 11.
3. Augustine, *On Christian Doctrine*, Book 1, p. 27.

In book 13 of *Confessions*, Augustine speaks of man's final end as a kind of rest, writing, "In Thy gift we rest; . . . Our rest is our place. . . . In Thy good pleasure lies our peace." Just as fire, stone, and oil have natures, which tend to natural ends, so too do humans. Our selfish loves mislead us, however. "Out of order, [we] are restless; restored to order, [we] are at rest." The weight of our loves, for self or for God, either drags us down or elevates us upward as if set aflame. God is the good fire, says Augustine, by which "we go upwards to the peace of Jerusalem; for glad was I when they said unto me, 'Let us go into the house of the Lord.' There hath Thy good pleasure placed us, that we may desire no other thing than to dwell there forever."[4] Desire of any other kind—intellectual desire included—must cease for heaven to be heaven from Augustine's standpoint.

Likewise, in a later portion of this same book, Augustine comments on how to interpret Genesis by describing the gift of the Sabbath as a rest from change.

> O Lord God, grant Thy peace unto us, for Thou hast supplied us with all things,—the peace of rest, the peace of the Sabbath, which hath no evening. For all this most beautiful order of things, "very good" (all their courses being finished), is to pass away, for in them there was morning and evening.[5]

Put in the terms of this chapter, Christians should pray for an intellectual Sabbath that knows no morning or evening, in which our knowledge (perfect and complete, once and for all) and mental lives become changeless.

An Eastern Orthodox Strain of Thought

On the classical Western view (as I have interpreted it), open-mindedness ceases in heaven, because it no longer serves a purpose. Gregory of Nyssa, however, represents a different strand of theology. In *Against Eunomius* he writes:

> The First Good is in its nature infinite, and so it follows of necessity that the participation in the enjoyment of it will be infinite also, for more will be always being grasped, and yet something beyond that which has been grasped will always be discovered, and this search will never overtake its Object, because its fund

---

4. Augustine, *Conf.* 13.9.
5. Augustine, *Conf.* 13.35.

is as inexhaustible as the growth of that which participates in it is ceaseless.[6]

Thus, the virtue of open-mindedness remains necessary in the theatre of the beatific vision, on this view, since there is always more to be learned and experienced about God.

Theologian Paul Blowers helps explain what motivated Gregory (and Maximus the Confessor) in thinking this way. They were rejecting the Origenist idea that "an intellectual being [or mind] already united with God" (as in a pre-fallen order) "could become sated in the contemplation of God, thus stalling out in its spiritual progress to the point of falling away through boredom or negligence"—as they argue is inevitable, assuming such total unity even possible.[7] Instead, the true vision of God is "never to be satisfied in the desire to see him. But one must always ... rekindle his desire to see more. Thus, no limit would interrupt growth in the ascent to God, since no limit to the good can be found."[8] The logic appears to make sense.

Nyssa's notion of *epektasis*, or a never-ending "stretching forward," a "stretching out," or unending movement toward a finish line never reached is, however, fundamentally at odds with the Augustinian description of heaven given above. Nyssa begins with the assumption that, because God is infinite, he can never be truly known. As a result, any progress towards knowledge of or unity with God can never be complete. If it were, whatever was assumed to be known would not (*could* not, by definition) *be* God. As Nyssa says,

> Therefore, he who thinks God is something to be known does not have life, because he has turned from true Being to what he considers by sense perception to have being. True being is true life. This Being is inaccessible to knowledge. If, then, the life-giving nature transcends knowledge, that which is perceived certainly is not life.[9]

Note how this contrasts with the intellectualism of Aquinas to be discussed below, in which seeing and knowing God is the true end of

---

6. Gregory of Nyssa, *Gregory of Nyssa*, 62.

7. Blowers, "Maximus the Confessor," 153–54. Special thanks to Jeremy Wallace for suggesting this article to me.

8. Gregory of Nyssa, *Life of Moses*, 106.

9. Gregory of Nyssa, *Life of Moses*, 105.

man. Loving and enjoying God naturally occur along with achieving this true final end, but they are not themselves the actual goal.

Nyssa continues, "Whoever pursues true virtue participates in nothing other than God," and "since this good has no limit, the participant's desire itself necessarily has no stopping place but stretches out with the limitless. It is therefore undoubtedly impossible to attain perfection."[10] Note, again, that the direction of movement described by Nyssa here is that of humans moving toward God as they increase in saintliness, a depiction of heaven that contrasts with those of Aquinas and Dante to be discussed in subsequent parts of this chapter. It is also worthy of notice that, even if one disagrees with Nyssa about such continuing open-endedness and open-mindedness in heaven, he lends his implicit support to the notion that there can be a kind of intellectual hunger and desire which is not based in or motivated by any kind of strong fallibilism, an argument made previously in chapter 5.

The belief that humans could ever stop in their progress toward God and their growth in virtue strikes Nyssa as not only unbefitting of heaven but actually vicious. He writes, "[S]topping in the race of virtue marks the beginning of the race of evil." There is an ontological assumption common to the Christian West (found in Plato, Origen, and Augustine, among others) that is not shared by Nyssa and helps explain the divergent East-West beliefs about this aspect of the afterlife for Christians. Nyssa denies the premise that changeability must be a bad thing, a form of degeneration, which is a consequence of original sin. As Bowers explains, Nyssa's problem with Origenism is that, from his perspective, "it confused moral and ontological stability."[11] Where we go, which ontological direction, is up to us, our own moral decisions. The evermore and evermore ascent towards God implies change on our part but not any kind of imperfection in our heavenly existence.[12]

10. Gregory of Nyssa, *Life of Moses*, 31.

11. Blowers, "Maximus the Confessor," 157.

12. Interestingly, Maximus the Confessor, following in the tradition of Nyssa, tried to work out some sort of halfway compromise regarding this never-ending desire in which a kind of stationary movement or static progress occurs. Historian of philosophy Endre von Ivánka observantly "sees Maximus aiming at 'higher synthesis' of Aristotelian and Platonic perspectives, wherein the realization of a creature's very essence entails both the fulfillment of a natural course of movement and the attainment of the higher supernatural destiny. The 'essence' expresses itself in the perpetual striving in time for achievement of the eternal plan pre-ordained before the creature was ever even brought into being." von Ivánka, "Der philosophische Ertrag," 25–26.

Mental Peace and the Catholic Tradition

For Augustine, as mentioned earlier, peace means desiring everything one already has and nothing one lacks. And perfect peace, including mental peace, is part of what must characterize heaven in order for it to be truly blissful. It is the conclusion of this chapter that such an understanding of paradise (and the consequences it has for open-mindedness and intellectual diversity in the afterlife) is philosophically and theologically preferable to the alternative offered by figures like Nyssa.

Aquinas, in his *Compendium of Theology*, comes to the same conclusion by way of logic slightly different than Augustine's, derived from the axiom that a natural desire cannot be in vain. He begins by pointing out that man's final end cannot consist in the cognition of sensible objects because "once the ultimate end has been reached, natural desire ceases." But no matter how much we may advance in this kind of understanding—the kind we gain through our senses—"there still remains a natural desire to know other objects. For many things are quite beyond the reach of the senses."[13] Even the sensible things within our reach are not known completely or with total certainty, says Aquinas. Thus, "our natural desire for more perfect knowledge ever remains" in this life. But, he repeats, "a natural desire cannot be in vain."[14] Note, again, how this last premise, which Aquinas (following Aristotle) seems to regard as simply self-evident, directly conflicts with Gregory's description of a natural desire (for knowledge and moral growth) that continues to exist in the afterlife but is very much not, therefore, proven to be in vain.

Aquinas, of course, believes that God is man's final end. And that this last end can only be reached when "our intellect is actualized by some higher agent than an agent connatural to us," one "capable of gratifying our natural, inborn craving for knowledge. So great is the desire for knowledge within us that, once we apprehend an effect, we wish to know its cause."[15] This cause, finally, is God, who is ultimately the cause of all other causes. Or as Aquinas puts it, "This first cause is God. Consequently the ultimate end of an intellectual creature is the vision of God in His essence."[16] When this vision is had, all desire on the part of the

---

13. Aquinas, *Light of Faith*.

14. Aquinas, *Light of Faith*. Special thanks to Denys Turner for pointing me to this passage.

15. Aquinas, *Light of Faith*, 116–17.

16. Aquinas, *Light of Faith*, 116–17.

human ceases. "Once this end is reached," says Aquinas, "natural desire must find its full fruition."[17] Our intellects, finally united to the divine essence as we see God, are at rest for the first time, as they have always naturally desired to be. Believing that God can be known in such a way, with such a response on the part of humans, does not, importantly, imply or require that God is not infinite, as it seems to in Nyssa's thought. Aquinas admits as much:

> Of course, we shall never comprehend Him as He comprehends Himself. This does not mean that we shall be unaware of some part of Him, for He has no parts. It means that we shall not know Him as perfectly as He can be known, since the capacity of our intellect for knowing cannot equal His truth, and so cannot exhaust His knowability. God's knowability or truth is infinite, whereas our intellect is finite.[18]

Lastly, Aquinas does not assume that this comprehension of God on our part is for the sake of loving or enjoying God in heaven. In the *Compendium*, Aquinas states that "the ultimate end of an intellectual creature is the direct vision of God, but not delight in God."[19] Delight will naturally accompany, supervene upon, or even "perfect" such a vision. But it is not itself the last end. As Aquinas points out, "desire or love [cannot] be the ultimate end, because they are present even before the end is reached."[20]

Dante's *Paradiso*

The poet Dante lends further credence and illustration to the arguments made by Aquinas above and the sentiment he shares with Augustine. All share a form of what is often called "intellectualism," or the belief, described in the previous section, that while love drives us to God, what unites us finally to God and so to our ultimate happiness is the vision of God, an act of the intellect of a person who loves. As Dante remarks, "I see well that our intellect is never satisfied unless the truth enlighten it beyond which no truth can range. In that it rests as soon as it gains it, like a beast in its lair; and it can gain it, else every desire ware vain. Doubt, therefore, like a shoot, springs from the root of truth, and it is nature that

---

17. Aquinas, *Light of Faith*, 118.
18. Aquinas, *Light of Faith*, 119.
19. Aquinas, *Light of Faith*, 119.
20. Aquinas, *Light of Faith*, 123.

urges us to the summit from height to height."[21] An alternative translation to the same verse reads, "The mind is satisfied only with that truth which contains within itself every other truth."[22] In either case, the spirit of Dante's thought is in accord with that of Augustine and Aquinas regarding the unsatisfying nature of the human intellect. Translator John Sinclair, glossing this same passage in his commentary, writes, "The striving intellect, reaching the truth, 'rests like a beast in its lair,' and meantime it carries in itself the assurance that it can reach it; its ever-new doubts spring from the truth, like the shoots of a tree-trunk, by its very vitality; it is driven by its nature, like a mountain-climber, from one height to another up to the great summit."[23] The image of a mountain-climber is particularly compelling as it captures the notion that people reach intellectual summits only to realize, as often happens to climbers, that what they thought was the summit was actually a lower peak.

For Dante, as for Aquinas, heaven offers relief to such intellectual climbing and labors. Beatrice, speaking in front of the circles of Seraphim and Cherubim, observes how such a shared rest can occur with some members, nevertheless, knowing more than others: "[A]ll have delight in the measure of the depth to which their sight penetrates the Truth in which every intellect finds rest; from which it may be seen that the state of blessedness is founded on the act of vision, not on that which loves, which follows after."[24] How deep we will be able to gaze into the depths of God's wisdom will be a function of our respective natures, not dependent on any continual effort on our parts. In heaven, everyone is happy where they are assigned to be because being there leaves no margin of dissatisfaction. Beatrice speaks of knowledge as being given to each nature according to its lot, "wherefore they move to different ports over the great sea of being."[25] Dante, reflecting on this, suddenly realizes "that everywhere in Heaven is Paradise, even if the grace of the Supreme Good does not there rain down in one same measure." The buckets may be different sizes, but all are full, as the trope goes.

Importantly, in heaven we do not resent or envy those who are higher up or know more. Piccarda Donati, who Dante depicts as in paradise

21. Dante, *Paradiso*, 4.124–38.
22. Singleton, *Paradiso Commentary*, 94.
23. Sinclair, *Divine Comedy*, 71–72.
24. Dante, *Paradiso*, Canto XXVIII, vv. 106–111.
25. Dante, *Paradiso*, Canto I, v. 112.

by the skin of her teeth, is in the lowest circle thereof. She knows others are higher up and further in than she, so Dante asks her: Is there not some measure of sadness or even frustration in knowing that there are higher places in heaven than hers—in other words, don't you resent your lowly place? To which she famously replies: "[I]n his will is our peace."[26] Far from being unhappy where she is, she could not be happy higher up in heaven, for justice is what has her in this lowly place, and there would be nothing just about her being any higher up. Everything would be wrong were she anywhere but where she is. Likewise for what this project has called intellectual justice (or knowing what we deserve to know).

As with Augustine, Dante envisions the reunification with God as resulting in a kind of perfect and therefore *changeless* state on the part of the human participants. Beatrice, in the second sphere of heaven, remarks:

> Whate'er from this immediately distils
> Has afterwards no end, for ne'er removed
> Is its impression when it sets its seal.
> Whate'er from this immediately rains down
> Is wholly free, because it is not subject
> Unto the influences of novel things.[27]

Novelty of any kind—intellectual newness or change included—is not present here. Enraptured by the presence of God, we desire nothing else than to remain there.

It is, finally, intriguing that in describing the ancient philosophers born before Christ (e.g., Aristotle, Socrates, etc.) stuck in limbo, Dante observes them as continuing to engage in the great conversation (Dante sees them still "discoursing"), the big questions forever unresolved (and, if not freed from limbo, forever unresolv*able*) for them, stalled in a kind of cognitive limbo. Intellectual diversity, it seems, persists for the souls in limbo, according to Dante, as yet one more *apparent* punishment. And yet, Dante depicts this continued open-mindedness and intellectual diversity among the great pagan philosophers as occurring without "lamentations," though not without an element of longing; it entails no pain, but it does entail desire and sorrow. Dante observed them in the following way:

26. Dante, *Paradiso*, Canto III, v. 85.
27. Dante, *Paradiso*, Canto VII, v. 105.

> There, as it seemed to me from listening,
> Were lamentations none, but only sighs,
> That tremble made the everlasting air.
> And this arose from sorrow without torment . . .[28]

A few lines later, Virgil remarks:

> For such defects, and not for other guilt,
> Lost are we and are only so far punished,
> That without hope we live on in desire.[29]

The "defect" refers to the great handicap under which these philosophers labored: having lived before Christ. Whether it is possible to imagine (as Dante does) a form of painless sorrow, or non-punitive hopelessness, is an open question. For the purposes of this chapter, it is enough to observe that these noble, thoughtful pagans have not reached their final end (their true happiness) because they remain in a state in which they still want answers. Since they have a desire to know more that will never be put to rest, their souls can never enjoy true rest either, even if, as is the case, they do not truly realize what they are failing to experience in paradise.[30]

---

28. Dante, *Inferno*, Canto IV, vv. 25–27.

29. Dante, *Inferno*, Canto IV, vv. 41–42.

30. Interestingly, Socrates himself did not imagine that such continued postmortem philosophizing without closure would be in any way "sorrowful." In the *Apology*, he speaks of death as being a blessing for the just man, explaining: "Again, what would one of you give to keep company with Orpheus and Musaeus, Hesiod and Homer? I am willing to die many times if that is true. It would be a wonderful way for me to spend my time whenever I met Palamedes and Ajax, the son of Telamon, and any other of the men of old who died through an unjust conviction, to compare my experience with theirs. I think it would be pleasant. Most important, I could spend my time testing and examining people there, as I do here, as to who among them is wise, and who thinks he is, but is not. What would one not give, gentlemen of the jury, for the opportunity to examine the man who led the great expedition against Troy, or Odysseus, or Sisyphus, and innumerable other men and women one could mention? It would be an extraordinary happiness to talk with them, to keep company with them and examine them." Plato, *Five Dialogues*, 198040a–c.

Jonathan Edwards

Theologian Jonathan Edwards offers evidence that the picture of heaven attributed above to Augustine, Aquinas, and Dante can be shared by a self-understood Protestant figure as well. Writing about saints and angels in heaven, Edwards says, "They are all united, with one mind, to breathe forth their whole souls in love to God their eternal Father, and to Jesus Christ their common Redeemer, and head, and friend."[31] Being of one mind, "There is not a single secret or open enemy among them all."[32] In other words, in the terms of this project, intellectual diversity is no more. Indeed, Edwards shares in the belief with Aquinas that some saints know more than others but that those of lesser knowledge are not any less at peace or less fulfilled because of this comparative deficiency:

> They that are highest in degree in glory will be of the highest capacity; and so having the greatest knowledge, will see most of God's loveliness.... And on this account those that are lower in glory will not envy those that are above them, because they will be most beloved by those that are highest in glory. And the superior in glory will be so far from slighting those that are inferior, that they will have most abundant love to them—greater degrees of love *in proportion to their superior knowledge* and happiness.[33]

Edwards refers to yet more univocity in heaven in describing what verges on a kind of shared intellect by all present. As has been argued throughout this book, such a union should be a goal for Christians, and its opposite, intellectual diversity, should be cause for lament. Put differently, to be united with one another in Christ entails an intellectual component: to be collectively of one mind. Edwards writes:

> There shall be no wall of separation in heaven to keep the saints asunder.... Nor shall there be any want of full acquaintance to hinder the greatest possible intimacy; and much less shall there be any misunderstanding between them, or misinterpreting things that are said or done by each other. There shall be no

---

31. Edwards, *Jonathan Edwards in the Pulpit*, 118. Special thanks to Robert Jenson for recommending this text.

32. Edwards, *Jonathan Edwards in the Pulpit*, 118.

33. Edwards, *Jonathan Edwards in the Pulpit*, 121, emphasis added.

> disunion . . . from various opinions, or interests, or feelings, or alliances.[34]

This is true communion. Short of it, we are not yet fully united with each other. It is also the real objective of Christian intellectual charity. Without it, there can be no rest. Perfect intimacy with each other. Full acquaintance with God. At long last, we are united in and with a Truth forever changeless and forever satisfying. It is this finality that Christians may rightly hope and pray for. In the spirit of Augustine, "You made us for yourself, O Lord, and our minds are restless until they rest in thee.

---

34. Edwards, *Jonathan Edwards in the Pulpit*, 125.

Bibliography

Abadeer, Adel. "Seeking Redemptive Diversity in Christian Institutions of Higher Education." *Christian Higher Education* 8.3 (2009) 187–202.
Abley, Mark. *Spoken Here: Travels Among Threatened Languages*. New York: Mariner, 2005.
Abrams, Samuel. "Think Professors are Liberal? Try School Administrators." *The New York Times,* October 16, 2018.
Academic Association of University Professors. "Academic Bill of Rights." December 2003. http://www.aaup.org/report/academic-bill-rights.
Agresto, John. "The Suicide of the Liberal Arts." *The Wall Street Journal*, August 7, 2015.
Alighieri, Dante. *The Divine Comedy: The Inferno, the Purgatorio, and the Paradiso*. Translated by John Ciardi. New York: New American Library, 2003.
Aquinas, Thomas. *The Disputed Questions on Truth*. 3 vols. Chicago: Henry Regnery, 1954.
———. *Light of Faith: The Compendium of Theology*. Manchester, NH: Sophia Institute, 1993.
———. *The Literal Exposition on Job*. Translated by Anthony Damico. New York: Oxford University Press, 1989.
———. *Summa Contra Gentiles*. Translated by Anton C. Pegis. Notre Dame: Notre Dame University Press, 1991.
———. *Summa Theologica*. Translated by the Fathers of the English Dominican Province. New York: Benziger Bros., 1947.
Aristotle. *Nicomachean Ethics*. Translated by Terence Irwin. Indianapolis: Hackett, 1999.
———. *Physics*. Translated by Robin Waterfield. New York: Oxford University Press, 2008.
Augustine of Hippo. *The City of God*. Translated by Marcus Dods. Peabody: Hendrickson, 2009.
———. *Confessions*. Translated by Albert Cook Outler. Mineola, NY: Dover, 2002.
———. *De Fide et Symbolo*. Translated by E. P. Meijering. Amsterdam: Gieben, 1987.
———. *The Essential Augustine*. Edited by Vernon J. Bourke. Indianapolis: Hackett, 1974.
———. *The Haeresibus of Saint Augustine*. Translated by Liguori G. Müller. Washington, DC: Catholic University of America Press, 1956.
———. *Homilies on the Gospel according to St. John*. Translated by Edmund Hill. The Works of Saint Augustine III/12. Hyde Park: New City, 2009.

———. *Instructing Beginners in the Faith*. Translated by Raymond Canning. Edited by Boniface Ramsey. Hyde Park: New City, 2006.

———. *Letters of Saint Augustine*, Translated by J. G. Cunningham. Edinburgh: T. & T. Clark, 1875.

———. *Of the Morals of the Catholic Church*. Translated by Richard Stothert. Self-published, CreateSpace, 2015.

———. *Our Lord's Sermon on the Mount*. Translated by Richard Stothert. Self-published, CreateSpace, 2012.

———. *The Retractions*. Translated by Sister M. Ingez Bogan. The Fathers of the Church 60. Washington, DC: Catholic University Press, 1999.

———. *The Trinity*. Translated by Edmund Hill. Edited by John Rotelle. The Works of Saint Augustine I/5. 2nd ed. Hyde Park: New City, 2012.

Barnes, Julian. *Nothing to Be Frightened Of*. New York: Vintage, 2009.

Barth, Karl. *Church Dogmatics*. Translated by G. W. Bromiley and T. F. Torrance. London: T. & T. Clark, 2010.

Batson, Daniel C., et al. "Immorality from Empathy-Induced Altruism: When Compassion and Justice Conflict." *Journal of Personality and Social Psychology* 68.6 (June 1995) 1042–54.

Bede. *Ecclesiastical History of the English People*. Translated by Leo Sherley-Price. Edited by D. H. Farmer and Ronald Latham. New York: Penguin, 1991.

Bilgrami, Akeel. *Secularism, Identity, and Enchantment*, Cambridge: Harvard University Press, 2014.

———. "Truth, Balance, and Freedom." In *Who's Afraid of Academic Freedom?*, edited by Akeel Bilgrami and Jonathan R. Cole, 10–26. New York: Columbia University Press, 2015.

Bishop, Bill. *The Big Sort: Why the Clustering of Like-Minded America is Tearing Us Apart*. New York: Mariner, 2008.

Blowers, Paul. "Maximus the Confessor, Gregory of Nyssa, and Embracing the Concept of 'Perpetual Progress.'" *Vigiliae Christianae* 46.2 (June 1992) 151–71.

Blumberg, Antonia. "China On Track To Become World's Largest Christian Country By 2025, Experts Say." *Huffington Post*, April 22, 2014. https://www.huffpost.com/entry/china-largest-christian-country_n_5191910.

Bonhoeffer, Dietrich. *Ethics*. New York: Touchstone, 1995.

Borges, Jorge Luis. *Jorge Luis Borges: Collected Fictions*. Translated by Andrew Hurley. New York: Penguin, 1999.

Bottum, Joseph. "The Death of Protestant America." *First Things*, August 2008.

Bowlin, John. "Jesus and Baseball, Or, How Sacrifice Works." Talk given at Princeton Reunions, Princeton, NJ, 2015.

Braceland, Lawrence, trans. *Aelred of Rievaulx: Spiritual Friendship*. Edited and with an introduction by Marsha L. Dutton. Collegeville: Cistercian, 2010.

Brooks, David. *Bobos in Paradise: The New Upper Class and How They Got There*. New York: Simon & Schuster, 2001.

———. "Why Partyism is Wrong." *The New York Times*, October 27, 2014.

Bryant, Alyssa N., and Christy M. Craft. "The Challenge and Promise of Pluralism: Dimensions of Spiritual Climate and Diversity at a Lutheran College." *Christian Higher Education* 9.5 (2010) 396–422.

Calvin, John. *Institutes of the Christian Religion*. Translated by Ford Lewis Battles. Edited by John McNeill. Philadelphia: Westminster John Knox, 1960.

Charry, Ellen. "Preface: Same-Sex Relationships and the Nature of Marriage: A Theological Colloquy." *The Anglican Theological Review* 93.1 (Winter 2011).
Chesterton, G. K. *Orthodoxy*. Louisville: GLH, 2016.
Christ, Oliver, et al. "Contextual Effect of Positive Intergroup Contact on Outgroup Prejudice." *Proceedings of the National Academy of Science* 111.11 (March 18, 2014) 3996–4000.
Christensen, Clayton. *The Innovator's Dilemma*. New York: Basic, 2011.
Chua, Amy. *Political Tribes: Group Instinct and the Fate of Nations*. New York: Penguin, 2018.
Contreras-Huerta, et al. "Racial Bias in Neural Empathic Responses to Pain." *PLoS One* 8.12 (2013) e84001. https://doi.org/10.1371/journal.pone.0084001.
Cowling, Maurice. "Exchange with Bernard Williams." *London Review of Books* 3.6 (April 2, 1981) 22–23.
Dante. *Dante's Paradiso (The Divine Comedy, Volume II, Paradise)*. Translated by Henry Wadsworth Longfellow. Digireads.com, 2017.
Davidson, Donald. "Three Varieties of Knowledge" In *A.J. Ayer Memorial Essays: Royal Institute of Philosophy Supplement*, edited by A. Phillips Griffiths, 153–66. Cambridge: Cambridge University Press, 1991.
de Botton, Alain. *The Art of Travel*. Reprint, New York: Vintage, 2004.
Deneen, Patrick. *Why Liberalism Failed*. New Haven: Yale University Press, 2018.
Deresiewicz, William. *Excellent Sheep: The Miseducation of the American Elite and the Way to a Meaningful Life*. New York: Free Press, 2014.
Douthat, Ross. "Who Are We?" *The New York Times*, February 4, 2017.
———. "Why I Am a Catholic." *The New York Times*, October 28, 2014.
Dreyfus, Hubert, and Sean Dorrance Kelly. *All Things Shining: Reading the Western Classics to Find Meaning in a Secular Age*. New York: Free Press, 2011.
Duarte, José, et al. "Political Diversity Will Improve Social Psychological Science." *Behavioral and Brain Sciences* 38 (2015) e130.
Edwards, Jonathan. *Jonathan Edwards in the Pulpit: Famous Sermons*. Minneapolis: Curiosmith, 2012.
Eisenach, Eldon. *The Next Religious Establishment: National Identity and Political Theology in Post-Protestant America*. Lanham: Rowman & Littlefield, 2000.
Eliot, T. S. *The Complete Prose of T. S. Eliot: The Critical Edition*. Edited by Anthony Cuda and Ronald Schuchard. Baltimore: Johns Hopkins University Press, 2014.
Episcopal Church. *The Book of Common Prayer and Administration of the Sacraments and Other Rites and Ceremonies of the Church Together with the Psalter or Psalms of David*. New York: Episcopal Church, 1979.
Florida House of Representatives. "Florida House Bill 837." http://archive.flsenate.gov/data/session/2005/House/bills/billtext/pdf/h083700.pdf.
Franklin, James. *The Science of Conjecture: Evidence and Probability before Pascal*. Baltimore: Johns Hopkins University Press, 2001.
Fricker, Miranda. *Epistemic Injustice: Power and the Ethics of Knowing*. New York: Oxford University Press, 2009.
Garvey, John, and Mark W. Roche. "What Makes a University Catholic? An Exchange on Mission & Hiring." *Commonweal*, February 10, 2017.
Graham, Gordon. *Evil and Christian Ethics*. New York: Cambridge University Press, 2001.

Gregory of Nyssa. *Gregory of Nyssa: Dogmatic Treatises.* Vol. 5, *Nicene and Post-Nicene Fathers, Second Series,* edited by Philip Schaff and Henry Wace. New York: Cosimo, 2007.

———. *The Life of Moses.* San Francisco: HarperOne, 2006.

Griffiths, Paul. *Intellectual Appetite: A Theological Grammar.* Washington, DC: Catholic University of America Press, 2009.

———. "Theological Disagreement: What It Is, and How to Do It." *Proceedings of The Catholic Theological Society of America* 69 (2014).

Grisez, Germain. "Academic Freedom and Catholic Faith." *NCEA Bulletin* 15.17 (November 1967).

Gros, Frédéric. *A Philosophy of Walking.* Translated by John Howe. Brooklyn: Verso, 2014.

Gumbrecht, Hans. *The Production of Presence: What Meaning Cannot Convey.* Stanford: Stanford University Press, 2004.

Haidt, Jonathan. "About Us." Heterodox Academy. https://heterodoxacademy.org/about-us/.

Hamburger, Philip. *Separation of Church and State.* Cambridge: Harvard University Press, 2004.

Hardy, G. H. *A Mathematician's Apology.* Self-published, CreateSpace, 2011.

Hart, David. *The Beauty of the Infinite: The Aesthetics of Christian Truth.* Grand Rapids: Eerdmans, 2003.

Harvard Divinity School. "History and Mission." https://hds.harvard.edu/about/history-and-mission.

Hayes, Christopher. *Twilight of the Elites: America after Meritocracy.* New York: Broadway, 2012.

Hector, Kevin. *Theology without Metaphysics: God, Language and the Spirit of Recognition.* Cambridge: Cambridge University Press, 2011.

Heraclitus. *Fragments.* Translated by Brooks Haxton. Penguin Classics. New York: Penguin, 2003.

Hirschman, Albert O. "The Principle of the Hiding Hand." *National Affairs* 39 (Winter 1967).

Holmes, Oliver Wendell. *Selections from the Letters, Speeches, Judicial Opinions, and Other Writings of Oliver Wendell Holmes.* Chicago: University of Chicago Press, 1922.

Horgan, John. "Gravity Quantized?" *Scientific American* 267.3 (September 1992) 18–20.

Hume, David. *Essays: Moral, Political, and Literary.* Indianapolis: Liberty Fund, 1985.

———. *The Philosophical Works of David Hume.* Boston: Little, Brown, 1854.

———. *A Treatise of Human Nature.* Edited by David Norton. Oxford: Oxford University Press, 2000.

Hunsinger, George. "Robert Jenson's *Systematic Theology*: A Review Essay." *Scottish Journal of Theology* 55.2 (May 2002) 161–200.

Iyengar, Shanto, and Sean J. Westwood. "Fear and Loathing Across Party Lines: New Evidence on Group Polarization." https://pcl.stanford.edu/research/2015/iyengar-ajps-group-polarization.pdf.

Iyengar, Shanto, et al. "Affect, Not Ideology: A Social Identity Perspective on Polarization." *Public Opinion Quarterly* 76.3 (Fall 2012) 405–31.

Jacobs, Alan. "Embrace the Pain: Living with the Repugnant Cultural Other." Lecture delivered at Duke University, January 29, 2018.

———. *How to Think: A Survival Guide for a World at Odds*. New York: Currency, 2017.
Jenkins, John. "Notre Dame Principles of Diversity and Inclusion." https://diversity.nd.edu/together-at-notre-dame/#diversity-inclusion.
Kant, Immanuel. *The Critique of Pure Reason*. 2nd ed. New York: Macmillan, 1915.
Kaveny, Cathleen. "No Academic Question: Should the CTSA Seek 'Conservative' Views?" *Commonweal Magazine*, June 16, 2014. https://www.commonwealmagazine.org/no-academic-question.
Kelly, Thomas. "Disagreement, Dogmatism, and Belief Polarization." *The Journal of Philosophy* 1 (forthcoming).
———. "The Epistemic Significance of Disagreement." In *Oxford Studies in Epistemology*, edited by John Hawthorne and Tamar Gendler, 1:167–96. Oxford: Oxford University Press, 2005.
Kitcher, Philip. "Things Fall Apart." *The New York Times*, September 8, 2013.
Kubizek, August. *The Young Hitler I Knew*. Translated by Geoffrey Brooks. Yorkshire: Greenhill, 2006.
Lear, Jonathan. *Open Minded: Working out the Logic of the Soul*. Cambridge: Harvard University Press, 1998.
Lee, Kyongjoon, et al. "Does Collocation Inform the Impact of Collaboration?" *PLoS One* 5.12 (2010) e14279.
Levi, Primo. *If This Is a Man*. New York: Abacus, 2003.
Liberty University. "Master of Arts Marriage and Family Therapy."
Lilla, Mark. "The End of Identity Liberalism." *The New York Times*, November 18, 2016.
Liu, Stephanie. "99% of Donors Give to Obama." *The Daily Princetonian*, November 6, 2012.
Lorenz, Konrad. "Kant's Doctrine of the A Priori in the Light of Contemporary Biology." In *Philosophy After Darwin: Classic and Contemporary Readings*, edited by Michael Ruse, 231–46. Princeton: Princeton University Press, 2009.
Lowrie, Walter. *Memoirs of the Rev. Walter M. Lowrie, Missionary to China*. Philadelphia: Carter & Bros., 1849.
Marocco, Joe. "Climate Change and the Limits of Knowledge." In *The Virtues of Ignorance: Complexity, Sustainability, and the Limits of Knowledge*, edited by Bill Vitek and Wes Jackson, 307–22. Lexington: University of Kentucky Press, 2008.
Mason, Lilliana. "'I Disrespectfully Agree': The Differential Effects of Partisan Sorting on Social and Issue Polarization." *American Journal of Political Science* 59.1 (2015) 128–45.
"Master of Arts Marriage and Family Therapy (Online) Handbook." http://www.liberty.edu/media/1118/MA_MFT_Handbook_2015-2016_Online_Revised_7_7_2015.pdf.
McCormack, Bruce. "Let's Speak Plainly: A Response to Paul Molnar." *Theology Today* 67 (2010) 57–65.
McSorley, Joseph. "Open-Mindedness." *Catholic World* 83.2 (April 1906) 18–31.
Medina, José. *Epistemology of Resistance: Gender and Racial Oppression, Epistemic Injustice, and Resistant Imaginations*. New York: Oxford University Press, 2013.
Mill, John Stuart. *On Liberty and Other Writings*. Cambridge: Cambridge University Press, 1989.
Miller, James Grier. *Living Systems*. Boulder: University Press of Colorado, 1995.

Morse, Marston. "Mathematics and the Arts." *Bulletin of the Atomic Sciences* 15.2 (1959) 55–59.

Murray, Charles. *Coming Apart: The State of White America, 1960–2010*. New York: Crown Forum, 2013.

Musil, Robert. *Five Women*. Boston: Verba Mundi, 1999.

———. *The Man Without Qualities*. New York: Vintage, 1996.

Napier, William. *History Of General Sir Charles Napier's Administration Of Scinde*. London: Chapman & Hall, 1851.

Nehamas, Alexander. "The Good of Friendship." *Proceedings of The Aristotelian Society* 110 (2010) 267–94.

———. *Only A Promise of Happiness*. Princeton: Princeton University Press, 2010.

Neuhaus, Richard John. *The Catholic Moment*. New York: Harper & Row, 1987.

Newman, John Henry. *Discourses Addressed to Mixed Congregations*. London: Longmans, Green, 1906.

Nietzsche, Friedrich. *Notes on the Eternal Recurrence*. Living Time Thought. Living Time Media, 2007.

Nozick, Robert. *Anarchy, State, and Utopia*. New York: Basic, 1974.

Nussbaum, Martha. "The Professor of Parody." *The New Republic*, February 22, 1999. https://newrepublic.com/article/150687/professor-parody.

O'Neill, Edward. "Consortial Book Circulation Patterns: The OCLC-OhioLINK Study." *College & Research Libraries* 75 (2014) 791–807.

Oppenheimer, Daniel. *Exit Right: The People Who Left the Left and Reshaped the American Century*. New York: Simon & Schuster, 2016.

Orwell, George. *A Collection of Essays*. New York: Harvest, 1981.

———. *Homage to Catalonia*. New York: Mariner, 1980.

Packer, George. *The Unwinding: An Inner History of the New America*. New York: Farrar, Straus & Giroux, 2013.

Pardue, Stephen. *The Mind of Christ: Humility and the Intellect in Early Christian Theology*. New York: T. & T. Clark, 2013.

Pascal, Blaise. *Pensées*. Translated by A. J. Krailsheimer. New York: Penguin, 1995.

Paulsen, Michael. "Dirty Harry and the Real Constitution." *University of Chicago Law Review* 64.4 (1997) 1457–91.

———. "The Uneasy Case for Intellectual Diversity." *Harvard Journal of Law & Public Policy* 37.1 (2014) 145–64.

Peirce, C. S. "The Fixation of Belief." *Popular Science Monthly* 12 (November 1877) 1–15.

Peterson, Anna L. "Ignorance and Ethics." In *The Virtues of Ignorance: Complexity, Sustainability, and the Limits of Knowledge*, edited by Bill Vitek and Wes Jackson, 109–34. Lexington: University of Kentucky Press, 2008.

Pettit, Philip. "When to Defer to Majority Testimony—and When Not." *Analysis* 66.291 (July 2006) 179–87.

Pieper, Josef. *Faith, Hope, and Love*. San Francisco: Ignatius, 1997.

———. *Leisure, The Basis of Culture*. South Bend: St. Augustine's, 1998.

Placher, William. *A History of Christian Theology*. Philadelphia: Westminster John Knox, 1988.

Plato. *Five Dialogues*. Edited by John M. Cooper. Translated by G. M. A. Grube. Indianapolis: Hackett, 1980.

Polanyi, Michael. *Personal Knowledge*. London: Routledge, 1962.

Prinz, Jesse. "Against Empathy." *Southern Journal of Philosophy* 49.1 (September 2011) 214–33.
Putnam, Robert D. "*E Pluribus Unum*: Diversity and Community in the Twenty-first Century." *Scandinavian Political Studies* 30.2 (June 2007) 137–74.
Quash, Ben. "Prologue." *Heresies and How to Avoid Them*, edited by Ben Quash and Michael Ward, 1–12. Grand Rapids: Baker, 2007.
Quine, W. V. "Carnap and Logical Truth." In *Ways of Paradox and Other Essays*, 107–32. Cambridge: Harvard University Press, 1956.
———. *The Web Of Belief*. New York: McGraw-Hill, 1978.
Ratzinger, Joseph Cardinal. *Introduction to Christianity*. San Francisco: Ignatius, 2000.
Rieff, Phillip. *Freud: The Mind of the Moralist*. Chicago: University of Chicago Press, 1979.
Roberts, Robert Campbell, and Jay Wood. *Intellectual Virtues: An Essay in Regulative Epistemology*. New York: Oxford University Press, 2010.
Rose-Wiles, Lisa. "Are Print Books Dead? An Investigation of Book Circulation at a Mid-sized Academic Library." *Technical Services Quarterly* 30.2 (2013) 129–52.
Ruse, Michael. "The Two Cultures Revisited." Presentation given at the University of Dayton, February 14, 2001.
Saracino, Michele. "Response to Paul Griffiths' 'Theological Disagreement: What It Is And How To Do It.'" *Proceedings of the Catholic Theological Society of America* 69 (2014) 37–39.
Schellenberg, J. L. "Time Out of Mind: Remembering the Future in the Debate Over Science and Religion." Paper presented to a colloquium of the Institute for the History and Philosophy of Science and Technology at the University of Toronto, February 2, 2011.
———. *The Wisdom to Doubt: A Justification of Religious Skepticism*. Ithaca: Cornell University Press, 2007.
Schmitt, Carl. *Dictatorship*. Malden, MA: Polity, 2014.
———. *Political Theology: Four Chapters on the Concept of Sovereignty*. Chicago: University of Chicago Press, 2006.
Scruton, Roger. *Education and Indoctrination: An Attempt at Definition and a Review of Social and Political Implications*. Self-published, Education Resource Center, 1985.
Sidgwick, Henry. *The Methods of Ethics*. Cambridge: Cambridge, 1981.
Sinclair, John. *The Divine Comedy*. Vol. 3, *Paradiso Commentary*. New York: Oxford, 1961.
Singleton, Charles. *Paradiso Commentary*. 3 vols. Princeton: Princeton University Press, 1991.
Steiner, George. *Real Presences*. Chicago: University of Chicago Press, 1991.
Stewart, Christopher. "An Overview of ACRLMetrics." *The Journal of Academic Librarianship* 37.1 (January 2011) 73–76.
Strauss, Leo. "Relativism." In *The Rebirth of Classical Political Relativism*, edited by Thomas L. Pangle, 13–26. Chicago: University of Chicago Press, 1989.
Sullivan, Winnifred. *The Impossibility of Religious Freedom*. Princeton: Princeton University Press, 2007.
Sunstein, Cass. "Partyism." https://chicagounbound.uchicago.edu/cgi/viewcontent.cgi?article=1543&context=uclf.
Swidler, Leonard. "Understanding Dialogue." In *Interfaith Dialogue at the Grass Roots*, edited by Leonard Swidler, 9–24. Philadelphia: Ecumenical, 2008.

Taylor, Charles. *A Secular Age*. Cambridge: Belknap, 2007.
Taylor, Mark C. "The Devoted Student." *The New York Times*, December 21, 2006.
Theunissen, Bert. "Darwin and his Pigeons: The Analogy between Artificial and Natural Selection Revisited." *Journal of the History of Biology* 45.2 (Summer 2012) 179–212.
Thiel, Peter. *Zero to One: Notes on Startups, or How to Build the Future*. New York: Crown, 2014.
Thucydides. *History of the Peloponnesian War*. Translated by Rex Warner. New York: Penguin, 1954.
University of Dubuque. "Mission, Vison, and Values." https://www.dbq.edu/AboutUD/MissionVisionValues/.
University of Notre Dame. "Undergraduate Admissions." https://admissions.nd.edu/discover/student-life/inclusion/.
von Ivánka, Endre. "Der philosophische Ertrag der Auseinandersetzung Maximos des Bekenners mit dem Origenismus." *Jahrbuch der Österreichischen Byzantinischen Gesellschaft* 7 (1958) 23–49.
Wampole, Christy. "How to Live Without Irony." *The New York Times*, November 18, 2012.
Westberg, Daniel. "Did Aquinas Change His Mind about the Will?" *The Thomist* 58.1 (January 1994) 41–60.
Wetzel, James. "Absolute Augustine: Post-Hegelian Reflections on Eternity and the End of Time." Presentation given at Princeton University, March 8, 2014.
Whitcomb, Dennis, et al. "Intellectual Humility: Owning Our Limitations." *Philosophy and Phenomenological Research* 94.3 (2017) 509–39.
Whitman, James. "The Origins of 'Reasonable Doubt.'" https://digitalcommons.law.yale.edu/fss_papers/1/.
Wilbur, Richard. *Anterooms: New Poems and Translations*. New York: Houghton Mifflin, 2010.
Wilkes, Kathleen. *Real People: Personal Identity without Thought Experiments*. Oxford: Clarendon, 1988.
Wittgenstein, Ludwig. *On Certainty*. New York: Harper & Row, 1972.
———. *Tractatus Logico-Philosophicus*. Mineola: Dover, 1998.
Wolterstorff, Nicholas. "The Significance of Inexplicable Disagreement." In *Religious Faith and Intellectual Virtues*, edited by Laura Callahan and Timothy O'Connor, 317–30. New York: Oxford University Press, 2014.
Wordsworth, William. *The Complete Poetical Works*. London: Macmillan, 1888.
Xu, Xiaojing. "Do You Feel My Pain? Racial Group Membership Modulates Empathic Neural Responses." *The Journal of Neuroscience* 29 (July 1, 2009) 8525–29.
Zagzebski, Linda. Paper delivered at the fourth annual CCT conference, Biola University, 2015.

www.ingramcontent.com/pod-product-compliance
Lightning Source LLC
Chambersburg PA
CBHW021728220426
43662CB00008B/755